on track ...
Beck

every album, every song

Arthur Lizie

sonicbondpublishing.com

Sonicbond Publishing Limited
www.sonicbondpublishing.co.uk
Email: info@sonicbondpublishing.co.uk

First Published in the United Kingdom 2023
First Published in the United States 2023

British Library Cataloguing in Publication Data:
A Catalogue record for this book is available from the British Library

Copyright Arthur Lizie 2023

ISBN 978-1-78952-258-7

Typeset in ITC Garamond & ITC Avant Garde
Printed and bound in England

Graphic design and typesetting: Full Moon Media

Dedications

This book is dedicated to everyone who didn't have the money to spend on that import record just to get one hard-to-find song, who spent the money on that import record just to get that one song.

Follow us on social media:
Twitter: https://twitter.com/SonicbondP
Instagram: https://www.instagram.com/sonicbondpublishing_/
Facebook: https://www.facebook.com/SonicbondPublishing/

Linktree QR code:

Foreword

In the spring of 1993, I was working a crappy job on a radioactive military base somewhere in the American Southwest. My most vivid memory is being tasked by the boss to get a coffee in a Styrofoam cup. There were no Styrofoam cups, so I brought his java in what was available. Soon I had my 'that's not a Styrofoam cup!' ass handed to me in front of a room of colleagues. Well, not colleagues so much as people I worked with who had much better paying, permanent jobs – but other human beings, nevertheless.

Around the same time, I traveled to Seattle to visit a friend. Strolling around University Ave., I noticed a handmade sign in the Tower Records window updating passersby on the in-stock status of Beck's 'Loser' 12" – Beck? 'Loser'? Should I know about this? The record was out-of-stock, but I soon located the song, gave it a listen, and fell in love. I wasn't a 'slacker' as much as grievously underemployed, but nevertheless made a connection with the song's upbeat pessimism – and I'm still here 30 years later.

on track ...

Beck

Contents

Introduction 8
Golden Feelings (1993) 10
A Western Harvest Field by Moonlight (1994)............................. 14
Stereopathetic Soulmanure (1994) 17
Mellow Gold (1994).. 23
One Foot in the Grave (1994) 32
Odelay (1996) 39
Mutations (1998) 55
Midnite Vultures (1999) 62
Sea Change (2002).. 73
Guero (2005)... 79
Guerolito 86
The Information (2006) 91
Modern Guilt (2008) 100
Morning Phase (2014) 115
Colors (2017) 124
Hyperspace (2019).. 132
Early Recordings 140
Compilations and Live Collections 142
Collaborations.. 145
Sideman, Songwriter, Producer, Remixer 150
Sources 157

Introduction

Beck was born Bek David Campbell on 8 July 1970, early on adopting the Beck spelling. His father, David Campbell, has worked in the music industry since the late 1960s. He has made thousands of appearances as a musician, arranger, and conductor on recordings by Carole King, Adele, U2, and hundreds of other artists, including Beck. Beck took his last name from his mother, Bibbe Hansen, who is an artist, actor, and musician.

The other backstory person in Beck's life is Bibbe's father, Al Hansen. The elder Hansen was part of the Fluxus art community, which included such luminaries as John Cage, Yoko Ono, and Nam June Paik. Fluxus artists often engaged in time-based events and lived-art experiences, emphasizing the importance of the art process rather than the art product, much like early Beck. When Al lived with the family in the late 1970s, he and Beck didn't have much contact, but Beck claims to have learned from him that an education isn't something that has to happen in a school.

Beck's family struggled financially early on, although Beck has said: 'Where I come from financially doesn't inform my music'. His parents divorced in 1984 and soon after, he was moving around Los Angeles with his mother and her future husband, Mexican artist Sean Carrillo. The new family settled in predominantly Hispanic East Los Angeles. According to Beck, his new high school was gang-ridden and he didn't feel safe. He applied to the public art school but was rejected. He left school at the age of 14; his education didn't happen in a school.

Beck soon got hooked on music by checking out records from the public library (which subsequently burned down). He felt a connection with the American roots music of Mississippi John Hurt, Woody Guthrie, The Carter Family, and others. He taught himself to play guitar and then set out to play live wherever he could, which was generally not in money-producing venues. In 1988 he looked to change his fortune by moving to New York City, riding cross-country on a $30 Greyhound bus ticket. While in NYC, Beck fell in with the anti-folk scene, which sought to rejuvenate a Greenwich Village folk scene still under the spell of Bob Dylan's early 1960s persona (which Dylan himself had long ago shed). Beck began to write his own songs, many of which would end up on his first self-released cassette, *Banjo Story* (1988). He enjoyed mild success on the East Coast but grew tired of being cold and getting beaten up, so he moved back to L.A.

Beck's 1990 West Coast return found him working his way into the burgeoning alternative music scene by playing clubs, recording music on his four-track, and releasing cassettes – the standard life of a struggling musician. Things began to change in August 1991 when Bong Load Records leaders Tom Rothrock and Rob Schnapf saw Beck live and decided they wanted to work with the unusual folk artist. This led to the release of 'Loser' about 15 months later in spring 1993, an interval which saw more self-released cassettes, Beck's first vinyl single 'MTV Makes Me Want to

Smoke Crack', and his first album, *Golden Feelings* – this is where our story begins.

Notes on the chapters

The chapters follow chronologically in order of commercial Beck album releases. Each chapter includes album liner-note information, background on LP recording and reception, and a dive into individual tracks. If the album was re-issued with additional tracks, bonus tracks are covered before 'related tracks', such as singles and songs on various artist LPs. This can make it difficult to understand the integrity of singles and EPs (a three-track single might have one track in the album section, one in the bonus section, and one in the related section), but it should be clear in the text how the songs were released.

I have pulled some material out of the strict chronology. The handful of early self-released cassettes are not covered in depth and share a later chapter with compilations and live collections, many of which are promotional only. Collaborations also get their own chapter, although collaborations on which Beck receives a 'featuring' shoutout as artist or in the song title appear in the main narrative as Beck songs.

What's not here? First, I have purposefully avoided discussing Beck's personal life, such as Scientology, Judaism, and his relationships, unless the information informs a better understanding of his music. Second, this text doesn't cover live performances, unreleased live songs, or bootleg studio songs. It doesn't cover album art or Beck's art projects (save, glancingly, *Song Reader*). It also doesn't methodically cover live television appearances, TV broadcasts, or music videos and web clips. Each of these areas, covered thoroughly and properly, would require its own book – maybe that's the sequel.

All songs are written by Beck Hansen, except where noted.

All mistakes are written by me.

Golden Feelings (1993)

Personnel
Beck Hansen: vocals, acoustic guitar, harmonica, percussion, bass
Steve Hanft: spoken vocals on 'Heartland Feeling'
Produced by: Beck Hansen
US Release Date: January 1993
Label: Sonic Enemy
Highest chart places: did not chart
Running Time: 42:35

Sonic Enemy was a Claremont, CA-based label that issued about a dozen cassettes and a vinyl 7" in an early 1990s incarnation. Among those tapes was Beck's debut album, *Golden Feelings*. The label catalog advertised the collection of four-track recordings as such:

'Like Neil Young on cough syrup' says his lawyer, and who am I to differ? Genuine and genuinely fucked-up, straight from the heart of spooky folky noisy unaffected tales of poverty and lucklessness, fast food & bad trips. Thirty-five or more minutes ... $3.00

Sonic Enemy released a few thousand copies, then went out of business in 1995. The label returned in 1999 and pressed 2000 CDs. Beck was not amused, and Sonic Enemy shut down production, sharing this website message:

Hey, where's Beck?

Beck doesn't live here anymore. Mommy says the mean lawyer people took him away to live with his other family, even though he lived with us first. Mommy says I'll understand someday.

The cover art is a black-and-white picture of Raggedy Ann and Teddy Bears at a tea party. The j-card includes the song titles and an untitled verse. Original versions included a piece of paper stating: 'EVERYTHING IN THIS BOX IS FALSE'.

Beck ran out of copies of the tape and duplicated it privately for his 1 April 1994 show at New York City's The Grand, opening for Evel Knievel. Two titles, referenced below, were misspelled.

It's unclear if the album was reviewed at the time of release, but multiple Beck album-ranking articles place it among his least successful LPs. Neither *Golden Feelings* nor *Stereopathetic Soulmanure* are acknowledged on *Beck.com*.

'The Fucked Up Blues' 2:11
This song sets the pace for the whole album. There are two snippets of found sound, followed by two minutes of barely hanging together reverbed drums,

guitar, and vocals, eventually tagged by a short harmonica solo. The lyrics mainly repeat the title with a few existential lamentations thrown in. As with many early projects, this is meta-Beck: the song IS fucked-up blues.

'Special People' 1:42
This chorus-less acapella is, more-or-less, 16 rhyming couplets featuring monotone, high-and-low non-harmonizing Beck vocal tracks. It's the type of song that makes people say either 'turn this off, it's not even music'! or 'there's a whole album on this stuff? – Great!' This is one of three *Golden Feelings* tracks 'evacuated' onto 1994's 'Pay No Mind' UK maxi-single.

'Magic Stationwagon' 1:36
If someone's walking down the Tesco aisle humming Beck, it's probably not this song. The core is a call-and-response battle of throbbing, percussive guitars alongside some screechy vocals lurking under the surface. The title evokes an idyllic California youth, but the lyrics evoke confusion.

'No Money No Honey' 2:35
It's an earworm as Beck nonchalantly repeats the title phrase over an increasingly distorted and gradually more mariachi-like guitar. The last portion of the track is a sound collage, including the 'c'mon motherfucker' clip that would be extended on 'Truckdrivin' Neighbors Downstairs', some classical music, and some rock music. An alternate version appears on *Stereopathetic Soulmanure*.

'Trouble All My Days' 2:07
This menacing track features percussive, foot-stomping blues. Lyrically it doesn't venture far beyond the title, but opens with extended dialogue from Los Angeles-area TV pitchman Ed Vanton about the past as a 'cancelled check' that Beck would find lyrically memorable. This version appeared on singles and the *Odelay* deluxe edition.

'Bad Energy' 1:39
This loosely assembled track begins with an unidentified song sample over which Beck eventually strums a guitar and mumbles. No one can dispute his assertion that it's like 'a big empty city full of toasters'.

'Schmoozer' 2:38
This guitar/bass/drums number with harmonica and double-tracked Beck vocals recalls numerous churning pleasures from Velvet Underground and reverberates in contemporaneous Beck tracks such as 'Thunder Peel'. The lyrics seem like a standard kiss-off to a girlfriend. Beck's second run of the cassette alternatively called this track 'Feeling Hurter'. There appears no connection with the 'Snoozer' subtitle of 'Pay No Mind', although it is the title Weird Al Yankovic wanted to use for a rejected 'Loser' parody.

'Heartland Feeling' 7:11

After a minute-long opening that includes a Steve Hanft monologue about a heartland feeling (it involves the true American music of Mellencamp, Springsteen, and Seger), Beck delivers the collection's centerpiece. In five mock-strident verses, Beck offers snapshot biographies of heartland people before concluding each observation with the rejoinder chorus: 'only a person / who didn't know shit / anything happening / that's about it'. The song features Beck and acoustic guitar with multi-tracked vocals on the choruses and a distorted fadeout, which is followed by a sound collage that includes a portion of The Tokens' 'I Hear Trumpets Blow' (1966). Beck opened a 1995 episode of *The Larry Sanders Show* with a performance of the song.

'Super Golden Black Sunchild' 2:11

This echoey number about scepters, flames and fate recalls portentous late 1960s/early 1970s English acoustic folk-rock tunes by the likes of Jethro Tull, Led Zeppelin, and Pentangle. Not to mention Tenacious D, the faux-metal duo featuring Jack Black, brother-in-law of Beck-collaborators Rachel and Petra Haden. The track appears on the 'Pay No Mind' UK maxi-single as 'Supergolden (Sunchild)'.

'Soul Sucked Dry' 1:50

The serene, fey leanings of the previous song are joined here by hard rock acoustic blues – Zeppelin or a touch of Jon Spencer Blues Explosion. There's a second Beck deep in the mix of this brief, dark yowl. The second edition cassette titled the track 'Sould Sucked Dry'.

'Feelings' 1:35

The title emotions aren't of the golden variety in this lighter acoustic track which, in retrospect, almost seems like a *Sea Change* parody.

'Gettin' Home' 4:15

Pretty, untarnished acoustic Delta blues, this is one of the few songs in which you can't hear Beck's tongue in his cheek. Although lacking their complexity lyrically or musically, it points toward more mature songs from *Mutations* onwards. Beck recorded multiple versions, most without the long guitar intro.

'Will I Be Ignored by the Lord?' 2:00

Gospel/blues acapella with some occasional tapping, this is a fairly serious, if not typically cryptic rhyming exercise – until the third verse when 'the flapjacks will flap back / Off the ceiling on to my head'.

'Bogus Soul' 1:14

The near-sanctimoniousness of the previous few tracks is quickly dissipated with the *in medias res* appearance of perhaps the most strained falsetto ever recorded. Chugging along like the 16th minute of a half-hour version of VU's 'Heroin', the lyrically distressed song also cuts out mid-thought.

'Totally Confused' 2:00

A slight, loping acoustic track that doesn't develop lyrically beyond its title. A marginally different version appears on demos, but the song would be reworked to greater effect on *A Western Harvest Field by Moonlight*.

'Mutherfuker' 2:16

Although it's common for fans to favor non-Geffen versions of songs for their perceived authenticity, here authenticity is good only as far as it goes, with the sludgy, compressed sound failing to match the manic dynamics of the *Mellow Gold* version.

'People Gettin' Busy' 2:34

A bass-heavy, multi-tracked vocal goof, this is the closest that Beck gets to the funk he'd start exploring in earnest on *Midnite Vultures* – it's fun.

Related Tracks
'To See That Woman of Mine' 2:22

Often discussed as Beck's first commercial release, it shares the A-side with the following song on a limited edition flipside 7" vinyl, with actor Steve Moramarco's band Bean holding down the B-side. Played straight, it's a driving folk rock song that bears more than a passing resemblance to 'Sweet Little Sixteen', among other Chuck Berry tunes.

'MTV Makes Me Want to Smoke Crack' 3:49

One of Beck's best early songs, it's a funny, upbeat acoustic folk song with harmonica. Beck shows off his more studied singing chops on the first verse before goofing on the rest of the tune. An earlier version on 1992's *Don't Get Bent Out of Shape* cassette is just as good – urgent and driving, sounding like a lost *Blonde on Blonde* outtake. The song also showed up in a 'Lounge Version' (3:29); the cocktail piano may be a nod to the Los Angeles' hip swinging bar scene of the early 1990s. The single version appeared on Geffen promo releases, while the 'Lounge' version was on the 'Loser' CD.

A Western Harvest Field by Moonlight (1994)

Personnel:
Beck Hansen: vocals, acoustic guitar, electric guitar, percussion, SK-1
Rachel Haden: drums, background vocals on 'Totally Confused'
Anna Waronker: background vocals on 'Totally Confused'
Petra Haden: violin, background vocals on 'Totally Confused'
Produced by: Beck Hansen, Tom Grimley
Recorded at: Poop Alley Studio and wherever Beck set up his four-track
US Release Date: January 1994
Label: Fingerpaint Records
Highest chart places: Did not chart
Running Time: 22:46

In a January 2002 *Record Collector* interview, Beck said he considered this his first proper release. It came about when the independent Fingerpaint label approached him to release an EP (while he was working on three LPs). He pulled together some songs he had lying around and spent two weeks recording them on his four-track and at Tom Grimley's Poop Alley Studio. The 10" EP was pressed multiple times. Each copy of the original 3,000 included a unique fingerpainting created by Beck and his friends at what he called 'one of those Fellini-esque all-night painting melees'. The spine is mislabeled 'A Western Harvest Moon by Moonlight' and the sides were named 'Bic' and 'Beek', both label executives mispronunciations of his name.

'Totally Confused' 3:23
A more mature reworking of the *Golden Feelings* song, this dispenses with audio gimmicks and effects, laying bare a beautiful, honest love song. The track is notable for the use of a full band – bassist Ann Waronker (daughter of Warner Bros. Record's president Lenny), drummer Rachel Haden, and, shining, violinist Petra Haden, all from the Los Angeles band that dog. This version wound up on 'Loser' and 'Beercan' maxi-singles and compilations.

'Mayonaise Salad' 1:08
Feedback and then a minute of pulsating electric rock with some vocal sounds. Not essential, but not totally forgettable.

'Gettin' Home' 1:56
Another *Golden Feelings* reworking, this Delta blues number highlights Beck's sweet fingerpicking.

'Blackfire Choked Our Death' 1:46
In an early career of offbeat recordings, this might be the most offbeat. Beck's voice is pitched high through effects (it doesn't sound like the tape

is sped up), made to sound like a girl singing and the apocalyptic lyrics eventually reveal that the singer has a husband. And then the catchy, grim Dust Bowl saga breaks character, with a 'snowman all in flames' and 'Black Sabbath playing' – just another day at the office for early 1990s Beck.

'Feel Like a Piece of Shit (Mind Control)' 1:27
The first of three versions of this tune, this one starts with 20 seconds of noise before hitting an electronic keyboard groove overlayed with distorted vocals.

'She Is All (Gimme Something to Eat)' 1:15
The continued 'piece of shit' lyrical motif opens this song, which morphs into a restrained acoustic guitar and drum track that features Beck on lead vocals and, presumably, background sound effects. The track ends with an Ozzy-like 'Oh yeah!'

'Pinefresh' 1:23
Opening the 'Beek' side, this acoustic instrumental doesn't build to the level of 'song'. Perhaps the air freshener was needed to clear the air of the shit motif of the previous two songs.

'Lampshade' 4:04
The track starts with an unidentifiable snippet from a female vocal group, then offers a slow, gentle, three-verse acoustic gem. The rueful lyrics are patented Beck, searching for an end rhyme that's on-the-nose sonically but a click off thematically. The song would find its way onto Geffen's *The History of Beck* cassette.

'Feel Like a Piece of Shit (Crossover Potential)' 1:34
The second of three versions, this sound collage opens with a (sampled?) cello and acoustic guitar with what sounds like a werewolf howl. This is followed by a faster, almost plaintive electronic keyboard groove with less distorted title vocals. The track closes with the question 'Are you my butterfly?', followed by a heavily modulated response.

'Mango (Vader Rocks!)' 2:49
Accompanied by acoustic guitar and atmospheric modulations, this is what happened when Darth Vader gets up the courage to present his sparse spoken word poetry at open mic night.

'Feel Like a Piece of Shit (Cheetos Time)' 0:58
The third version of the tune is more spacey and dance-like but even more slight.

'Styrofoam Chicken (Quality Time)' 0:01 / 2:24

Not a song as much as an electronic sound, infinitely repeated on the original 1994 10" through a locked groove, a technique best known for ending side two of The Beatles' *Sgt. Pepper's Lonely Hearts Club Band* (1967). Subsequent pressings curtailed the infinity groove into a more manageable yet still frenzy-inducing length.

Related Tracks

'Steve Threw Up' 3:35

The three members of that dog. once again accompany Beck on the A-side of this three-track Bong Load Records early 1994 follow-up to 'Loser'. A lilting acoustic number (until the explosive end), it's a kid-like litany of foods that Steve Moramarco (of the band Bean) hurled after a bad tab of acid. A different version of the song appears on *Fresh Meat + Old Slabs*, co-produced by Tom Grimley.

'Mutherfuker' 2:06

Same as on *Golden Feelings*.

'Untitled (Cupcake)' 0:47

Some distorted yelling about what the fuck is up over some wah-wah guitar. The lyric 'cocktail cupcakes on fire' probably tells you all you need to know about the song.

Stereopathetic Soulmanure (1994)

Personnel:
Beck: vocals, guitar, bass, harmonica
Anna Waronker: bass on 'Pink Noise (Rock Me Amadeus)'
Rachel Haden: drums on 'Pink Noise (Rock Me Amadeus)'
Lisa Dembling: drums on 'Rowboat' and 'Modesto'
Ken: vocals on 'Waitin' for A Train' and 'No Money No Honey'
Leo LeBlanc: pedal steel guitar on 'Rowboat', 'The Spirit Moves Me', and 'Modesto'
Dallas Don Burnette (as Dallas): drums on 'Thunder Peel', 'The Spirit Moves Me', 'Total Soul Future (Eat It)', 'Cut 1/2 Blues', 'Satan Gave Me A Taco', and 'Tasergun'; drumification on 'Ozzy'
Bobby Hecksher (as Bobby): guitar on 'Total Soul Future (Eat It)' and 'Cut 1/2 Blues'; co-bassplosion on 'Tasergun'
Thomas Hendrix: vocals on 'Dead Wild Cat'
Johnny Cashmachine: backing vocals on 'Satan Gave Me A Taco'
Produced by: Beck Hansen, Tom Grimley
Executive Producer: Gus Hudson
Recorded at: The Latona House, Poop Alley Studio, and Wire Works Studio, 1988-1993
US Release date: 22 February 1994
Record label: Flipside Records
Highest charting: Did not chart
Running time: 64:35

Stereopathetic Soulmanure pulls together tracks recorded over a six-year period in numerous locations. Unsurprisingly, it's a ragged collection, but one that's rewarded by multiple listenings, even if some tracks seem purposefully undone by Beck's aesthetic choices. The album was poorly reviewed at the time, overshadowed by the more conventional and accessible subsequent albums – unsurprisingly, it is excluded from Beck.com's discography. Despite all this, for many long-time fans, this is the quintessential Beck album, the perfect expression of the artist's unrestrained creativity.

'Pink Noise (Rock Me Amadeus)' 2:57
The festivities open with a low-end punk screecher featuring the rhythm section from that dog, Anna Waronker and Rachel Haden. The song includes two angry and disconnected verses with no chorus. The title? The Austrian singer Falco's hair is streaked pink in the video for his 1985 global number one 'Rock Me Amadeus' and this song is noisy – okay, it's a stretch.

'Rowboat' 3:45
Unshackled from a noise aesthetic and gliding on Leo LeBlanc's pedal steel guitar, 'Rowboat' delivers Beck as a legitimate American folk singer-songwriter. Less abstract than many other early songs – but still

impressionistic – it appears to tell the tale of the jilted storyteller (fantasizing about?) burning his lover's corpse over a body of water. The song opened *Unchained*, the second of six Rick Rubin-produced Johnny Cash American Recordings albums.

'Thunder Peel' 1:48
Is it about farting on a Ferris wheel? Salmonella poisoning? An excuse to use the phrase 'cold-ass fashion'? Who knows? Who cares? It's Beck and drummer Dallas ripping loud and proud, hypnotically grooving over four verses, before a climax in which Beck's falsetto approximates what most people sound like in the shower – it's pure joy. Beck re-recorded the song in 1995.

'Waitin' for a Train' (Jimmie Rodgers)1:09
Beck doesn't appear on this track. It opens with an amusing spoken-word 'alien sound bite' by Ross Harris from Steve Hanft's short film *Normal*. Harris would work more with Beck, but is perhaps best known as Joey, the young boy who mixes it up with Kareem Abdul-Jabbar and Peter Graves in 1980's *Airplane*! The song proper is a version of the Jimmie Rodgers classic, which has been recorded over 100 times. This incomplete, yodel-less version is by Ken, a hobo Beck met and recorded. Beck has performed the song live and recorded Rodgers' 'Peach Picking Time Down in Georgia' with Willie Nelson.

'The Spirit Moves Me' 2:10
Another appealing early LP song that doesn't quite feel complete. Backed by Dallas on drums, Beck on slide guitar and Leo LeBlanc on pedal steel, Beck meanders through a series of rhyming observations. Legally blind, LeBlanc was an in-demand session musician who died in 1995 at the age of 55. He played with John Prine, Mac Davis, and Carole King, among others. He was also in the California Poppy Singers. The group released a handful of albums in 1969, mostly covers of current hits. LeBlanc shone on a cover of The Beatles' 'Why Don't We Do It in the Road?', which features a very Beck-like falsetto out of the instrumental bridge.

'Crystal Clear (Beer)' 2:30
Beck returns to fingerpicking blues on this LP highlight. According to whiskeyclone.net, the 'better not let my good girl catch you here' echoes 'don't let my good girl catch you here', which appears in John Hurt's beautiful 1928 'Ain't No Tellin'', a traditional tune that Hurt would later record under the song's better-known title 'Make Me a Pallet on Your Floor'. Looking like a contestant in an Emo Phillips lookalike contest, Beck performed the song on MTV's *120 Minutes* in 1994. The appearance also included an airing of 'Pay No Mind (Snoozer)' and a noise jam with the Beastie Boys' Mike D. and Sonic Youth's Thurston Moore, variously titled '120 Minutes Jam' and 'Fuck Up Session #2'. DGC released the show as a promo VHS in March 1994.

'No Money No Honey' 2:13

Beck reprises this one-line, on-the-dole (or prostitute's refrain) mantra from *Golden Feelings*. This unadorned acoustic version is a duet with hobo Ken. The song opens with a snippet (recorded from a boombox speaker?) of UK techno duo B12's 'Hall of Mirrors' (1992). The song appeared on the 1993 WaxTrax! Records promo cassette sampler *Artificial Intelligence* along with Olivine's 'Close Up and Over', which intros 'Today Has Been a Fucked Up Day'.

'8.6.82' 0:37

The first of three sped-up, spoken word pieces on the album. These came about when Beck was recording fake diary entries into a tape recorder and accidentally sped up the playback, creating a kid's voice.

'Total Soul Future (Eat It)' 1:49

Backed by Dallas on drums and Bobby Hecksher on guitar, this sounds like an insomnia-induced outtake from the Rolling Stones' *Some Girls* sessions.

'One Foot in the Grave' 2:14

One of Beck's top-ten most performed songs and always a concert high-point, this live, acoustic foot-stomper features some blow-your-face-off harmonica. As in many early Beck folk-blues songs, the Devil shows up here and, as in many other early Beck songs, the encounter involves food, this time with Satan 'out of mayonnaise'. The studio version appears on 2009's *One Foot in The Grave* expanded edition while an intimate version (4:07), recorded on 9 August 1997, appeared on the 1997 CD *WBCN Naked Disc: A Collection of Unreleased Performances*. Another live version (2:38) showed up on the *Dear Life* Words + Music Amazon Audible in July 2022.

'Aphid Manure Heist' 1:30

The track begins with chamber music of unknown origin before heading into a lyrically misremembered, uncredited cover version of songwriter Bob McDill's 'Amanda'. The entire song is sped up, resulting in a country waltz reminiscent of tunes from Kurt Weill's *Threepenny Opera*. It's unclear who's singing, but a last second, normal speed, 'Amanda' sounds like Beck. Waylon Jennings had a US country number one with 'Amanda' in 1974, but Don Williams' 1974 original, with slight wah-wah and pedal steel, wouldn't feel out of place on this LP. The title doesn't have any apparent meaning but would have been a sufficiently poop-oriented alternate album name.

'Today Has Been a Fucked Up Day' 2:29

Rightfully claimed by biographer Julian Palacios as an unpretentious little morsel of a song, this is another uncredited, traditionally arranged folk song. With profane alterations, this banjo story recalls the sentiments of the Carter

Family's 'Sad and Lonesome Day' (1936), at least in the first two verses, and follows its melody (which also appears in Blind Lemon Jefferson's 'See That My Grave is Kept Clean' and multiple other adaptations). If someone got it in their head to stage a musical based on the first few Beck LPs, I'd nominate this song as the overture. It begins with a lo-fi sample from Olivine's 'Close Up and Over', which originally appeared on the Black Dog Productions techno collection *Bytes* (1993).

'Rollins Power Sauce' 2:07
A plodding, lo-fi take on the muscular musical stylings of Henry Rollins, without the attendant energy. Rollins made his name in the early 1980s as the lead singer of Los Angeles punk pioneers Black Flag. As the band wound down, Rollins pivoted to macho spoken-word performances and fronting his metal group Rollins. By the time of this song's release, the former outsider was as well known for his ripped body (Beck jokes here that 'my throat muscles are completely shredded'!) and outspoken cultural commentary as his music, garnering *Details* magazine's 1994 Man of the Year award.

'Puttin It Down' 2:22
Most of Beck's early material embodies both the charm and the pitfalls of haste, never failing to capture the authenticity of the moment, but often neglecting to completely develop promising ideas. That's why it's often both fun and frustrating. This fast-paced acoustic song ranks high on the fun/ frustrating chart. The lovelorn lyrics are clever and full of Beck rhyming, and he's using a wider 'serious' vocal range but, in this case, the urgent arrangement feels more convenient than necessary. A bit more effort and this is an all-time classic.

'11.6.45' 0:32
The second spoken word piece, this mentions enjoying MTV and Pac-Man in 1945, but that's about as far as it goes.

'Cut 1/2 Blues' 2:36
This ragged, walking blues tune feels a little too on point, like the work of a stand-up comedian trying to create a novelty song. Beck wrote the song in the late 1980s during his time in New York and his performance of the song at Jabberjaw in Los Angeles in the late summer of 1992 convinced Bong Load co-owner Tom Rothrock that he wanted to work with Beck.

'Jagermeister Pie' 1:10
The LP's only instrumental, this slender tune, appears to be played on an accordion or a melodica-like organ, such as a Magnus Chord Organ. An Edinburgh bakery made Jägermeister pies in the summer of 2020 – no word if the bakers were Beck fans.

'Ozzy' 2:06
A live song with Dallas on drums, 'Ozzy' is a goofy tribute to the Black Sabbath singer. It's a funny track, with Beck addressing Ozzy on a keychain with 'mascara bleeding out of (his) eyes'. Beck's 'can I get a little echo on this?' request on the repeated title refrain beat *Saturday Night Live*'s 'more cowbell' skit by eight years.

'Dead Wildcat' (Steve Hanft) 0:25
An inconsequential soundbite by Thomas Hendrix from Hanft's *Normal* about a beer and...a dead wildcat. Also appears as 'Dead Wild Cat'.

'Satan Gave Me a Taco' 3:46
A mishap-filled story-song in the tradition of 'Bob Dylan's 115th Dream', this is Peak Beck. The first half is a food misadventure, the result of a devil-delivered gone-bad taco. As a result of the bad taco, in the only non-rhyming couplet of the song's 19, the singer is sentenced to death before realizing that he's a singer in a music video ... who ends up opening a taco stand. It's all very meta. And catchy, quirky, and hilarious.

'8.4.82' 0:25
The third and final 'kid' voice spoken word piece, it's a truncated series of observations from a 'really bored' day.

'Tasergun' 3:51
This sludgy low-end number is the third trio song on the LP, with Dallas on drums and Hecksher on 'co-bassplosion'. A somewhat monotonous portrait of a taser-gun totting neighbor, it lacks the humorous observations of surrounding songs (aside from the guy's 'greasy bathrobe') and instead provokes an unnerving vibe – an odd fit on an album of odd fits.

'Modesto' 3:27
Not the final track but the LP's closing song, this is a melodic acoustic number about a relationship gone wrong. Beyond the food (Frito-Lays, meatloaf, supermarkets) and domestic paranoia, this one seems a bit more autobiographical with a reference to 'subway trains'.

'Ken' 0:12
Some parting words from the 'No Money No Honey' vocal star. You can hear Beck say 'Yeah' in the background.

'Bonus Noise' 16:40
The first five minutes of the track are silent, while the next 11:40 are a sound collage akin to The Beatles' 'Revolution 9', albeit with much less Yoko. The mix includes a backwards vocal song, typically called '(Bend Over) In the

Clover', random sounds fading in and out, and a vocal interlude with the upper range 'dumbfounded' vocal that shows up on 'Beercan'. If you tune out during the silent five minutes or get a CD that doesn't include this track, you're not missing much.

Mellow Gold (1994)

Personnel:
Beck: vocals, guitars, bass, harmonica, synthesizers, percussion
Karl Stephenson: sitar on 'Loser'
Mark Boito: organ on 'Beercan'
David Harte: drums on 'Nightmare Hippy Girl', 'Pay No Mind (Snoozer)', and 'Mutherfuker'
Rob Zabrecky: bass on 'Blackhole'
Petra Haden: violin on 'Blackhole'
DJ Smash: turntables on 'Loser'
Produced by: Beck Hansen, Tom Rothrock, Rob Schnapf, Karl Stephenson
Recorded at: Karl's House, Rob's House, and Beck's four-track
Release date: 1 March 1994
Record label: DGC / Bong Load
Highest charting places: UK: 41, US: 13
Running time: 45:31

Beck prepped songs for a Bong Load album from 1992 through the summer of 1993. The album was ready in August 1993, but once 'Loser' hit and major labels came calling, the release was delayed. Beck eventually signed with David Geffen Company, enticed by a deal that allowed non-Geffen releases. The album finally hit the streets in March 1994, accompanied by a promotional blitz that leaned heavily on Beck's independent and alternative roots, including an array of creative promo compilations.

The album was generally well received, although many critics were put off as much by the 'slacker' hype as what was perceived as his juvenile musical flourishes. Paul Moody in *New Musical Express* (six out of ten) said that 'At his best Beck refuses to be what you assume he must be (i.e. an acid-fried LA novelty) and stretches way beyond all the usual singer-songwriter clichés. Pat Martino (*Musician*) was dismissive, but thought enough of three songs to say, 'however offhandedly delivered, it's genuine artistic expression, of which one suspects there'll be more to come'. *Rolling Stone* dismissed the album in a fit of exasperated, condescending finger-wagging at 'kids these days', but *The Rolling Stone Album Guide* now gives the LP five stars.

Beck toured *Mellow Gold* through the end of the year, mostly in the US, but also hitting 18 countries in Europe, East Asia, and Australia. He continued touring in 1995, including dates on the fifth edition of Lollapalooza. The album produced three singles and went Gold in the UK and Platinum in the US: his best-selling LP in both countries, save *Odelay*.

'Loser' (Beck Hansen, Karl Stephenson) 3:55
The National Anthem of Beck. Even if he had only released this song, he'd still receive warm applause playing it on nostalgia package tours into the 2050s.

The song came to life in the fall of 1991. While chatting with Bong Load Records owner Tom Rothrock, who had previously raved about 'this self-contained folk artist', Beck mentioned he was interested in rap. Rothrock set up Beck to record with producer Karl Stephenson, who had had success with the nasty hip-hop group Geto Boys. Beck went to Stephenson's house, they ate pizza and Doritos, and Beck played him a catchy slide guitar riff. Stephenson added some sitar and a sample of Johnny Jenkins' version of Dr. John's 'I Walk on Gilded Splinters'. Beck tried to rap like Chuck D., but didn't succeed, perhaps being the worst rapper ever: a loser.

Beck played the song live in 1992 (find the online video *5 Nights Out*), but Bong Load didn't release the single until March 1993. The single took off, first as a regional hit in Los Angeles, where he played his first live radio show on the 23 July edition of KCRW's *Morning Becomes Eclectic*, then in Seattle, and then around the US. This led to a bidding war among the major labels, with Geffen/DGC finally getting Beck's signature in the late fall, about two years after the original recording. The DGC single hit US stores in February 1994.

Lyrically the song is a cascade of wild and unfortunate observations and incidents, best summed up in the self-deprecating couplet 'With the rerun shows and the cocaine nose job / The daytime crap of a folksinger slob'. Of course, the enduring refrain from the song is the song's enduring refrain: 'I'm a loser baby / so why don't you kill me'. This chorus caused Beck to be lauded and loathed as the voice of the so-called slacker generation. In response, he said, 'Slacker, my ass…I mean that slacker stuff is for people who have the time to be depressed about everything'. In addition to the Jenkins loop, the song includes a sample from director Steve Hanft's 1994 feature-length debut *Kill the Moonlight* – 'I'm a driver / I'm a winner / Things are gonna change / I can feel it'. Hanft would direct 'Loser' and five other videos for Beck.

Peaking at number ten, 'Loser' was Beck's only sniff of the US top 60. It was certified (non-mellow) Gold and was the first of three Beck number one alternative tracks. In the UK, it hit number 15, bested only by 'The New Pollution', and went Silver, his only UK-certified single. It was the number one single in the 1994 *Village Voice* Pazz & Jop critics' poll and routinely makes 'top rock songs of all time' lists.

The song was released with a total of seven different B-sides and additional songs. Beck self-released an early version as 'Kill Me (Loser)'. The song has been officially remixed a few times, including the 'Pseudo-Muzak Version' below, and unofficially dozens of times, including the 2009 'Loser Vs. My Name Is' mash-up with the Eminem hit on the DJ Hero video game. Beck has released live versions on multiple promo CDs and a 2018 Japanese *Colors* DVD. It remains a standard in his live setlist. Beck re-recorded the song (2:49), more open and vocal-centric, for the Amazon Audible *Dear Life* Words + Music audiobook (2022).

'Pay No Mind (Snoozer)' 3:15

The anthemic 'Loser' melds into this laidback acoustic number that features a tight harmonica solo. In a KCRW interview, Beck said he used to live in a shed and this is 'about being bored and sitting in the shed'. But it seems like it's about the music industry ('I just got signed') and it sure ain't a pleasant vision ('the toilets are overflowing'). An alternate version with a different verse appears on some editions of *Mellow Gold*, and the song appears on self-released cassettes. The song appeared as the second *Mellow Gold* single in the UK, paired with three *Golden Feelings* tracks – it failed to chart. A live studio version (2:38) was on *The History of Beck* from a KCRW performance and the song shows up as 'Got No Mind' on the 'Beercan' single. Sonic Youth covered the song as The Sonik-Youth on a 2009 double B-side single, with Beck returning the favor on the band's 'Green Light'.

'Fuckin' With My Head (Mountain Dew Rock)' 3:41

Offering vague observational couplets that lead to the title chorus, this song defies deep lyrical analysis. But it is deep with sound, featuring a pile of instrumentation, punctuated by an almost hidden but very melodic bass and occasional romps into ZZ Top's 'La Grange' territory. The clean version, '%*!@?# With My Head', sounds like someone hepped up on a six-pack of Mountain Dew accidentally kneeing the turntable. This contains a sample of 'Save the World' (1974) by Southside Movement, as does 'Sweet Sunshine'.

'Whiskeyclone, Hotel City 1997' 3:28

A haunting, atmospheric anti-folk song, it's memorable for Beck's fingerpicking and the faux-mannered 'She can talk to squirrels / Coming back from the convalescent home' spoken word interlude. The 'whiskeyclone' in the title continues Beck's tendency to create compound words that imply meaning, such as 'soulmanure' or 'ghettochip', but don't really rise to the level of a portmanteau in which they'd actually mean something.

'Soul Suckin' Jerk' (Beck Hansen, Karl Stephenson) 3:57

The second of three collaborations with Stephenson, Beck goes full-tilt *Paul's Boutique* production on this posturing martial anthem about a put-upon fast-food worker. Filled with food imagery (chicken, bacon and eggs, barbeque sauce), the narrative rates high in online 'work sucks / I hate my boss' song lists. It contains a sample of Billy Squier's 'The Big Beat'. An alternate version, 'Soul Suckin Jerk (Reject)', appears on the US 'Loser' maxi-single.

'Truckdrivin' Neighbors Downstairs (Yellow Sweat)' 2:55

Beck chronicled a few problematic acquaintances in early songs, but this best captures the mixture of incredulousness and helplessness one experiences with horrible neighbors. Opening with a brief glass-smashing argument, Beck's acoustic guitar lays a foundation for him to play the dozens one-sided in a series of humorous insults, calling his nemesis a 'whiskey-stained bucktoothed backwoods creep' and a 'grizzly bear motherfucker'. The 'clean version' is just awkward. A re-recorded 35-second version showed up in 2022 on *Dear Life*.

'Sweet Sunshine' (Beck Hansen, Karl Stephenson) 4:14
With a belted-out chorus not dissimilar to the previous song, 'Sweet Sunshine' would have been a highlight of earlier collections, but here it's rightfully hidden at the end of vinyl side one. The first three minutes are a monotonous slog of bass and vocals, while the final minute shines with some guitar soloing. The cheery title stands in opposition to the lyrics, which read like the end of one bad trip and the start of the next. As with 'Fuckin with My Head', it contains a sample of 'Save the World' by Southside Movement.

'Beercan' (Beck Hansen, Karl Stephenson) 4:00
The album's second US single, 'Beercan', flips the perceived self-defeatism of 'Loser', replacing it with a confident (if boozy) party song that encourages you to 'just shake your boots and let it all get loose'. Centered by slinky bass and spicy percussion, the tune is bouncy and infectious, with a memorable organ break and an essential appearance from Beck's old-man voice ('Oh, my goodness'!). The track went Top 30 in the US Alternative charts. The song includes screeching guitar from The Melvins' 'Hog Leg' and the vocal sample, 'I'm sad and unhappy', is pulled from 'I Feel So Alone', which appears on The Care Bears LP *Adventures in Care-A-Lot*. The CD single featured four non-LP tracks.

'Steal My Body Home' 5:34
Although conceived much earlier, the longest song on the LP seems like a companion to 'Sweet Sunshine'. In both tracks, much of the song is a monotone drone, with the gnawing distortion replaced here by a gentler hum and a contemplative Eastern/Indian vibe. As with the mood-breaking close-out guitar in the earlier song, this song takes a left turn with a kazoo, sitar, and anvil(?) percussion: we're suddenly in the middle of a Mummers Parade. Lyrically the song is a series of disheartening observations, with each verse a rhyming couplet concluded by a non-rhyming final line, giving it the feel of a formal experiment.

'Nitemare Hippy Girl' 2:55
This is a lyrical highlight of Beck's early career. It's a poignant and witty portrait that nails both a common post-1960s character type and the moment in a doomed relationship – or even a brief encounter – when all those character traits that seem so appealing on first glance don't hold up to closer inspection. The first half of the song has two verses and two choruses; the two verses catalog the broken dream of the relationship – 'disappointment'

and 'letdown' – while the choruses describe the girl's qualities ('beauty', 'moody', and 'snooty'). The song kicks in with the second half, with 16 paradigmatic lines further describing the hippy girl. Echoing the 'she's a nightmare hippy girl' of the chorus, the lines begin with 'She's...', and variously offer 'got a thousand lonely husbands', 'a witness to her own story', and most memorably 'got tofu the size of Texas'. The technique of repeating initial words is called anaphora, used to devasting effect in Bob Dylan's 'A Hard Rain's A-Gonna Fall'. Like the Dylan anthem, the folk instrumentation here is incidental: acoustic guitar, David Harte's drums, and some oohing background vocals.

'Mutherfuker' 2:04

Pulsating with a fat and fuzzy bass, mocking falsetto, and a breakdown with a pile of random vocals, this is an empowering two-minute piece of noise punk. Another golden non-mellow slice of life, the exasperated singer taunts 'Mr. Asshole' (a boss? A drug dealer?) with the line 'everyone's out to get you, motherfucker!' It's fast, and fun, and the chorus is easy to remember. The earlier 'Mutherfukka' from *Golden Feelings* is more tame and tentative, whilst the clean version, '&*$^?#%*@#', is absurd.

'Blackhole' 5:14 (listed as 7:33)

Beck throws two curveballs at the end of *Mellow Gold*, both in the same track. The first is this disarmingly beautiful song that reads like the most precarious lullaby ever. In an album full of character portraits, it feels like Beck has reflected inward for this final song. Rob Zabrecky of Possum Dixon features on bass, alongside violinist Petra Haden. It's both a consolidation of early strengths and a view of the future. A new, abbreviated studio version (1:08) arrived on the *Dear Life* Words + Music release.

'Analog Odyssey' (1:45)

After about 30 seconds of silence, this uncredited track appears: an orgy of synth knob-twisting. It's also known as 'Bonus Noise'. It's non-essential and here either as a link with the 'include everything' ethos of the contemporaneous independent albums, or an attempt by a maturing artist trying to keep his street cred. Ultimately, it provides closure.

Related Tracks
'Corvette Bummer' 4:55

This is a live-feel, hip-hop track with talking-rap verses similar to 'Loser'. The choruses about what he's 'gonna' do contrast with a memorable melody. At least until a high-pitched silly voice comes out and he eventually breaks down laughing with 'Gonna get my walkie-talkie and some mustard and some mayonnaise / And a mermaid and some macaroni, bricks, and some telephone wires'. It's hard not to smile at the absurdity, or that Chevrolet used the song in their 2019 reveal of the 2020 Corvette Stingray. It appears on the US (recorded in '1996') and UK (recorded in '1997') 'Loser' maxi-singles and a ten-track 'clean' *Mellow Gold* promo CD for US in-store play, replacing the naughty titles.

'Alcohol' 3:51

The first two-and-a-half minutes is a simple acoustic number about the title subject, with a slightly double-tracked Beck vocal. The last 80 seconds feature heavy percussion with what sounds like guitar or vocals heavily distorted through a foot pedal. It was the vinyl B-side of 'Loser' and appeared on maxi-singles, falsely credited as recorded in 1988.

'Soul Suckin Jerk' (Reject) 6:10

For the first few minutes, this sparser, free-flow groove sounds like the LP original on quaaludes, then it opens up into a bass, organ, and sax jam that wouldn't be out of place during live revues of the late 1990s. On the 'Loser' maxi-singles recorded in '19666'.

'Fume' 4:28

'Fume' is two songs for the price of one. The first two minutes showcase Beck's adaptation of a true story he encountered about some kids who died after letting off some nitrous in their non-ventilated truck cab. This tragic story leads to a loose, rocking, first-person story about 'smokin' broken pencils and beating up kids'. The song ends and then there's a break with mostly unintelligible conversation. The music resumes, loud and angry, sounding like nothing so much as Beck's response to Nirvana and grunge, as the chorus 'There's a fume in this truck! / And I don't know if we're dead or what the fuck'! is yelled repeatedly. Two earlier versions of the song are in circulation. On the 'Loser' maxi-singles recorded in '19666'.

'Got No Mind' 4:22

A semi-rocking, band version of 'Pay No Mind', punctuated by a subdued exhortation to 'pump up the volume!' On the 'Beercan' maxi-single.

'Asskiss Powergrudge' (Payback! '94) 3:06

Not a big payback, but 'just a little grudge', with a gangsta-sounding Beck fronting new jack style, without the swing. The staccato acoustic strumming, which sounds like a plucked violin, and shotgun drums quickly wear out their welcome and eventually break down into cacophony. On the 'Beercan' maxi-single.

'Spanking Room' 5:21

A truly odd track: akin to the second part of 'Fume', this starts out as a melodic, balls-out grunge tribute. About two minutes in, it morphs into slow, distorted, dinosaur metal with a barely audible Beck repeating the phrase, 'Tell your parents and your teacher when something strange happens to you'. After about 20 seconds, the next, untracked song starts. On the 'Beercan' maxi-single.

'Loser (Pseudo-Muzak Version)' 3:26
This sounds like a live recording, with the muffled performance taking place in a locked room down the hall and up a flight of stairs. The guitar occasionally happens upon 'Loser' riffs over a drum click track, but the most notable melody is a synth picking out the African-American folk song 'Shortenin' Bread', most famously recorded in 1938 by the Andrews Sisters and most interestingly by the Beach Boys in 1979 – an unexpected treat. On the 'Beercan' maxi-single.

'In a Cold Ass Fashion' (Beck Hansen, Karl Stephenson)
Sitar, banjo, a tuneful bass, and Beck rapping some typically elliptical lyrics ('I'm trying not to look at Satan making love to a dishrag'): a perfect song. This slick tune with lyrical and musical similarities to 'Corvette Bummer' and 'Loser', would have been at home on the latter's B-side, but it showed up in the US in 1994 on Mammoth Records' *Jabberjaw: Good To The Last Drop* compilation LP, the promo disc, *Mammoth Educational Series Fall 1994 – Elements Of Mammoth*, and as a 7" B-side to Hole's 'Rock Star (Alternate Version)'. In the UK, it was on the electronica/trip-hop compilation *110 Below :: Trip To The Chip Shop Vol. 2*. And what's 'cold ass fashion?' We find out that 'It's like 45 horses running through the graveyard with yellow panties'.

'Bogusflow' 3:09
On more than one online publication's list of top-ten Beck songs, this acoustic talking blues is a swipe at the burgeoning alternative music scene, citing 'people with cordless personalities' and the 'California white boy sound'. This song appeared on the compilation *DGC Rarities: Vol.1*, with Beck offering the abstruse liner notes: 'Pulling up roots...again. Stranded in the decaying harbor. Surfing in the oil spillage'. Labelmates Nirvana ('Pay to Play') and Sonic Youth ('Compilation Blues') also took the opportunity to stick it to The Man with their tracks. A live-in-studio version (3:22) appears on the promo cassette *Live on KCRW's 'Morning Becomes Eclectic' with Chris Douridas*, along with the next four tracks and 'It's All in Your Mind' (see *One Foot in the Grave* chapter).

'Dead Man with No Heart' 2:10
Accompanied by Chris Ballew, this minor banjo run-through from KCRW mixes roots tropes (dead men missing body parts) with contemporary conveniences (helicopters and cash machines). Beck tries out a Dylan circa *Freewheelin'* accent.

'Hard to Compete' 3:01

With Ballew on bass and Beck picking an acoustic guitar, this sounds like an early aural stab at a Nick Drake vibe. Lyrically it's muted, early Beck ('And their eyes / And their gasoline hormones / Accessories accessorizing'). With some tweaks, it could fit on *Sea Change*.

'Howling Wolves (Bon Jovi in a Vacuum Cleaner)' (Beck Hansen, Chris Ballew) 3:02

A tape of this noise-jam Beck/Ballew side project was played over the radio during the KCRW session. It features difficult-to-distinguish vocals of hollowly portentous lyrics ('Severing the ties of God / covering their souls with masking tape'). It's perhaps best described by its lyrics: 'Lackadaisical/ fermented/elastic/comatose'.

'It's All Gonna Come to Be' 4:34

Aired on KCRW the day *Mellow Gold* was released, Beck dons acoustic guitar and harmonica to air his concerns about the major-label music industry, with fears of 'The same bad video for twenty years' and becoming an 'Optimistic Xerox of yourself'. Ballew joins the festivities as a 'Cyborg'.

'Death is Coming to Get Me' 2:21

This acoustic, talking folk song, conjures a mischievous Grim Reaper ('He's laughing at your diary / He's puking on your suits / He's dancing on your forehead in your hiking boots') who's ultimately the result of too much time on Beck's hands: 'And this is the kind of stupid song / You write when you're unemployed'. Also known as 'Death is Coming to Get You', this was recorded live at KCRW 23 July 1993. It appears on the US promo-only cassette *The History of Beck – A Selection of His Non-DGC Work*.

'Whimsical Actress' 2:48

This creaky falsetto lark traffics in the mock importance upon which Tenacious D would build a career. Lyrically, the song's an exercise in rhyming, with 'In the courtyard / There was a large cube of lard' a favorite. Same recording and release information as previous song.

'Bedroom Light' (Thurston Moore, Beck Hansen, Chris Ballew) 7:22
'Super Christ' (Thurston Moore, Beck Hansen, Chris Ballew) 2:12
'Super Funky' (Thurston Moore, Beck Hansen, Chris Ballew) 9:54

These three noise jams come from a rare Geffen US promo cassette, *Thurston/Beck KXLU*, released in March 2004. It captures the chaotic 3 March 1994 in-studio show at Loyola Marymount's radio station, KXLU. A stark contrast with the Beck-produced Moore LP *Demolished Thoughts* (2011)

'Mexico' 5:10

This is a well-realized story song in the style of 'The Times They Are A-Changin'' that tells the tale of a fed-up McDonald's employee who starts robbing fast food stores before everything goes all wrong – or all right, depending on your point of view. Also known as 'Ballad of Mexico', it appeared on a *Mellow Gold* double-disc Australian tour sampler in 1994 and on the US promo tape *The History of Beck*. A live-in-studio version recorded on 23 July 1993 appeared on KCRW's 1994 compilation *Rare on Air: Live Performances Volume 1* on Mammoth Records.

'Whisky-Faced Radioactive Blowdryin' Lady' 1:50

Recorded in-studio on 13 September 1993 at college radio station KXLU, Beck introduced this as 'a stupid song I wrote today'. Standard guitar-and-vocals, it's as serious as lines such as 'You can sauté my dollar bills and feed 'em to the dog while he's watching cable'. It was released in 1995 on the compilation *KXLU Live Vol. 1*.

Mr. Hansen 'Glut' 3:18

This rarity was officially released in 1995 as 'Mr. Hansen' on the B-side of *We Are Bacteria*, a 100-copy limited edition 7" single from the Honey Bear (Records) Fan Club's first singles club. The A-side features Beck tour guitarist Lance Hahn's band J Church and two tracks from London's The Phantom Pregnancies. No producer is listed, but the production here is clean and slick – Beck's most atypical, traditional pop-rock song of the early years. Joey Waronker plays drums.

Mr. Hansen 'Untitled' 2:49

The other Mr. Hansen B-side is another slick exercise in mid-1990s melodic alternative rock a la the Pixies. These two songs are so unusual for the period it seems like he may have recorded them to convince someone of his conventional songwriting skills and/or his production abilities.

Caspar and Mollüsk 'Twig' (Chris Ballew, Beck Hansen) 4:22

The A-side of the only Caspar and Mollüsk single, this 1994 track came together when guitarist Chris Ballew (Caspar) and Beck (Mollüsk) were living together prior to the *Mellow Gold* tour. Beck's un-Barry White-like monologue about his 'twig' frames Ballew's song, which was re-recorded to better effect for the Presidents of the United States of America's second album. The Cosmic Records ad sheet for the release identified it as 'ultra-rare recordings' from Ballew 'and his 'Loser' friend'.

One Foot in the Grave (1994)

Personnel:
Beck: vocals (sing), guitar, drums, bass
Chris Ballew: guitar, bass
James Bertram: bass
Sam Jayne: vocals (sing)
Calvin Johnson: vocals (sing)
Scott Plouf: drums
Mario Prietto: bongos
Produced by: Beck, Calvin Johnson
Recorded at: Dub Narcotic Studio, Olympia, Washington, October 1993 and January 1994
US Release date: 27 June 1994
Label: K Records
Highest chart places: Did not chart
Running time: 37:05

Beck met super-hip K Records head Calvin Johnson, leader of super-hip Beat Happening, in the super-hip indie music center of Los Angeles, and the two wanted to work together. Beck traveled to Johnson's Olympia, Washington, Dub Narcotic Studio (aka Johnson's basement) in October 1993 and January 1994 and recorded a bunch of songs that ended up as the 16 songs for the 1994 *One Foot in the Grave* release, the three-track 1995 'It's All In Your Mind' single, and the dozen tracks that would pad out the 2009 LP expanded edition.

At this point, Beck didn't have a steady backing band. For this mostly folky outing, he relied on members of enduring indie darlings Built to Spill (Bertram, Plouf), Sam Jayne from the defunct Love as Laughter, and his early guitarist/wingman Chris Ballew, lead singer of The Presidents of the United States of America.

The album was well received upon release, with many reviewers preferring Beck in what they considered a serious, dramatic role rather than a *Mellow Gold* comedic turn. David Browne (*Entertainment Weekly*) gave the album a B+, calling it 'a genial throwaway — both a loving tribute to, and a gentle mocking of, various folk musics'. Richard Cromelin (*Los Angeles Times*) gave three of four stars, calling the songs 'modestly engaging, minimalist tunes and a couple of experimental squalls'. Reissue reviews generally gave little consideration to the 'new' tracks, although those that did, such as *Uncut*, were unkind, offering two of five stars with little explanation.

The album was released on K Records as part of a then-unique deal with Geffen that allowed Beck to release independent material. In practical terms, this arrangement didn't render much in the way of 'independent' releases (the K Records follow-up never materialized) but did eventually result in lawsuits.

The album had no singles and didn't chart, although, with the expanded edition considered, it's estimated to have sold over one-quarter million copies.

'He's a Mighty Good Leader' (Skip James / traditional) 2:41
Marked by gentle foot tapping and acoustic fingerpicking, the subdued opening track is an adaptation of the traditional tune 'Jesus is a Mighty Good Leader'. The song is generally attributed to Delta Blues master Skip James, a major influence on Beck's acoustic tendencies. Beck would later record James' 'Devil Got My Woman' and 'I'm So Glad'.

'Sleeping Bag' 2:15
Always on the edge of falling apart, this airy, lo-fi band song tells a tale of being on the edge of falling apart. Beck's on-the-roam childhood often found him settling down for the night in a sleeping bag.

'I Get Lonesome' 2:49
Accompanied by lilting drums and acoustic guitar, this is an out-of-phase duet by baritone Beck and bass Calvin Johnson. The vocal discordance combined with lyrics of isolation makes this feel like a disavowed sea shanty.

'Burnt Orange Peel' 1:38
Not quite a TV party, but rather a punkish, bass-fuzz hootenanny that would have been at home on expansive mid-1980s SST Records by Hüsker Dü (*Zen Arcade*) and minutemen (*Double Nickels on the Dime*). It's not a song about nothing – but it's not about anything, either.

'Cyanide Breath Mint' 1:37
This restrained song uncannily captures being trapped in a bad decision. In the opening, Beck realizes it's 'the wrong place to be', with 'blood on the futon' and a 'kid drinking fire'. The wrong physical place later shifts to a professional place, when Beck bemoans the 'positive people' in the entertainment industry who want to 'suck your mind'. Accompanied by acoustic guitar, Beck's vocal range is narrow here, but there's presence in the performance that adds a layer of haunting authenticity here. The song meant enough to Beck that he named his publishing company Cyanide Breathmint Music. At a September 2021 LA performance, Beck tagged the song as 'protest music from the '90s, when we had nothing to protest'.

'See Water' 2:22
Played at a grave tempo and punctuated by a melodic bass and loose drumming, the proceedings here almost shift into neutral, foreshadowing the pace of future 'serious' efforts *Sea Change* and *Morning Phase*. Unlike other early portentous tunes, the unhappy imagining of the aquatic first verse isn't

offset with a lyrical turn that lightens the mood. Rather, the second verse grows more obscure, but still ends in the observation that 'no one's gonna miss you' – a rare, early, straight-out sad song.

'Ziplock Bag' 1:44

Loud, distorted, and pushing the limits of tunefulness, this sounds like a 1960s blues power trio not quite getting the song back together after the 15-minute drum solo. Beck yells the song's four lines and plays some mean harmonica – but otherwise insignificant.

'Hollow Log' 1:54

Beck returns to acoustic fingerpicking on this blues song that captures the 'do what you want – I don't care' pain of unfulfilled love. The song appears on multiple self-produced cassettes. While Beck traffics in the 'hollow log' blues trope here, and in 'Soul of a Man' from *Modern Guilt*, beyond picking style, there is no direct connection between this song and 'Hollow Log Blues' by almost-mythic Mississippi Delta bluesman Robert Petway.

'Forcefield' (Beck Hansen, Sam Jayne) 3:30

Opening vinyl side B, 'Forcefield' is the longest and most weighty song on the LP. With slight accompaniment, it features Beck on lead vocals, accompanied by Sam Jayne. The Beck part is about not being pulled into bad decisions that 'turn you into the things you hate the most', while in Jayne's co-equal part, the forcefield has already pulled him in because of 'the stance I took on that' – but what is 'that'? According to Wiskeyclone.net, Beck has claimed that there is no story behind the song. That being said, it must be mentioned that force fields are mentioned in a negative light in L. Ron Hubbard's 1952 publication *Scientology 8-80*: 'A heavy force field can utterly nullify the entire personalness of a being'. For all this, one wishes the song had been a bit more fully realized: tighter production and, for the period, maybe the addition of Petra Haden on violin. Still, as is, in 2019, *Slant* magazine counted it among the top 25 Beck songs, calling it the centerpiece of the album.

'Fourteen Rivers Fourteen Floods' 2:54

It's not hard to imagine Beck sitting on the banks of the Mississippi, paddleboat in the background, grinding out this song. It's his take on the traditional blues song 'You Got to Move', first put to record by The Willing Four in 1944 and most famously set to vinyl by The Rolling Stones. As with the *Sticky Fingers* track, Beck's version strains to hold together, compelling and weary simultaneously. And it's in that tension, along with the mythic title and the shifting point of view, that the song takes its place among his greatest blues tracks. Beck would re-record the track as a choral experiment (2:41) in 2017 for *The American Epic Sessions* documentary film.

'Asshole' 2:32
A soft, two-verse acoustic number, the highlight here is Beck's beautiful multi-tracked harmonies, in particular on the thrice-repeated 'she'll do anything' refrain that builds to the big reveal: 'to make you feel like an asshole'. While the song includes typical left-turn lines ('the cigarettes were smoking by themselves'), the tale of being humiliated by a girlfriend finds Beck more clearly in pop-artist angst territory than other early relationship songs. A live version recorded on 16 June 1996 at San Francisco's Golden Gate Park appears on the 1997 double-CD collection *Tibetan Freedom Concert*. Tom Petty and the Heartbreakers released the song on 1996's *Songs and Music from 'She's the One'*, although the performance did not feature in Edward Burns' film.

'I've Seen the Land Beyond' 1:41
This sounds and feels so much like a traditional folk gospel song, or something written for the Coen Brothers' *O Brother Where Art Thou?*, that it's hard to believe it's a Beck original. Quick, with Beck's double-tracked vocals, it's a dispiriting vision of the afterlife, where 'the lord is strange and strong' and 'the gravestones never cease'.

'Outcome' 2:10
Buoyed by a smooth slide guitar and a bouncy bass, this Beck/Sam Jayne duet grooves like a Presidents of the United States of America outtake, although it's unclear if Beck or Ballew is on guitar. There are many nouns here that pop up in other Beck lyrics ('static', 'pistols', and a 'fly'). As with many songs on this collection, this one's about disappointment: 'Outcome is different than I expected'.

'Girl Dreams' (The Carter Family, Beck Hansen) 2:04
This solo acoustic song is a slowed-down lyrical adaptation of The Carter Family's 'Lover's Lane' (1937). Once again, romantic frustration is the order of the day as 'it seems my dreams never come true'. Backed by that dog., the teetering tune threatens to break out into 'Totally Confused' at any moment. Beck recorded a superior version of the song as 'Girl of my Dreams' (3:12) for 1995's *The Poop Alley Tapes: A Compilation Of 31 Los Angeles Bands*, and recorded The Carter Family's 'The World May Loose Its Motion' at the same 1994 session (see below).

'Painted Eyelids' 3:06
In a 2021 *Rolling Stone* interview, Tom Petty and the Heartbreakers keyboardist Benmont Tench remarked that 'Beck has such an amazing harmonic sense'. Beyond the hummable stanza melody, which recalls 1967 Ray Davies, the one-click-off duet between Beck and Sam Jayne on this unheralded gem is proof positive of this truth. Lyrically, it's one of Beck's most

directly dystopian love songs, finding comfort in a relationship while living in a world in which 'there's a police siren singing like a tiger with no skin'.

'Atmospheric Conditions' (Beck Hansen, Calvin Johnson) 2:10
The LP closes with its oddest track, another Beck-high / Johnson-low vocal duet. Although there's a deceptive musical hopefulness grounded in Ballew's slunky electric guitar, Johnson's opening lines – 'There's nobody, there's no mountain, there's no tunnel / You can't get from there to here, you can't get from here to there' – synthesize the album's main theme of romantic disappointment almost as a direct rejoinder to the bursting-out optimism of Marvin Gaye and Tammi Terrell's 'Ain't No Mountain High Enough'. The song's an earworm if you don't watch out.

Related Tracks
All but the last track are outtakes from the *One Foot in the Grave* sessions and appear on the 2009 Expanded Edition. The first three tracks were released on the 'It's All in Your Mind' single in 1995 and appeared on a Japan-only *One Foot* release in 1996.

'It´s All in Your Mind' 2:54
This yearning song about a missed chance 'to be your good friend' is simple: acoustic-and-vocals with the melody repeated as a fingerpicking guitar solo coda. The single A-side was part of K Records' International Pop Underground 7" single series. A 1 March 1994 recording (2:35) appeared on the promo cassette *Live on KCRW'S 'Morning Becomes Eclectic' With Chris Douridas*, featuring Ballew on his custom-made bassitar. A live, solo acoustic version recorded 28 October 1995 at Neil Young's annual Bridge Benefit concert, appeared in 1997 on *The Bridge School Concerts Vol. One*. Beck re-recorded the song for 2002's *Sea Change*.

'Feather in Your Cap' 1:13
With jangly acoustic and near-amelodic vocals, this feels like either a brief inventory of lines to use in other songs or one of the worst internal pep talks ever. Beck would re-record a fleshed-out version of this vinyl B-side in late 1994, the result released during the *Odelay* era.

'Whiskey Can Can' (Beck Hansen, Calvin Johnson) 2:12
A three-piece band song (Bertram and Plouf, but no Johnson), the highlight here is Beck's Byrds-like electric guitar.

'Mattress' 2:31
This is a fun, upbeat folk song about sexual yearning ('your body on the mattress') that would be at home on the Violent Femmes debut LP. No direct connection but it includes the lyrics 'I'm a loser'.

'Woe on Me' 3:10

Sounding like early Donovan, this fully realized three-verse, rambling folk song is an acoustic delight. On a 6 January 1995 KCRW *Morning Becomes Eclectic* appearance, Beck played the song and discussed it as being about a character from 'about a hundred years ago'. This song's wandering narrator mentions 'fourteen rivers', so it's possible it shares a mythic origin with 'Fourteen Rivers Fourteen Floods'. The song is also known as 'Feel the Strain of Sorrow Never Ceasing'. Along with 'Sweet Satan', the track (As 'Woe unto Me') was released as a 7" B-side to Grandaddy's 'John Deere' as part of a 2015 *Monster Children* magazine box set assembled by actor Jason Lee.

'Teenage Wastebasket' 2:28 (electric) and 1:27 (acoustic)

With a title echoing the chorus of The Who's 'Baba O'Riley', this appears here in a demo-like acoustic and a solo electric version with an additional verse. Although it's got the expected folk roots, musically, the song is more 1960s pop-inflected, with almost doo-wop vocal interludes. Lyrically, it's a not-so-radio-friendly song about a girl whose 'Life is a commercial for being fucked up', edging it into 'Nightmare Hippy Girl' territory. There's a 1993 video online of Beck performing the song in a driveway.

'Your Love is Weird' 2:27

As with several expanded edition tracks, this feels like Beck test-driving a different genre. The vampy pop verses, mostly four-line rhymes, contrast and buoy the repetitive chorus. Beck had self-released earlier versions, but the song reached its dramatic potential at an Olympia, Washington KAOS radio session on 26 January 1994. He's backed by that dog. on bass, drums, and kazoo.

'Favorite Nerve' 2:05

A slow, abrasive electric grind, this is Beck at Peak Grunge, especially evident in the whispered/sung call-and-response chorus lines: 'Rise you up (tell me your story) / Make it all up (I'll be the judge)'. Everything except the lyrics is the same as the unreleased song 'Make It Up'.

'Piss on the Door'2:05

Channeling the Legendary Stardust Cowboy, Mojo Nixon, and a touch of VU, Beck lets his psychobilly flag fly on this way-out tune that channels food (pickles, pies, donuts, tea, chicken, soda) and flat-out energy. The electric guitar burst at the end is worth the price of admission. The lyrics 'Out on the highway / I'm doing it my way' resurfaced in 'Electric Music and the Summer People'.

'Close to God' (Beck Hansen, Calvin Johnson) 2:28

Beck and Calvin Johnson go old-school punk, channeling the slower, ominous side of the 1969/1970 Stooges. While Beck on drums and vocals isn't exactly a ringer for Iggy, Johnson's electric guitar wah-wah stylings clearly echo the work of Ron Asheton. Recorded on 28 October 1993, the song first appeared on the 1998 K Records compilation *Selector Dub Narcotic*, a collection of songs recorded at Johnson's studio. The *One Foot* expanded edition removes some of Beck's highly distorted vocals.

'Sweet Satan' 1:45
Just acapella vocals and foot-stomping, this brief run-in with an evil 'band of brothers' ends up in another meeting with Satan, although the imagery isn't as amusingly vivid as in other songs. It seems like a companion piece to 'Fourteen River Fourteen Floods' and 'Woe on Me' and appeared with the latter song as the second B-side on the 2015 *Monster Children* single.

'Burning Boyfriend' 1:12
Simple acoustic guitar and vocals about 'this guy who wanted to kick my… ass', Beck sings as the boyfriend in the first verse and the boyfriend's tormentor in the second. The song first showed up as 'Beck Will Die', in which it's clearer that the narrator is talking to the girlfriend, on the 1994 KAOS radio broadcast. It was called 'Axe Ex' in initial *One Foot* expanded press materials.

'Black Lake Morning' (Beck Hansen, Sam Jayne, James Bertram) 2:25
A New Age-like instrumental, Beck and Jayne duet on acoustic guitars and Bertram joins on a rumbly, resonant bass.

'One Foot in the Grave' 3:18
An energetic, studio version of the crowd-pleasing foot-stomper, first released in a live version on *Stereopathetic Soulmanure*. Some mean harmonica playing here.

'I Get Lonesome' 1:56
An acoustic version of the LP original. Here, less of a duet and more Beck with Johnson on backing vocals.

'The World May Loose its Motion' (A.P. Carter, Beck) 3:10
Backed by that dog., this is the second Carter Family tune recorded during the June 1994 Poop Alley sessions, a rewrite of the 1928 hit 'The Storms Are on The Ocean'. An unbalanced mix with heavy vocals marks the sauntering gospel tune. The song appeared on the 1994 compilation album *Periscope: Another Yo Yo Compilation*.

Odelay (1996)

Personnel:

Beck Hansen: vocals, electric guitar, slide guitar, acoustic guitar, bass guitar, organ, Clavinet, electric piano, Moog synthesizer, harmonica, drums, percussion, thumb piano, rhumba box, xylophone, turntables, echoplex

The Dust Brothers: turntables, drum machine

Joey Waronker: drums, percussion, chimes

Mike Millius: scream

Mike Boito: organ, Clavinet, trumpet

David Brown: saxophone

Money Mark: organ

Greg Leisz: pedal steel guitar

Charlie Haden: upright bass

Ross Harris: The Enchanting Wizard of Rhythm

Produced by: Beck Hansen, The Dust Brothers (John King, Michael Simpson); Beck Hansen, Mario Caldato Jr., Brian Paulson ('Minus'); Beck Hansen, Tom Rothrock. Rob Schnapf ('Ramshackle'); Beck Hansen, The Dust Brothers, Jon Spencer ('Diskobox')

Recorded at PCP Labs, G-Son Studios, Conway Studios, The Shop, Sunset Sound Studios

Release date: 18 June 1996

Label: DGC / Bong Load

Highest chart places: UK: 17, US: 16

Running time: 54:13

Beck began work on a *Mellow Gold* follow-up in early 1994. Recording spread over two years as Beck dealt with fame, touring, and tinkering with his sound. He started with *Mellow Gold* producers Tom Rothrock and Rob Schnapf, writing more acoustic-type songs such as 'Cancelled Check'. He soon decided to think about the next LP 'as a sound project and not as a performative thing'. Translation: back to the drawing board. The next drawing board was Beastie Boys engineer/producer Mario Caldato Jr. This collaboration produced 'Minus' and a few bonus tracks, but Beck said, 'that stuff wasn't really turning me on'. Finally, Beck turned to The Dust Brothers, DJs John King and Mike Simpson, the production masterminds behind the Beasties' landmark *Paul's Boutique*. Beck worked with the duo before and after the 1995 Lollapalooza festival and another landmark LP was born: *Odelay*.

The title comes from the engineer's mishearing of the Los Angeles-Spanish word 'orale', the original name of 'Lord Only Knows'. The engineer heard the word, which sort-of translates as 'Ok! or 'Right on!', as 'odelay' and Beck, in readymade mode, embraced the error. Reflecting the place-based vibes of the title, in a 2019 *New Yorker* interview, Beck described the LP as 'me trying to Fellini the neighborhood where I grew up'.

The album was extremely well-received at the time. *Rolling Stone* jumped on the bandwagon with Mark Kemp's review: '*Odelay* takes Beck's kitchen-sink approach to new extremes while also managing to remain a seamless whole; the songs flow together with intelligence and grace'. Keith Cameron writing in *New Music Express* (eight out of ten) claimed that 'Genius means never having to think too hard'. Among the negative reviews, David Stubbs' in *Melody Maker* still stands out: 'It might be that I'm missing something here, but to me this lo-fi, facetious, arbitrary pick'n'mix of styles all presided over by Beck's whiny 'Mom! I'm booorrrreeed'! vocals sum up the still-abiding slacker psyche which governs the output of the American leftfield'. And get off my lawn, you damn kids!

Beck toured *Odelay* for a year, from late June 1996 through to late June 1997, then toured the LP off-and-on until the middle of January 1998. He hit the road again in the summer of 1998, mixing in a few songs from *Mutations* prior to its November release (and pimping crowd favorite 'Debra'). The core band included Justin Meldal-Johnsen on bass, Smokey Hormel on guitar, and Joey Waronker, with DJ Swamp (Ronald K. Keys Jr.) added in early 1997.

The album went double Platinum in the US and Platinum in the UK. It was the top LP in both the critically prestigious *The Village Voice Pazz & Jop* poll and *NME*'s annual poll. Beck was named *Rolling Stone* #1 Artist of the Year, *Spin* readers tagged him as Best Artist and Best Male Singer, and he was tagged Best Solo Artist in both *NME* and *Melody Maker*. 'Where It's At' won 1996 MTV Video Music Award for Best Male Video, and Beck picked up another five statues at the 1997 awards. He won a 1997 Grammy for Best Male Rock Vocal Performance and the album won that year's Best Alternative Music Album, his first of three wins in this category.

The album produced five singles: the first, 'Where It's At', reached 35 in the UK and 61 in the US; 'Devils Haircut' did better in the UK, number 22, but only hit 94 in the US; 'The New Pollution' hit number 14, his highest UK charting song, and went to 78 in the US; 'Jack-Ass' hit 73 in the US but 'Sissyneck' failed to chart in either country.

The 2008 deluxe edition added 19 songs, some previously unreleased and some in different versions.

'Devils Haircut' (Beck Hansen, John King, Michael Simpson) 3:14
An enduring classic, one of Beck's top three most-performed live songs, 'Devils Haircut' is a thrilling barrage of sampled drums and repurposed melodies. It finds Beck nodding toward the dance floor, as he dips his toes in the 120+ bpm of techno, and offers a slew of body-groovin' remixes.

The song is a jumble of sound, Beck everywhere on bass, electric guitar, harmonica, and organ. The core is a sample of the drums from Them's cover of James Brown's 'Out of Sight', layered with a looping Beck-replayed electric guitar motif from Them's version of the Phillip Coulter and Tommy Scott tune 'I Can Only Give You Everything'. Both appear on 1966's *Them Again*. Most memorably, the chorus samples the infectious drumbeat from Pretty Purdie's 1967 single 'Soul Drums', featuring legendary drummer Bernard Purdie. The tune also includes a sample from 'Climax One', the first side of 1971's 'For Adults Only' LP *Music for Sensuous Lovers* by 'Z', aka Moog-master Mort Garson.

Lyrically, the song is a kaleidoscopic explosion of near-apocalyptic imagery: 'Leprous faces', 'Smilin' eyes whippin' out of their sockets', and a most evocative line, 'discount orgies on the dropout busses'. Equally evocative is the (plural, not possessive) title – you don't know exactly what it is, but you know exactly what it is.

Beck has discussed the song as 'A really simplistic metaphor for the evil of vanity' and in a 2001 episode of the animated series *Futurama*, alluded to the elusive nature of the song: 'I was feeling really ...really ...what's that song about'?

He's also indicated that he was influenced by the Stagger Lee folk story in which, most simply, the title character kills Billy over a gambling argument. Stagger Lee was convicted of murder, served time, and was paroled. Beck imagines Stagger Lee as a revived Rumpelstiltskin or Lazarus character who returns and sees that 'everywhere I look, there's a dead-end waiting'. Since the early 1920s, 'Stagger Lee' has been recorded hundreds of times. Lloyd Price hit the top of the US pop and R&B charts with the tune in 1959, and lent his name to the 'Devils Haircut' 7" B-side, 'Lloyd Price Express' a remix of 'Where It's At'. Beck released a 1994-recorded version, 'Stagolee', in 2001.

For all that, it's hard not to think this is Beck's lyrical response to Hieronymus Bosch's fantastical *The Garden of Earthly Delights*. In a 2020 *New York Times* interview, he discusses wanting to write an album based on the painting, which he first encountered at Madrid's Prado whilst on tour in his early 20s (he played Madrid on 5 November 1994). He was struck by Bosch's technique and how he could 'make something so crazy and get away with it' – sort of like Beck.

The song was called 'Electric Music and The Summer People' on early *Odelay* promo cassettes. The title would be recycled for a different song.

'Devils Haircut' was the second *Odelay* single. It hit number 22 in the UK but stalled at 94 on the US top 100. There were nine unique B-sides spread across different configurations. 'Clock', 'Trouble All My Days', and '.000.000' all appear on the 2008 *Odelay* deluxe, as do the 'Devils Haircut' remixes 'American Wasteland' and 'Richard's Hairpiece'. 'Devils Haircut' remixes/B-sides 'Dark and Lovely', 'Devils Haircut (Noel Gallagher Remix)', and 'Groovy Sunday' didn't make the 2008 cut, nor did two Gallagher promo-only mixes, 'Single Version' and 'Rock & Roll Edit). All songs are discussed below.

The original song appeared on multiple various artists' collections. A 1997 live-in-studio version (3:13) appeared on the 2008 DVD collection *Later... With Jools Holland – The First 15 Years*, and the 2018 Japanese *Colors* reissue featured a 2017 live version.

'Hotwax' (Beck Hansen, John King, Michael Simpson) 3:49

Following the manic opener, this lolling 'backwash song' slows the tempo. It's another Dust Brothers collaboration, but Beck is in command: vocally slick and laying the sound thick with often distorted slide guitar, harmonica, and various keyboard instruments. According to Simpson, the song started out with Beck's 'nice solid guitar riff' and then built 'collage style', with Beck bringing in 'walkie-talkies and all kinds of weird instruments that he found at thrift stores'.

Beck says 'Hotwax' was influenced lyrically by 'traditional folk songs', which doesn't distinguish it from much of his early work. It seems to be the musings of an observant, self-aware but slightly self-deprecating player: he's 'still the mack' and someone who notices 'Silver foxes looking for romance / In their chain smoke Kansas flashdance ass pants' (the latter part featuring some wonderful assonance, pun intended). The Spanish chorus translates as 'I'm a broken record. I have bubblegum in my brain', which seems like standard ramblings from a poser who thinks he knows Spanish, but really doesn't.

The song has two credited samples: after the second chorus, Pretty Purdie return on 'Song for Aretha', from 1972's *Soul Is... Pretty Purdie*, and the coda features 'Up on The Hill' hand drums, from Monk Higgins & The Specialties' 1972 LP *Heavyweight*. There are claims of at least half a dozen more samples, mainly drumbeats. Some, such as Freda Payne's 'The Easiest Way to Fall' (1970) are spot on; others, such as Black Sabbath's 'Behind the Wall of Sleep' (1970), are more questionable. What's not questionable is that the end of the song includes re-recorded dialogue between a girl and 'the Enchanting Wizard of Rhythm' from Mandrill's 1972 track 'Universal Rhythms'. Beck collaborator and photographer Ross Harris features as the Wizard.

The 2008 deluxe *Odelay* includes unique, double-tracked vocals on the verses. A live version, recorded on 12 October 1996 at the Majestic in Ventura, CA, appears on Belgian (*Most Wanted Festival Acts '97*) and Dutch (*1997 Pinkpop Sampler*) 1997 festival sampler CDs.

'Lord Only Knows' 4:15

Identified by one reviewer as 'microwaved country', this well-crafted tune serves as the heart of the LP. Featuring a sweet, almost optimistic chorus, the song is notable for Beck's display of guitar styles, from full-bodied acoustic to harmonious slide to a deep-chuckle pass at some eruptive guitar-whiz antics a la Eddie Van Halen.

The song starts with an ominous sampled yell from Mike Millius' 'Lookout for Lucy', found on his 1969 LP *Desperado*. Although Joey Warnoker provides percussion, the main drum riff is sampled from Edgar Winter Group's 'When It Comes' from the double-Platinum 1972 LP *They Only Come Out at Night*.

The coda's 'going back to Houston / do the hot dog dance' is a version of a childhood rhyme Beck created with the encouragement of his grandfather

Al Hansen. Beck performed 'Lord Only Knows' at his grandfather's 1995 memorial service.

'The New Pollution' (Beck Hansen, John King, Michael Simpson) 3:40
Clinical in its pop precision, Beck almost jettisoned this track, dismissing it as a 'lightweight tune' and 'very fluffy to me at the time'. At 132 bpm, it's a heart-pumper sped along by Beck's mix-forward drums, a sampled sax, and intermittent organ blasts. Not lacking Beck-like lyrics ('She's got a carburetor tied to the moon'), the song decries contemporary consumer and technological noise, although Beck claims it is 'almost a love song'.
   The song includes two major samples: the core of the drum sound, layered over Beck's guitar and bass, is pulled from 'Hallelujah, Alright, Amen'! by Gus Poole, found on his early 1970s album *Soul Revolution*. The memorable sax appears in Joe Thomas' (aka 'The Ebony Godfather') 'Venus', found on his 1976 LP *Feelin's from Within*.
   'The New Pollution' was the third LP single. At 14, it is Beck's highest charting UK single. The US 12" vinyl included remixes by Mickey P. and by Mario C. & Mickey P., as well as the 'Devils Haircut' remix, 'Richard's Hairpiece' and 'Lemonade'. The former two aren't collected on the deluxe release and all are discussed below. An in-studio soundcheck version (3:32) is on 2000's *Y-100 Sonic Sessions 4* CD. The deluxe edition included the song's synthesizer beeps at a different pitch.

'Derelict' (Beck Hansen, John King, Michael Simpson) 4:13
Although not relaxing, this song offers a breather from the LP's frantic pace, as a slow, resonant Moog underpins a whirling mixture of Eastern-tinged sounds. The song's solemn nature is buffeted by lyrics that describe foul air and sacrifice on the 'funeral fire' – an L.A. boy's trip to the Ganges? The song includes tabla by Pablo Diaz and a sped-up drum sample from Rare Earth's 1972 hit 'I Just Want to Celebrate'.

'Novacane' (Beck Hansen, John King, Michael Simpson) 4:38
Sung through what sounds like a CB radio, Beck cranks up the macho as a 'full-tilt chromosome cowboy' for this fist-pumping trucker's anthem. Originally performed on 1995's Lollapalooza tour as 'Novacane Expressway', Beck claims the song invokes 'a concatenation of brakeless trucks… speeding towards an invisible doom'. According to co-producer Simpson, Beck constantly asked during the sessions, 'What can we do to this song to make it more fucked up?' The song includes at least three samples, including a horn blast from Freedom's 'Get Up and Dance' (1978), some drums from Lee Michaels' '(Don't Want No) Woman' (1969), and some Yoko-like vocals from French avant-folk group Catherine Ribeiro + Alpes' 'Poème Non-Epique N° III' (1975). The US CD promo of *Odelay* uses a different mix of the song, the 1996 vinyl edition included a 3:17 edit, and a

live version appeared on the 1996 CD-ROM *Blender Volume 2.2*. 10-4, good buddy.

'Jack-Ass' (Beck Hansen, John King, Michael Simpson, Bob Dylan) 4:12
A calm folk song secured by a loop of Them's 1966 version of Dylan's 'It's All Over Now, Baby Blue' – this is perfection. Playing with pronouns and time, this appears to be about feeling lost after (when?) a lover can't quite take advantage of the singer's giving their 'real' self ('where the puzzles and pagans lay'). The middle section's remembrance of initial love as weightless freedom – 'when the gravity shackles were wild' – is tempered by the void of loss when remembering this moment ('something is vacant when I think it's all beginning') – it's heartbreaking.

Structurally the song is an oddity; depending on how you figure, it either has three verses and no chorus, or three two-line verses each followed by four-line choruses. The vocal portion ends about two-thirds way through, as Beck then impresses on guitar and harmonica, punctuated by some braying.

This fifth and final single appeared on vinyl and CD in the US and UK; B-sides included 'Brother' and the Skip James cover 'Devil Got My Woman', 'Jack-Ass' reworkings 'Burro' and 'Strange Invitation', all of which appeared on the deluxe edition, and two Butch Vig remixes. The song's original title, 'Millius', appeared on a pre-release promo CD.

'Where It's At' (Beck Hansen, John King, Michael Simpson) 5:31
Beck spent a lot of his early years looking back to a folk past while dabbling in rock, funk, and electronic music. This track is his forward-looking look-back valentine to 'old-school rap house parties'. From the LP's B-side opening needle-drop and vinyl crackle onward, this smooth, anthemic track is designed to get asses out of seats and on the dance floor.

The lyrically identical first and (vocally distorted) third verses set the mood ('get-fresh flow') and location ('a little up the road'), while the middle rap highlights the DJ's dance floor observations ('Members Only, hypnotizers / Move through the room like ambulance drivers') –no Hollywood freaks tonight. For all that, the song is best remembered for its much quoted 'Two turntables and a microphone'! choral chant.

The album's longest song at over five minutes, includes, as Beck has said, 'a lot of experimenting going on'. Some of that experimentation is still in the song, including longish instrumental breaks and the inclusion of an organ and a sax-and-trumpet mini horn section, while some of it didn't make the final cut, such as 'twelve keyboard parts'.

What did make the song were numerous rich musical and lyrical samples; the most apparent, and the only one credited on the original release, is the computer-generated 'We've got two turntables and a microphone' from Mantronix's 1985 song 'Needle to the Groove'. 'That was a good drum break' was pulled from The Frogs' 'I Don't Care if U Disrespect Me (Just So

You Love Me)' (1989). Drums from Grand Wizard Theodore and DJ Kevie Kev Rockwell's 'Military Cut – Scratch Mix', from 1983's *Wild Style* Original Soundtrack, and Les Baxter's 'Hogin' Machine' (1969), pop up periodically. Snippets of Word of Mouth feat. DJ Cheese's 'Coast to Coast' (1986) show up a few times. And we have the spoken word 'What about those who swing both ways / AC-DC's'? from the 1969 health-ed album *Sex for Teens (Where It's At)* – yes, it's also where Beck got the title.

The outro spoken word part is by Eddie Lopez, who created the *Mellow Gold* cover art, *Last Man After Nuclear War*.

The first single from *Odelay*, the song didn't storm the charts as Geffen had hoped. Six remixes were spread across multiple international platforms, with only one, 'U.N.K.L.E. Remix', finding its way to the deluxe edition. Mashups of 'Where It's At' with DJ Shadow's 'Six Days (Remix ft. Mos Def)' (3:10) and with Public Enemy's 'Shut 'Em Down' (3:22) appear on 2009's DJ Hero video game, and numerous quasi-official and unofficial remixes are in circulation. An epic 9:34 version recorded live on 20 April 1997 in Dallas was released in 1998 on *Live Edge Sessions Volume II*, while a much shorter 1997 version appeared on the DVD *Saturday Night Live: 25 Years of Music Volume 5*. Beck re-recorded and released the song in 2019 on *Paisley Park Sessions*, and again (4:33) as part of the July 2022 Amazon Audible *Dear Life* Words + Music release. Live, it is Beck's most performed song.

'Minus' 2:32

'Minus' is a breakneck rocker that harks back to earlier guitar-based, grunge-era songs. The original promo release gave the song the parenthetical title 'Karaoke Bloodperm', a seemingly meaningless but evocative juxtaposition that points toward earlier naming conventions. The song opens with intriguing rhyming and consonance ('The last survivor of a boiled crown / Another casualty with the casual frown'), but ultimately the song is more an impressionistic portrait of decay (of 'minus') than anything concrete.

'Sissyneck' (Beck Hansen, John King, Michael Simpson) 3:53

Lyrically the song is a humorous snapshot of male pride, a guy enjoying a 'rhinestone life and some good ol' boys'. He's another of the string of *Odelay* guys who's fronting macho. Musically, this song has a reputation as a country-funk tune, but it's got much more in common with the country of 'Lord Only Knows' than the funk of, say, Parliament's 'Little Ole Country Boy'. And it's got some sweet pedal steel, a discordant computer breakdown, and some of the best production on the LP, especially the vocals: headphones are a must. Beck is (at least) duetting with himself, with the two vocals mostly off from one another by a fraction. On the verses, the vocals wrap from ear to ear across the top of your head and spread from front to back. In the choruses, the vocals come back to earth with a layer of sound cradling the bottom of your ears.

The production mastery continues with the samples, which are as essential to the body of the song as they are on 'Jack-Ass'. After some undistinguishable talking, the song opens with whistling from Dick Hyman's 'The Moog and Me' (1969) and soon samples bass from Country Funk's 'A Part of Me' (1970). This is soon joined by the recurring circus organ from Sly & The Family Stone's 'Life' (1968). It all chugs along 'like a three-dollar bill in the evening time'.

The song was released as the fourth single in the UK, with no exclusive B-sides. The pre-release promo included a 4:09 version with an unlicensed Cell Phone Barbie doll sample and different bongo work at the song's end. The deluxe edition version runs 3:57 and includes a slightly different computer presentation in the song's middle break.

'Readymade' (Beck Hansen, John King, Michael Simpson) 2:37
Slight among all the heavy hitters on the LP, 'Readymade' feels like an afterthought, and that, succinctly is what the song is about, according to Beck: being an afterthought as a human working in a business that sucks your soul dry. Perhaps this is best illustrated by the fact that in a 2011 interview, producer Mike Simpson forgot he worked on this track. This song has always reminded me of a toilet, specifically Marcel Duchamps' 'readymade' Fountain, which I often saw on display at the Philadelphia Museum of Art when this song was released. The song includes a drum sample of Rory Gallagher's 'Admit It' (1973) and relies on Laurindo Almeida and The Bossa Nova All Stars' 1963 version of 'Desafinado' for its Brazilian vibe.

'High 5 (Rock the Catskills)' (Beck Hansen, John King, Michael Simpson) 4:11
Recorded during the first sessions with The Dust Brothers, too many ideas caused production to drag on for three weeks, encouraging Beck to work quicker (one-day songs) when they got back together. For all its studio wizardry, the song's sheer bombast was a benefit as a frequent 1996-97 set closer.

The song is definitely about someone enjoying some tunes, but with the state of the singer ('wheelchair ways', 'more dead than alive', 'in my cot sweating like a dog'), it's unclear if it's all happening physically or mentally or in the present or past. Whenever or however it's happening, it's clear that, once again, there's a disconnect between self-image and reality.

Surprising for the sheer variety and quantity of sound, just a few samples have been identified. The only credited grab is a flourish of 'no jive / give me five' lyrics from 1971's 'Mr. Cool' by Rasputin's Stash (one of the best band names ever). The song begins with a 'High 5' shout-out over the South American sounds of Walter Wanderley's 'Baia' (1980) and is later interrupted by the First Movement of Franz Shubert's Unfinished Symphony (1822). Perhaps most famously, Beck interpolated the 'designer jeans' rap from the

Fantastic Five's performance at the Harlem World 1981 MC Battle. Tapes of the battle circulated widely before appearing on a 1998 CD *Afrika Bambaataa & The Universal Zulu Nation in Conjunction with Music of Life Presents Hip Hop Funk Dance Classics Volume 1* – for all the ladies in the house.

'Ramshackle' 4:40
Just as Beck ended *Mellow Gold* with a quiet, introspective number (followed by a barrage of noise), so he ends *Odelay*. The song is most often read as a portrait of homelessness ('The bargains you drag / In buckets and bags / And all your belongings'). However, based on the unattractive portrait of a consumer life offered to this point of the LP, it's just as likely that the stuff that's accumulated is as much mental as physical and that we're all in the same place at the final moment: 'We will go / Nowhere we know'. The musical highlight is the upright bass of jazz legend Charlie Haden, father of Beck collaborators Petra and Rachel Haden.

As much as it might put a philosophical cap on the LP, it's an outlier. Along with the two tracks discussed below, it's all that's left of Beck's immediate *Mellow Gold* follow-up attempt with Tom Rothrock and Rob Schnapf. According to Beck, 'It was a whole record's worth of stuff, somewhere between Big Star and Pavement, Nirvana', but he wasn't happy with the album's direction, hence The Dust Brothers pivot. The song was originally titled 'Marty Robbins'. Robbins enjoyed 17 Country number ones in the US and is credited with popularizing fuzz bass on 1961's 'Don't Worry'. When the fuzz kicks in about halfway through Robbins' song, you're suddenly in a *Golden Feelings* outtake.

'Hidden Track' 0:45
Also known as 'Computer Rock' on the deluxe edition, it's a barely melodic computer loop that sounds like the lost instrumental track for the 'Track Records' inner groove on *The Who Sell Out* (1967).

'Diskobox' (Beck Hansen, John King, Michael Simpson, Jon Spencer, Russell Simins, Edward Green) 3:34
This slinky, blues-based sound collage sounds more like a Jon Spencer Blues Explosion track (such as 'Do You Wanna Get Heavy') than a Beck one, but no one's complaining. Beck rifles off first-verse non-sequiturs ('About to shout / Nasty distortion / Animal toejam'), heads toward a chorus ('Get that brand new action / Gonna lubricate with the jet effect'), and then briefly introduces one of *Odelay*'s searching characters before the second chorus and a 'diskobox'! chant. Spencer is credited with playing keychain. The song includes a number of samples, most notably a piano riff from The Ramsey Lewis Trio's 'Upendo Ni Pamoja (Love Is Together)' (1972). 'Diskobox' appeared as a bonus track on the original *Odelay* in most non-North American markets, but was left off the deluxe edition.

Deluxe Edition (2008)

'Deadweight' (Beck Hansen, John King, Michael Simpson) 6:12
Elaborating on nodding South American elements in 'Ramshackle' and 'High 5', this is the first of Beck's 'Brazilian Trilogy', along with 'Tropicalia' and 'Missing'. The down-on-your-luck verses, grim at times ('Oh, this life seems like the gristle of loneliness'), are countered by the somewhat believable 'don't let the sun catch you crying' pick-me-up choruses. The core song, released as a 4:10 single, is expertly honed Bossa Nova – it's pretty close to perfection as a single. The full-length version is great, too, as a faded-out piano and fuzz-guitar counterpoint gives way to a longer guitar solo and about a minute of mellotron fun. The song was recorded with The Dust Brothers after *Odelay* for the *A Life Less Ordinary* soundtrack. It was released as a single, accompanied by 'Erase the Sun' and 'SA-5'.

'Inferno' (Beck Hansen, John King, Michael Simpson) 7:06
This epic number plays like a mash-up of 'Novacane' and 'High 5'. There's a little bit of everything in here – power-rapping, crushing echoed guitar, tambura, sitar, an exercise interlude, and an anthemic yelled chorus: 'Inferno!' In a 2007 *Record Collector* interview, Beck called the song 'The Dust Brothers and I's *magnum opus*', although he left it off *Odelay* because he thought it would completely alienate the record label. One of two previously unreleased tracks on the deluxe edition, along with the next song, it was tinkered with in the early 2000s, with samples swapped and Matt Mahaffey adding instrumentation. The original version remains unreleased.

'Gold Chains' (Beck Hansen, John King, Michael Simpson) 4:59
This is another character study of a mid-1990s would-be stud trying to make the scene. Sonically it's unpolished in comparison with the original LP, and there's not really a coffin nail to throw your hat on in the repetitive 'I'm going back home with my gold chains swinging' chorus. Nathalie Merchand, who's credited as a technician on *Modern Guilt*, provides spoken vocals here. Dare I say this is boring?

'Where It's At' (U.N.K.L.E. Remix) (Beck Hansen, John King, Michael Simpson) 12:21
The first half is a Big-Beat-ish remix of the song by hot 1990s remixer unit U.N.K.L.E., while the second half is the group's trippy instrumental extrapolation.

'Richard's Hairpiece' (Aphex Twin Remix Of 'Devils Haircut') (Beck Hansen, John King, Michael Simpson) 3:21
One of the more distinct remixes of the era, techno legend Aphex Twin (Richard James – it's his haircut in the title) speeds up the original music by 25%, tweaks Beck's vocals with David Seville acumen, and adds synthetic strings – hard to forget.

'American Wasteland' (Mickey P. Remix Of 'Devils Haircut') (Beck Hansen, John King, Michael Simpson) 2:44
This is a hardcore punk reimaging of the song. Remixer Mickey Petralia, who'd produce on *Midnite Vultures*, added thrash guitar, while Sean Ross, liner note writer extraordinaire on Rhino Records' essential *In Yo' Face!: The History of Funk* series, added bass. The tune is bookended by clips from the mid-1990s punk band Urbicide. The opening clip ends their song 'Barney Miller was a Cop' and introduces their 'American Wasteland', while the end leads to their 'Go to Hell'. The excerpts are from the band's self-produced cassette *They Finally Let Us Have a Gig*, recorded in May 1984 at CBGBs.

'Clock' (Beck Hansen, John King, Michael Simpson) 3:18
A solid, bass-heavy sound collab with The Dust Brothers nailed down by a drum sample from Lee Dorsey's 1966 'Get Out of My Life, Woman'. The meaning is impenetrable ('Is it comes in lovely bones that put their shirts on ice' – what?) and there's not an obvious hook beyond the bass. This appeared on singles and in some markets as a bonus on the original CD, and showed up as a 'rare' Beck track on various artists collections.

'Thunder Peel' 2:42
Smells like grunge as Beck returns to this *Stereopathetic Soulmanure* rocker. Accompanied by Joey Waronker on drums, there's a freshness and lack of import in this performance that winds up in bubbling feedback. It's one of the few tracks from the intermediary Mario Caldato Jr. sessions.

'Electric Music and the Summer People' 4:40
A breezy surf song with a fat punk bass – basically a Ramones song with more melodic vocals, at least until it devolves into the musings of a rambunctious drum machine. Future Beck bassist Justin Meldal-Johnsen plays keyboards. The deluxe edition version is a different mix than the original 'The New Pollution' B-side, campier with extra echo on the vocals. 'Devils Haircut' used this title on the *Odelay* promo CD. Beck re-recorded the track during the *Mutations* sessions.

'Lemonade' 2:23
A UK 'Jack-Ass' B-side coproduced by Brian Paulson ('Minus'), this features a noise barrage on the two yelled verses and gentle melodies on the two choruses, where Beck is backed on vocals by Rebecca Gates of Sub Pop's The Spinanes.

The line 'Revolution purple fists' doesn't seem to refer to Prince's band and it's unclear if the lyrics actually refer to anything. As the contemporaneous duo Bevis and Butthead would say aloud when reading books: 'Words, words, words'.

'SA-5' 1:53
A brief but catchy rhyming exercise that's reminiscent of Syd Barrett's psychedelic solo work, such as 'Octopus'. The title refers to the Casio synth model that bolsters the tune.

'Feather in Your Cap' 3:45
Beck revisited this 'It's All in Your Mind' B-side during the mostly scrapped late 1994 *Odelay* sessions with Tom Rothrock and Rob Schnapf. This version is fuller, longer, and generally more determined. It was released as a B-side and on the soundtrack to Richard Linklater's *Suburbia*.

'Erase the Sun' 2:58
A 'Deadweight' B-side culled from the Mario Caldato Jr. sessions, this song, with its 'Hairy fairies spinning their golden looms', sounds like the fanciful ramblings of a power-hungry Dungeons and Dragons dungeon master. The music is slow, almost sludgy, mock-heroic folk. The sludge was alleviated on the sped-up (and maybe remixed) deluxe edition version (2:56), cutting the sharp edges and rendering a more buoyant and well-rounded pop(ish) song.

'.000.000' 5:27
Attractive like rubbernecking a car crash, this is a slow, uneven, low-register drone, with sounds phased in and out, backwards and forwards, opaque even by early Beck standards. The lyrics, when audible, are up for debate. There are disagreements about how to say the title. Recorded during the Caldato sessions.

'Brother' 4:46
A slow, pensive ballad with a wailing underbelly that eventually disrupts the calm. It seems a simple reading, but the song appears to be straightforwardly about making peace with a departed brother. Ending up on *Odelay* B-sides, it's also culled from the truncated January 1995 Rothrock / Schnapf sessions.

'Devil Got My Woman' (Skip James) 4:36
A faithful version of Skip James' 1931 acoustic classic, Beck recorded this at Sun Studios in March 1994, at the same time as 'Stagolee', which wouldn't be released until 2001. He previously released James' 'He's a Mighty Good Leader'. If Beck had only had a career as a folk interpreter, he would have had a brilliant career. The song was released on two *Odelay* B-sides.

'Trouble All My Days' 2:25
This adaptation of Mississippi John Hurt's 'Trouble, I've Had All My Days' first surfaced on *Golden Feelings* before appearing on the 'Devils Haircut' single, although this version is in compressed mono.

'Strange Invitation' (Beck Hansen, John King, Michael Simpson) 4:09
From the 'Jack-Ass' single, this total reworking of the A-side is spectacular,
although it's always had a mid-1990s unplugged vibe. The track shines with
a string arrangement by David Campbell, Beck's dad, and Jon Clarke on
English horn and bass clarinet. The band is rounded out with co-producer
Meldal-Johnsen on bass and our first appearance of guitarist Smokey Hormel.
Beck's vocals are less processed and more forward in the mix than usual.

'Burro' (Beck Hansen, John King, Michael Simpson) 3:14
Another 'Jack-Ass' redo with David Campbell, this track heads south of the
border for a mariachi mix. Singing in Spanish, Beck is backed by Mariachi
Los Camperos de Noti. The band is best known for supporting Linda Ronstadt
on two of her Spanish-language albums. Beck came across the group playing
in leader Nati Cano's L.A. restaurant La Fonda. The song is a treat.

Related Tracks
Ending below with 'Jack-Ass (Lowrider Mix by Butch Vig)', these remixes
and edits, in addition to those that appeared on the deluxe edition, appeared
across multiple versions of the LP's five singles

'Make Out City' (Remix by Mike Simpson) (Beck Hansen, John King,
Michael Simpson) 3:06
Simpson's 'Where It's At' remix swings the house-party vibe with a joyous
brass sample from Freedom's 'Get Up and Dance' (1978), a tune also sampled
in 'Novacane'.

'Bonus Beats' (Beck Hansen, John King, Michael Simpson) 4:09
King produced and remixed this selection of 'Where It's At' drumbeats and
vocal tweaks.

'Lloyd Price Express' (Remix by John King) (Beck Hansen, John King,
Michael Simpson) 5:00
The 'Where It's At' party atmosphere has dissipated, replaced by an unending
guitar riff that sounds swiped from an Average White Band song.

'Where It's At' (Remix by John King) (Beck Hansen, John King, Michael
Simpson) 3:43
King's third mix is rhythm-dominated but not bass-heavy.

'Where It's At' (Remix by Mario C. And Mickey P.) (Beck Hansen, John
King, Michael Simpson) 3:26
Trippy but not quite trip-hop, notable for a sample from Biz Markie's old
school 'The Do Do' (1988).

'Dark and Lovely' (Remix by The Dust Brothers) (Beck Hansen, John King, Michael Simpson) 3:38
This 'Devils Haircut' has a downbeat, chilling out-after-the-Saturday-night-party feel, with some opera singing thrown in.

'Groovy Sunday' (Remix by Mike Simpson) (Beck Hansen, John King, Michael Simpson) 3:16
And this 'Devils Haircut' is later the same day, featuring some peppy keyboards and horns, while fixing a Sunday brunch.

'Devils Haircut' (Remix by Noel Gallagher) (Beck Hansen, John King, Michael Simpson) 3:47
Oasis guitarist/songwriter Gallagher adds some heavy guitar in what feels more like his reaction to the song than a remix.

'Devils Haircut' (Single Version) (Beck Hansen, John King, Michael Simpson) 3:55
It is likely the same track as above.

'Devils Haircut' (Rock N Roll Edit) (Beck Hansen, John King, Michael Simpson) 4:45
This is what a remix should be. Gallagher reimagines the song as a manic drums, harmonica, and guitar assault, punctuated by 'Got rock and roll in my mind' vocals.

'The New Pollution' (Remix by Mickey P.) (Beck Hansen, John King, Michael Simpson) 4:08
Petralia's second solo remix foregrounds the drums but bypasses the energy of the original.

'The New Pollution' (Remix by Mario C. Mikey P.) (Beck Hansen, John King, Michael Simpson) 3:49
Caldato and Petralia's second remix adds some sitar sounds and highlights the sampled sax.

'Jack-Ass' (Butch Vig Mix) (Beck Hansen, John King, Michael Simpson) 3:23
Celebrity producer Vig gets the song to single shape and size, foregrounding the swirling melody and chopping up the ending.

'Jack-Ass' (Lowrider Mix by Butch Vig) (Beck Hansen, John King, Michael Simpson) 4:14
If I were cruising in a lowrider to one of these songs, it would be 'Make Out City'. However, this funky remix is perfect for the dancefloor. The new

groove sounds heavily influenced by U2's 'Mysterious Ways' from *Achtung Baby*, one of the ten most important records for Garbage drummer Vig.

'Title Unknown, Sleeping Bag' 3:02

'Title Unknown' is a 0:58 burst that appears with 'Sleeping Bag' on the 1996 *Yoyo A Go Go* compilation. Recorded in July 1995 at the Capitol Theater in Olympia, Washington, it's a fast, shouted noise song that could be a cover of Black Flag's 'Rise Above' or it could be Beck getting electrocuted by the mic. The hillbilly version of *One Foot*'s 'Sleeping Bag' is sweet.

'The Little Drum Machine Boy' (Beck Hansen, John King, Michael Simpson) 7:02

Beck's contribution to Geffen's *Just Say Noël* charity holiday CD, released on 29 October 1996. The tune mixes up robot-voice Hanukkah blessings ('Baruch atah Adonei Elohenu Melech ha'olom') and disses ('Hanukkah pimp') with 'Hotwax' 'I get down' chants, and a flowing verse that would sound at home on *Midnite Vultures*. The song appears on a handful of other collections, while a 3:15 edit showed up on KCRW's *A Family Christmas in Your Ass* collection.

'Untitled' 3:12

An acoustic tale about going to prison for shooting a gun in a gas station bathroom, with some background vocals and sound effects. Released on 1996's *KXLU Demolisten Volume 2*.

'Leave Me on the Moon' 2:17

Beck sings this like a Vegas singer starting the night's second set after a few too many drinks backstage. Backed by Jon Spencer Blues Explosion drummer Russell Simins, this song appeared on the 2003 compilation *Root Damage*. With the next two, it appeared on the 1997 soundtrack to Steven Hanft's *Kill the Moonlight*. An earlier take appears on Beck self-released cassettes.

'Last Night I Traded My Souls Innermost for Some Pickled Fish' 1:58

This instrumental, akin to 'One Foot in the Grave', includes slide acoustic with harmonica.

'Underwater Music' 0:58

This instrumental features guitar feedback with some water sounds.

'Funky Fanfare' (Keith Mansfield)
'Allegretto Per Signora' (Ennio Morricone)

These two instrumentals were often played as set-opening music during the *Odelay* tour. Both were broadcast in the US on 6 September 1997 on PBS's

Sessions at West 54th. The former is a standard funk riff that goes by a few different names, including 'The House of Jack' and 'Soul Thing'. It was often used in the late 1960s/early 1970s to introduce movie trailers. The latter comes from The Italian maestro Morricone's 1970 soundtrack *Foto Proibite Di Una Signora Per Bene (The Forbidden Photos of a Lady Above Suspicion)*.

'I'm So Green' (Can, Beck Hansen) 4:08

This is a very liberal interpretation of the 1972 Can single that also appeared on the Germans' LP *Ege Bamyasi* (which means Aegean okra). Beck mainly keeps the chorus of the loose funk tune but uses a Nirvana-like buildup to get to his own 'Devils haircut in my mind' chorus. Beck recorded the song before signing to Geffen, but a minute-long clip showed up on The Dust Brothers' website in April 1998. The producers had teamed with music promoter Mitchell Frank to create a Can tribute LP, *Can Forgery Series*, that never came to fruition.

Mutations (1998)

Personnel:

Beck Hansen: vocals, guitar, piano, harmonica, glockenspiel, slide guitar
Justin Meldal-Johnsen: bass, double bass
Joey Waronker: drums, percussion
Smokey Hormel: guitar
Roger Joseph Manning Jr.: organ, piano, synthesizer
David Ralicke: trombone
Larry Corbett: cello
Fred Sesliano: esraj
Warren Klein: sitar, tambura
David Campbell: arranger, conductor
Produced by: Beck Hansen, Nigel Godrich
Recorded at: Ocean Way Studios, 19 March–3 April 1998
Release date: 3 November 1998
Label: Geffen Records / Bong Load Records
Highest chart places: US: 13, UK: 34
Running time: 49:17

Beck ended *Odelay* festivities in early 1998, ready to jump into a new album. He wanted to work with Nigel Godrich, best known at that point for producing Radiohead. Godrich happened to be in town, Beck's touring band happening to be hanging around, and over a few spring weeks, they pulled together *Mutations*. Some of the songs date back to early 1994, but some were written on the spot.

Beck intended the LP to also be released quickly on Bong Load, as it wasn't 'really' the follow-up to *Odelay*. But once Geffen heard the album, they wanted to release it. The dispute quickly resolved, resulting in Geffen releasing the CD and Bong Load the vinyl, but caused the release to be delayed until November. Beck sued both labels in spring 1999 over this incident as a breach of contract. The issues were resolved in October 1999, with Beck bowing out of the Bong Load relationship after *Midnite Vultures*.

The album was very well received, although several critics were skeptical about this being a 'parenthetical' follow-up to *Odelay* (a 'betweenie' in *The Village Voice*). Jim Irvin (*MOJO*) gushed more in the description of individual songs than in general: '*Mutations* has a focus missing from the frantic, funky-trash free-for-alls of Beck in computer mode; it's languid, easy, sometimes eerie and often very beautiful'. Ian MacDonald in *Uncut* (five out of five stars) went further, saying: 'This could be Beck's masterpiece'. JR Smith's review in *The Village Voice* was the most perceptive in contextualizing the import of the LP, deciding: 'This album's definitely a rainy Saturday afternoon home with the cats, but sometimes it's like that, you know?' *Q* gave the LP four out of five stars, as did *Rolling Stone*. Still, in a *Midnite Vultures* review, Tom Cox (*The Guardian*) called *Mutations* 'the career low that everyone was too afraid to slag off at the time'.

Beck didn't engage in a full-scale *Mutations* tour, although he did go on a nine-date Japanese jaunt in April 1999. The album went Gold in the US and UK. There were three global singles, all of which failed to chart. The CD was initially released in HDCD (High-Definition Compatible Digital), which meant increased dynamic range on decoding-ready hardware (such as most new Microsoft-based computers of the time). Beck discussed the LP on *The Mutations Conversations*, an 18-minute promo interview CD.

'Cold Brains' 3:41
Called by one critic 'acoustic-based gloom', 'Cold Brains' is a wonderful but disheartening opener. The song is filled with loss, from ideas ('No thoughts / No mind') to life ('abandoned hearse') and limb ('corroded to the bone'). Dispensing with the character-based songs of the first two Geffen albums, this signals a shift to a more obviously confessional singer-songwriter mode, which shows in his voice, as Beck is more studied (and slightly nasal). For all this, the sound is hopeful – deliberate and anthemic, not elegiac. The highlights are Beck's harmonica and glockenspiel as well as the production, beginning with the left/acoustic and right/electric stereo separation as the song unfolds.

Beck originally intended this for the K2 Records follow-up to *One Foot in the Grave*. That never happened, but he brought this song to Ocean Way Studios on 21 February 1998 for a getting-to-know-you recording session with producer Godrich. Beck's decision, heard at the end of the song, was 'Yeah, I like that a lot' – two weeks later, they were recording the LP.

The song was released as an Australian single with four additional songs. A live version (3:34), recorded on 25 November 1999, was released in 2000 on Austin radio station 107.1 KGSR's *Broadcasts Vol. 8*.

'Nobody's Fault but My Own' 5:02
Beck once again plays the self-loathing card, taking the fall for a relationship in which 'the tongues are full of heartless tales that drain on you'. But the split is not all bitter, as, in a marvelous turn of a phrase, the singer suggests that 'When the moon is a counterfeit, better find the one that fits / Better find the one that lights the way for you'. Beck brushed aside this as a reflection of real anguish, saying of this composition: 'Well, I went down to my basement. It was raining outside, and I wrote it'. But the song did give him pause. In a 2014 interview, he noted, 'I was really wary of recording that one. It seemed too precious or something, not at all like the more confrontational stuff going on'.

The song sticks out musically in Beck's oeuvre as his 'Indian' song, doing the sitar on 'Loser' one better. Over a traditional rock foundation, the song features not only cello and viola from his dad but a trio of Indian stringed instruments: the esraj, sitar, and tambura (which Beck had played on 'Inferno'). It's exotic and impressionistic without being fetishistic.

The song was released as a Japan-only single edit (4:45) with two B-sides. A live version (4:57) appeared in 1999 on *SNL25 – Saturday Night Live, The Musical Performances | Volume 2*. Marianne Faithfull covered the song on 2002's *Kissin' Time*, along with two songs Beck co-wrote and co-produced: 'Sex with Strangers' and 'Like Being Born'.

'Lazy Flies' 3:43

'Lazy Flies' is an excessively tuneful acoustic waltz punctuated by fuzz guitar solo. Beck said the song is 'this imaginary movie about some futuristic, colonial backwater. But it also contains elements of the barrio I grew up in'. Either way, it's a song of moral (slavery) and literal disease (syphilis), punctuated by a hideous game. The 'futuristic' line 'The skin of a robot vibrates with pleasure' wows and resonates.

'Canceled Check' 3:14

This is one of the older songs on the LP, written in the late summer of 1994 in Tokyo. The song is inspired by a Tony Robbins self-help infomercial that insisted 'The past is a canceled check: your maximum point of power is now!' Beck previously included a 'canceled check' infomercial sample in *Golden Feelings*' 'Trouble All My Days'. The song is a kiss-off to someone who's a canceled check, someone for whom 'it's crystal clear your time is nearly gone'. The shuffling acoustic song is punctuated by Greg Leisz's pedal steel and a horn section of David Ralicke on trombone and Elliot Caine on trumpet. The song degrades into the cacophony of the band throwing instruments around the room, which extends longer (4:28) on an early promo of the album. An early version was allegedly slated for *The One Step* follow-up.

'We Live Again' 3:04

Another waltz, part looking back, part reckoning with 'the end', this is most often interpreted as being about Beck's recently deceased grandfather. The upright bass and Roger Manning Jr.'s harpsicord highlight the instrumentation. Some reviewers mention a Beatles quality to this song, which I don't agree with except in the use of an exceptionally strong bridge. And, notably, there's even an unexpected touch of sentiment: 'When will children learn to let their wildernesses burn / And love will be new / Never cold and vacant' – almost brings a tear to the eye.

'Tropicalia' 3:20

Following 'Deadweight', this is the second of Beck's Brazilian Trilogy. The lyrics address the social inequity between resort employees ('misery waits in vague hotels') and guests ('They're anabolic and bronze / They seem to strut in their millennial fogs'). Much is made of the fact that the song isn't Tropicalia but more a bossa nova/samba. However, Beck gets it mostly right, as Tropicalia was originally a progressive ideology as well as a musical style. Members of the late 1960s Brazilian Tropicalia movement included Os Mutantes, who likely contributed their name to this LP's title.

Beck didn't play on this piece. According to producer Godrich, the band had some troubles recording this track as it was Meldel-Johnson's first time on upright bass and Hormel encountered difficulties with the quica (or cuica, aka monkey drum, the song's most distinct sound).

The song was released as a limited edition 7" single in the UK on 7 December 1988 and as a multi-track CD in international markets. A live version (5:05) appeared on 2000's *Live at The World Café Volume Ten*. More than a decade later, 'Tropicália (Mario C 2011 Remix)' (3:24) appeared on the HIV/AIDS awareness album *Red Hot + Rio 2*. Producer Mario Caldato Jr.'s version adds himself on marimbas and Money Mark on keyboards and electric tres, originally a Cuban three-stringed instrument, now typically played as a Cuban or Puerto Rican six-stringed instrument. Brazilian legend Seu Jorge adds lyrics, vocals, and receives a co-songwriting credit.

'Dead Melodies' 2:35

This is the album's briefest song. It's about disconnection, from both the creative process ('doldrums are pounding') and other people ('Seasons of strangers that come and go'), resulting in the bleak title situation. There's a 1965 Beatles vibe, especially in the harpsicord-like guitar break, and the monk-like background vocals are a refreshing approach to filling out the sound.

'Bottle of Blues' 4:55

This upbeat blues song was laid down in half a day. This efficiency is due in part to Beck's belief that he 'didn't need to get bogged down in any technology' on this LP and also that he's using a band. This lends a bit more humanity, if not warmth, to this LP and especially this song. Although the song deals with impotence and brothels, it's unlikely the title refers to Viagra, the bottle of blues that was also released in 1998. As usual, there's some wonderful wordplay: 'Egos drone and pose alone / Like black balloons all banged and blown'. Musically the highlights are Beck's harmonica and the shaky synth on the instrumental break. An earlier version (5:07) exists with a longer spoken introduction.

'O Maria' 4:00

On an album of lyrical downers, this might be the nadir. It's a weary reflection on loss ('the circus' 'My shadow') and failed expectations ('And I've been looking for a good time / But the pleasures are seldom and few'), and finally resignation ('The night is useless and so are we'). The resonant, t-shirt-worthy line, 'The fabric of folly is falling apart at the seams', is a stunning metaphor for self-deception. But who is the singer? It seems from a woman's point of view, and, perhaps from a washed-up prostitute: 'I've been looking for a new friend / And I don't care if he's decrepit and grey'. The barroom piano and trombone edge this last interpretation toward a Marlene Dietrich-type character (or at least the 'tired' Lili Von Shtüpp of *Blazing Saddles*).

'Sing It Again' 4:19
A light, country waltz, this closing-time song was written for Johnny Cash in 1994. Beck thought the result 'a piece of shit' and the song remained unused until he started shaking the trees for *Odelay* follow-up material. Cash instead got 'Rowboat', which is less abstract and downcast. The star here is Hormel, with a pretty and precise acoustic solo.

'Static' 4:20
The anthemic 'Static' returns to the unhurried pace of the album's opening songs, albeit with a more rock-oriented approach. The song is about being down on yourself and the creeping suspicion that those rumors about you may be true ('Who you fooling if the fools are right'). The solution to this problem is to isolate, to 'lock yourself inside' and 'drown in a convalescent bliss'. The song pivots on the concept of static; most apparently, static is the feedback/noise of those rumors, which 'leaves you hollow and unkind'. Although the relationship is not readily apparent in the song, it's worth noting that the concept of 'Static' is central to Scientology, as the first axiom states: 'Life is basically a Static', that 'has no mass, no motion, no wavelength, no location in space or in time. It has the ability to postulate and perceive'. 'Static' shares a name with an unreleased acoustic song that is often mistitled 'Baby'. That song was penciled in for a 1995 EP release before being abandoned.

'Diamond Bollocks' 6:03
After an album of what Beck called 'waltzes and dirges', this hidden, Bach-meets-Rush headbanger, is a heart-pounding revelation. The song was mostly composed in the studio and stitched together from between four and eight other songs (depending on who you believe). It moves in and out of Manning's breathy harpsichord sections, four-on-the-floor rock outbursts (including lyrics from 'Erase the Sun' and a guitar riff from 1994's most grungy, unreleased 'Megaboob'), bird sounds, and some of Beck's most wonderfully pretentious prog-rock lyrics – 'A tearful gaze turns away, emoting cold and grey / Scented eunuchs clothe our wretchedness'. And it all resolves in some ominous sci-fi puzzlement: 'Looking back at some dead world that looks so new'. The title comes from a quickly corrupted accolade Beck and the band received after a European show, approximately 'That was top bollocks, you diamond geezer'. The track does not receive cover credit on UK and US releases.

Related Tracks

The non-duets here are an old Beck-only track ('Black Balloon'), the first and last song recorded with Godrich in 1998 ('Electric Music and the Summer People', 'Runners Dial Zero'), and three collaborations with Mikey Petralia that seem like a test-run for his co-producing *Midnite Vultures*. The latter three would have made a tidy standalone single.

'Runners Dial Zero' 4:02

The last song recorded in the two-week mad dash, it's muted and atmospheric. Godrich describes it well: 'basically we got a fucked-up vocal sound and a fucked-up piano sound'. The song seems to be about a lover's pact. The title was literally pulled out of thin air: it's the PA announcement when the studio was directing gophers to call the office. It appeared on some international versions of the LP and on US and Australian 'Cold Brains' promo CDs.

'Halo of Gold' (Skip Spence) 4:29

Not as many moving parts as 'Diamond Bollocks', but similar in aural dynamism from quieter tinkling keys to brawny rock bombast. The song is a cover of Skip Pence's 'Furry Heroine (Halo of Gold)', an unreleased 1999 addition to Spence's 1969 release *Oar*. The original version from the Jefferson Airplane (drummer) and Moby Grape (guitarist) member Spence is more folky/pastoral, a la Donovan. Although included on international versions of *Mutations* and 'Tropicalia' and 'Cold Brains' singles, Beck worked on the track with *Midnite Vultures* producer Mickey Petralia. The song also appeared in February 1999 on *More Oar: A Tribute to Alexander 'Skip' Spence* and on a Japanese Beck B-sides CD. Beck covered the original *Oar* LP for his online Record Club in 2009.

'Black Balloon' 3:30

A funky Beck-only keyboard and bass instrumental, this sounds like the part in a Blaxploitation movie when the hero is looking through filing cabinets trying to put all the clues together. This appeared on the UK 'Tropicalia' single and the German *Mutations*.

'One of These Days' 4:48

Not the Pink Floyd song, but then again, the light dream-pop isn't far away from Pink Floyd. And it's almost a straightforward love song. Another collaboration with mixer/engineer Petralia, it appeared on an Australian 'Cold Brains' promo and the Japanese 'Nobody's Fault but My Own' single.

'Diamond in the Sleaze' 4:09

This Petralia-produced pop song with a repeated 'How could you let a good thing go' chorus has the feel of a single, a less bitter take on 'Deadweight'.

Featuring David Ralicke's flute and some fuzz guitar from Beck, it's polished but still feels incomplete. Same release history as the previous song.

'Electric Music and the Summer People' 3:34
Previously released as an *Odelay* B-side, Beck recorded this and 'Cold Brains' in late February 1998 as a speed date with producer Nigel Godrich. As Godrich explained: 'It had this sitar solo and four keyboard solos and timpanis and stuff'. The two agreed to work together, although to these ears, this 'surfing version' is flat compared with the original. This version appeared on the Japan *Mutations* CD, US and Australia 'Cold Brains' singles, and numerous compilations.

'Drivin' Nails in My Coffin' (Floyd Tillman) 2:47 by Willie Nelson & Beck
Beck and music legend Nelson wash away the break-up blues on this country-folk song that saw both Floyd Tillman and Ernest Tubb hit top five on the US folk charts in 1946. The song was recorded in Dallas in 1998 and released in January 1999 on the soundtrack to Steven Frears' Western *The Hi-Lo Country* and two various artist collections. The duo had joined forces in 1997 for performances of 'Peach Picking Time in Georgia' on Jay Leno's *The Tonight Show* and Farm Aid '97, the latter released in 2000.

Beck & Emmylou Harris 'Sin City' (Gram Parsons, Chris Hillman) 4:01
Beck is low in the vocal mix, reverential, and a bit studied in the presence of Harris on this country-rock tribute to singer-songwriter Gram Parsons. In addition to frequent collaborators Meldal-Johnsen, Waronker, and Hormel on bass, drums, and guitar, the duo is backed by Beck's Farm Aid augmentation, fiddler Gabe Witcher, pedal steel player Jay Dee Maness, and pianist Billy Payne. Maness was a member of Parsons' early International Submarine Band and Payne was a founding member of Little Feat. The original appeared on The Flying Burrito Brothers' 1969 LP *The Gilded Palace of Sin* and was written by band members Parsons and Chris Hillman. Beck and Harris' version appeared on 1999's *Return of The Grievous Angel: A Tribute to Gram Parsons* and a few compilations.

Midnite Vultures (1999)

Personnel:

Beck Hansen: vocals, keyboards, synthesizer, piano, vocoder, background vocals, handclaps, harmonica, marimbas

Smokey Hormel: guitar

Justin Meldal-Johnsen: bass, synthesizer F/X, handclaps

Roger Manning Jr.: synthesizer, piano, tambourine, shaker, Clavinet, vocoder, handclaps, acoustic guitar, Fender Rhodes

Joey Waronker: drums, percussion

DJ Swamp: scratching

Johnny Marr: guitar

Tony Hoffer: guitar

Jay Dee Maness: pedal steel

Greg Leisz: pedal steel

Beth Orton: background vocals

David Ralicke: trombone

David Brown: tenor saxophone

Jon Birdsong: trumpet

Herb Peterson: banjo

Jay Dee Maness: pedal steel

Arnold McCuller: background vocals

Valerie Pinkton: background vocals

Joel Derouin: violin

Eve Butler: violin

David Campbell: viola, conducted by

Larry Corbett: cello

The Dust Brothers: scratching

Arroyo Bombers: background vocals

Arroyo Tabernacle Mens Choir: background vocals

Fernando Pullum: horns

Steve Baxter: horns, background vocals

Joe Turano: horns, background vocals

Produced by: Beck Hansen, Mickey Petralia, The Dust Brothers (John King, Mike Simpson)

Recorded at: Soft Studios, PCP Labs, July 1998–June 1999

Release date: 23 November 1999

Label: DGC / Bong Load Records

Highest chart places: UK: 19, US: 34

Running time: 58:52

Beck started recording the 'official' *Odelay* follow-up in January 1998 but hit computer problems, which necessitated the more stripped-down *Mutations* sessions in spring 1998. He began recording again in June 1998, mostly at his home, Soft Studios, with veteran L.A. DJ Mickey Petralia acting as co-producer and engineer. He added some sessions with The Dust Brothers at their PCP Labs, wrapping up recording 11 months later. According to reports, it was a long, laborious project, with Beck saying they'd 'spend 16 hours on four seconds of music'.

The critical results of all this were, we'll say, 'mixed bizness' – some raves, some pans. *Uncut*'s Kit Aiken seemed to like the LP despite himself: '*Midnite Vultures*' frighteningly inventive and adept collage of rock/soul/pop/dancefloor clichés proves he can't really play dumb even when he's trying'. Keith Cameron (*NME*) went where a lot of other reviewers went, Minneapolis, saying it's 'the Prince of mid-80s purple patch legend, of raspberry berets, orgiastic funkfests and real, uninhibited, dropdown-dirty fun. Unsurprisingly, it's brilliant'. Tom Cox (*The Guardian*) was not amused, offering 3 of 5 stars: 'Beck doesn't continuously reinvent himself; he just continuously fiddles and throws more and more into the mix (this time more funk, swing and squeaky 80s electronica)'.

Beck expanded the live band to ten pieces, including a horn section, and toured for most of 2000 and into 2001. The most notable happening during this time was his breakup with longtime girlfriend Leigh Limon sometime in the first half of 2000.

The album went Gold in the US and UK and was nominated for Album and Alternative Album of the Year Grammys, losing both awards. As with initial mixed reviews, *Q* put it on a 2006 list of worst albums of all time, while *NME* put it on a 2013 list of best albums of all time. In interviews, Beck seems genuinely surprised when people tell him it's their favorite of his long players.

There were three singles, each with a dizzying array of B-sides and remix offerings. 'Sexx Laws' went to 27 in the UK, his last top 30 hit, and 21 on the US Alternative Charts, his new home as only 'E-Pro' and 'Girl' would hit the Top 100 after this. 'Mixed Bizness' went to number 34 on the UK chart, while 'Nicotine & Gravy' was only released in Europe. The CD was initially released in HDCD, as with *Mutations*.

'Sexx Laws' 3:39

After the generally downbeat *Mutations*, Beck returns as a freewheeling MC who wants to liven the party by denying the 'logic of all sex laws'; the song includes some of Beck's most evocative lyrics, as multiple possible sexual encounters are spun off, culminating in fantastical 'Bed and breakfast getaway weekends / With *Sports Illustrated* moms'. The couplet 'Coquettes bitch slap you so polite / Till you thank them for the tea and sympathy' pulls from the 1950s play and film *Tea and Sympathy,* a groundbreaking story about a female teacher who sexually pursues a teenage schoolboy who's being bullied for appearing too feminine/gay. The title phrase, which means a shoulder to cry on, was famously reworked as 'coke and sympathy' by the Rolling Stones in 'Let it Bleed'.

The music is upbeat R&B, brass-in-your-face fun...plus banjo and pedal steel guitar. The horn charts have been criticized as 'corny' and 'trite', but they're what Beck was aiming for. According to an interview quoted in whiskeyclone.net: 'I think it was the L.A. Rams. I used to watch them when I was growing up, and it just reminded me of *Monday Night Football* in 1978'. Find a 1978 *MNF* broadcast online and you'll hear that he nailed it. Ultimately, the musical highlight of the song is the out-of-leftfield banjo solo by veteran Herb Pedersen, who worked with Emmylou Harris and Gram Parsons, among others.

Numerous single configurations include multiple remixes and the non-LP tracks 'This is My Crew' and 'Salt in the Wound'. The single was released as a 7" picture disc in the UK and a clear vinyl 12" in the US. The song appeared as 'Sexxlaws' on some pre-release promos.

'Nicotine & Gravy' 5:13
Another song crafted in the studio from a handful of song ideas, this is among Beck's sonic masterpieces, with both syntagmatic and paradigmatic depth and intrigue. In terms of syntax, the grammar of the song, the four or five sections, from the bass rumble and vinyl hiss of the opening to the sex-me-up Prince middle interlude to the klezmer-like coda, shouldn't make sense together – but they do. Beck, channeling his inner Jean-Luc Godard, alluded to this, saying that the song has a beginning, middle, and end, just not necessarily in that order. In terms of paradigm, there are layers-upon-layers of sound, from strings arranged by his dad, synths and Clavinets, the Brass Menagerie, to banjo, and the first appearance of DJ Swamp and his turntables. You get caught following one audio layer and realize you're missing something else at the same time, especially in the fadeout. Lyrically, the song's POV is from one of the album's multiple playas. This one is ready to tell his lady every Prince-like thing he'll do for her, from 'leave graffiti where you've never been kissed' to 'turn you over to the highway patrol'.

The song includes a sample from Les Baxter's 'Hogin' Machine' (1969). It was released as a European single with the B-sides 'Midnite Vultures' and 'Zatyricon', with the German version including a video remix (3:22). The 2000 180-gram pressing features an early fade to accommodate vinyl time limitations, rendering the song about 4:30.

'Mixed Bizness' 4:10
This high-octane dance number with built-in call-and-response lyrics was made to play live. Its unrelenting rhythm is propelled by Meldal-Johnsen's bass, a bedding for Brass Menagerie horn punctuations, Beck's vocoder, and funky wah-wah guitar from co-producer Tony Hoffer. The song once again plays with sex/gender roles (it might be from a woman's POV) and ticks off things to do for a lover: 'I'll comb your hair / rewrite your diary'. The song includes a sped-up drum sample from the Rolling Stones' 'Honky Tonk

A youthful beck photographed
by Alison Dyer in 1996.'
(*Everett Collection/Alamy*)

Left: Beck's 1993 full-length commercial debut was a cassette-only affair with a kid-friendly cover. (*Sonic Enemy*)

Right: The spine on this 1994 10" vinyl EP is mislabeled 'A Western Harvest Moon by Moonlight.' (*Fingerpaint Records*)

Right: Beck's most eclectic release, this 1994 CD took six years to reach vinyl and almost 30 to hit streaming services. (*Flipside Records*)

Left: Beck's commercial breakthrough features cover art, 'Survivor from the Nuclear Bomb', sculpted by artist Eddie Lopez. (*DGC/Bong Load*)

Right: 'Loser' is the first of six Beck videos directed by his friend and one-time bandmate Steve Hanft.

Left: Beck channeled his middle-aged salesman self for 'Where It's At', winner of 1996's MTV Video Music Award for Best Male Video.

Right: Beck's not afraid to get down on his knees trying to get with Jenny and her sister 'Debra'.

Right: The original version of the Beck-directed 'Sexx Laws' video, which features actor Jack Black, was over 18 minutes long.

Left: The video for 2005's 'Girl' is an affectionate nod to *MAD* magazine and artist Al Jaffee's fold-in back covers.

Right: Beck joined Charlotte Gainsbourg for a 2010 radio session performing the Beck-penned track 'Heaven Can Wait.' (*KCRW*)

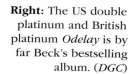

Left: The last of three 1994 album releases, *One Foot in the Grave* was expanded by 16 tracks and rereleased in 2009. (*K Records*)

Right: The US double platinum and British platinum *Odelay* is by far Beck's bestselling album. (*DGC*)

Right: Robert Fisher's *Mutations* artwork was photographed by Autumn de Wilde, who released the photo/interview book *Beck* in 2011. (*DGC/Bong Load*)

Left: 1999's *Midnite Vultures* was nominated for a 2001 Grammy Award for Album of the Year, his second of three nominations in this category. (*DGC/ Bong Load*)

Left: Considered by many as Beck's masterpiece, *Sea Change* was released with four different album covers created by artist Jeremy Blake. (*Geffen*)

Right: Hitting number two, 2005's *Guero* is Beck's highest-charting album in the US; it reached 15 in the UK. (*Interscope*)

Right: Each copy of 2006's *The Information* was released with a blank cover sleeve and one of four sticker sheets so fans could make 'customizable' covers. (*Interscope*)

Left: 2008's brief, punchy *Modern Guilt*, co-produced by Danger Mouse, was Beck's last album for over half a decade. (*DGC/XL*)

Left: Beck is feeling the love from a group of blue dancers in the video for the title track of 2017's *Colors*.

Right: The organic, country-tinged video for 'Wow', the second of five singles from 2017's *Colors*, contrasts with song's infectious electronic-hum.

Left: With 2019's *Paisley Park Sessions*, Beck was the first artist to record at Prince's home studio since The Artist's death in 2016.

Right: Released in conjunction with a TV commercial, Beck's 2022 cover of Neil Young's 'Old Man' endured criticism from Young and social media about the relationship between art and commerce.

Left: Beck never properly toured *Hyperspace* because of the COVID-19 pandemic, but he resumed a regular tour schedule in June 2022.

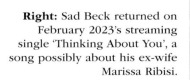

Right: Sad Beck returned on February 2023's streaming single 'Thinking About You', a song possibly about his ex-wife Marissa Ribisi.

Left: *Morning Phase* cleaned up at the 57th Annual Grammys in 2015, winning both Album of the Year and Best Rock Album, in addition to an engineering award. (*Capitol/Fonograf*)

Right: 2017's *Colors* featured five singles released from 2015 ('Dreams') through 2018 ('Colors'). (*Capitol*)

Left: Featuring Beck in front of a Japanese Toyota Celica, the title of 2019's *Hyperspace* is written katakana, one of two Japanese syllabaries. (*Capitol*)

Right: *Song Reader* features artists such as Sparks, Jack White, and Jarvis Cocker performing original Beck compositions. (*Capitol*)

Left: Beck has never released a full-length live performance in the US or UK, but live material has appeared on numerous promo CDs. (*Westwood One Radio Networks*)

Right: Record Club's front cover for *The Velvet Underground & Nico* presents an Andy Warhol-like twist on Warhol's original album art.

Left: Beck and Charlotte Gainsbourg bonded over debilitating injuries while recording *IRM* (French abbreviation for magnetic resonance imaging). (*Because Music*)

Right: Beck produced and appears on three tracks on *Demolished Thoughts*, the release of which coincided with the 2011 demise of Moore's band Sonic Youth. (*Matador*)

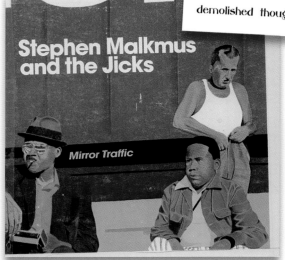

Left: Beck produced the fifth album from the Pavement frontman's group The Jicks, but doesn't appear on the record itself. (*Matador/Domino*)

Right: This fan-produced cover fronts an unofficial CD version of Beck's early country, blues, and roots collaborations with the mysterious Dava.

Above: Beck's self-released 1992 cassette features many otherwise unreleased songs and early versions of future commercial releases such as 'Fume' and 'Hollow Log'.

Right: Beck compiled the *Fresh Meat + Old Slabs* cassette for his mother, Bibbe Hansen. It functions as a greatest hits of his pre-label recordings.

Left: Beck's commercial breakthrough single is also his only gold 45 in both the US and UK. (*Bong Load/DGC*)

Right: *Odelay*'s 'The New Pollution' is Beck's highest charting single in the UK, hitting number 14 in 1997. (*DGC*)

Left: 2005's *Hell Yes* EP featured three tracks, including the imminently listenable 'Ghettochip Malfunction' remix of the title song. (*Interscope*)

Women' (1969). The song was the LP's second single, with multiple remixes and non-LP tracks 'Dirty Dirty' and 'Arabian Nights' spread over multiple US and UK formats. The 4:10 run time includes about 25-seconds of 'robot fucking' noise at the end, which tracks as 'Intro to 'Get Real Paid' on most streaming services, rendering the song length about 3:46. The song ends with a literal 'Fuck you' from a robot voice.

'Get Real Paid' 4:44
This is Beck channeling Kraftwerk, with a touch of Sparks for good measure. Beyond the quirky funk electronica, the song's most striking feature is the heavily modified monotone vocal of Beck's alter-ego Surrealius. Beck conceived of this character as the space between Prince and Serge Gainsbourg. This alter-ego side project consumed him at the time, and the *Midnight Vulture* project was originally conceived as a Surrealius album, but the idea was dropped. A la Prince's female alter-ego Camille, the song once again plays with sex/gender roles, with Beck singing 'Thursday night I think I'm pregnant again'. The song includes a Kraftwerk sample, from 1981's 'Home Computer', and one from Idris Muhammad's 'Crab Apple' (1977).

'Hollywood Freaks' (Beck Hansen, John King, Michael Simpson' 3:59
This is Beck's more-or-less straightforward shot at late 1990s R&B rap. The song slinks along musically while parroting the high-living braggadocio of satin sheets and champagne. Critics claim the song makes fun of the genre, but Beck claims it's not a parody (and it's not: it's more an inhabitation of the genre as in his early folk work). Further, in his imitation of a Black rapper, some have taken issue with his 'lisping, nasal drone that's part Truman Capote and part Sylvester the Cat'. Whatever the critical reaction, it's his most 'Los Angeles song' to this point. The Dust Brothers co-produced and scratched on the tune, which appeared as 'HLWD. Freaks' on some pre-release promos. The song bears some resemblance to 'California Rodeo', an unreleased track recorded with rapper Kool Keith during the *Midnite Vultures* sessions.

'Peaches & Cream' 4:54
The body of this track is Beck's most metaphorically obvious sex-u-up track, with luscious falsetto couplets such as 'Give those pious soldiers another lollipop / Cos we're on the good ship menage a trois'. As with the previous song, this isn't as much a parody of slow-jam seduction as an inhabitation/tribute to the genre, and especially Prince (who had songs named 'Peach' and 'Cream'). But with about a minute left, the (religiously named) Arroyo Tabernacle Mens Choir launch into the traditional gospel blues song 'Keep Your Lamp Trimmed and Burning'. This chant of 'Keep your lamplight trimmed and burning' weaves in and out of Beck's falsetto performance of the sexed-up chorus ('you make a garbage man scream'), moving it beyond a

simple sexual encounter into a spiritual or even sacramental realm. The chant is associated with Jesus' Parable of the Ten Virgins. Succinctly: attending a wedding, five of the virgins prepare for future happiness (husbands and heaven) by keeping their lamplights trimmed and burning while waiting for the groom to show up, while five don't prepare and end up alone. As with many of Beck's lyrics, the exact meaning is difficult to pin down, but this religious nod comes from the Jewish tradition, already invoked on the LP with 'she looks so Israeli' on 'Nicotine & Gravy' and Surrealius' Gainsbourgian bent.

'Broken Train' 4:11
Opening side two, this slightly funky track seems influenced by the mid-1990s exotica music revival. And the inhabitants of the song seem like they'd be hanging around worn-down 1950s tiki lounges – Hollywood area and zip codes far from the freaks' glamor. Some fat synth and harmonica highlight a song best remembered for its memorable lines, from the opening disorientation of 'The snipers are passed out in the bushes again', to the sad realization that 'beige is the color of resignation'. The song appeared as 'Out of Kontrol' on pre-release promos, with the name changed to avoid confusion with The Chemical Brothers' single.

'Milk & Honey' (Beck Hansen, Buzz Clifford) 5:18
Nirvana's 'Smells Like Teen Spirit' is a kissing cousin of Boston's 'More Than a Feeling', but this song holds its own in the mid-1970s/Boston bombastic (opening) and sensitive (outro) rock song department. But then there's the bridge, stand-up comedy, disco lasers, and a monotone recitation of espionage observations. Lyrically, the song seems to be about a US soldier adrift in Southeast Asia ('Bangkok athletes in the biosphere / Arkansas wet dreams') – but maybe not. The 'sensitive' coda is a joint guitar effort from Beck (acoustic) and The Smiths' Johnny Marr (electric). In Marr's telling of the sessions, when he 'turned up there were pictures of Prince all over the studio, so I was like, 'OK, this is what we're doing is it?'' According to Marr, the duo also recorded an unreleased tune, 'The Doctor'. It's believed to be the same as 'Let the Doctor Rock You', performed lived on 10 October 1998 during the *Midnite Vultures* sessions. 'Milk & Honey' includes a sample of Buzz Clifford's 'I See, I Am' (1969). Clifford had a top-ten US single in 1960, 'Baby Sittin' Boogie'. The song's 'break-in' baby gurgling would not be out of place on early Beck records. This is the third ampersand title on the LP. All contain food references.

'Beautiful Way' 5:44
Musically, this is the album's sore thumb, as this breezy, light psychedelia would seem more at home on *Mutations*. The song is almost hesitant to share its subdued riches – pedal steel from Jay Dee Maness and Greg Leisz,

Smokey Hormel guitar fills, Beck's harmonica, and Beth Orton's understated background vocals. Lyrically, as a love song, it's also out of place on this LP, although with its 'searchlights on the skyline', 'glittering shoals', and 'Egyptian bells', it continues the second side's vague international / soldier vibe, an alternative narrative to side one's Angeleno ambience. And, for further international intrigue, the song borrows liberally from the Velvet Underground's 'Countess from Hong Kong', a track from 1969 released in 1995. A promo single was released in the US, but there was no chart action. For many, the song is best remembered as a 30-second Microsoft Windows ME sample. This timing includes seven seconds of a spray can writing graffiti that appears as 'Intro to Pressure Zone' on streaming services.

'Pressure Zone' 3:14

As with the previous song, this hard pop-rock track feels like an LP interloper. Beck described it as 'a Cars-style blueprint of an alternative rock song', which is more-or-less accurate. Online lyric interpretations lean toward the sexual (which is the default when a song's not obviously about drugs), but I'll take the seemingly disconnected lines at face value and consider this as a stroll through a museum, with one-line descriptions of each piece of art ('Wrestling with butcher girls / She don't ever change her clothes'). Beck's art heritage might partially explain the chorus line 'Masterpieces liquidate in fertile tears' – or maybe it is a song about abortion.

'Debra' (Ed Green, Beck Hansen, John King, Michael Simpson) 5:38

For many fans who caught the *Odelay* tour, this IS Beck. Seemingly from nowhere, this folk/dance/alternative 'slacker' was throwing down a convincing sweet falsetto and sexy slow jam – it was heaven. This version doesn't live up to the live performances, but it hits the blue-eyed soul target somewhere between the Stones' 'Fool to Cry' (1976) and National Lampoon's 'Kung Fu Christmas' (1975). The song, an extended come-on to the name-tagged Jenny and her sister, Debra, is often criticized as a parody (as if that's bad) or for simply making fun of the genre and middle-class values. However, for its seeming absurdity in its use of everyday subjects to impress a woman (a 'fresh pack of gum', a Hyundai, a 'real good meal'), the character has a lyrical honesty and realism that's missing from the braggers and freaks on the LP's first side. Of course, that itself is undermined by the overblown, majestic music, highlighted by the one-time horn section of industry veterans Fernando Pullum, Steve Baxter, and Joe Turano. The song borrows from David Bowie's 'Win' (1975), which appeared on his blue-eyed soul LP *Young Americans*, and samples Ramsey Lewis' 'My Love for You' (1973) (written by Ed Greene, who gets co-writing credit). The CD track is 13:46. After a seven-minute silence, the next track starts. The song is referenced and used in the film *Baby Driver* (2017) and appears on the amazing soundtrack. A live version from the 19 November 1999 show at Felix Meritis, Amsterdam, Netherlands appeared on the Dutch CD *2 Meter Sessies, Volume 10* (2001) – it's a bit soft. 'Frontin' on Debra' (6:12), a mashup with Pharrell & Jay-Z's 'Frontin'', was released in 2004. A silkier, more atmospheric version (4:51) graced the 2022 *Dear Life* Words + Music Amazon Audible release. As with 'Mixed Bizness', the original 'Debra' ends with a 'Fuck you'.

'Untitled Track' (Justin Meldal-Johnsen) 1:03
Also known as *'Midnite Vultures* Bonus Noise', it's some hardcore bass and noise, then a funky synth groove, then back to hardcore with some sampled interludes. More pleasing than other bonus noise entries.

Related Tracks
'Arabian Nights' 4:02
With sound design and co-production by Tony Hoffer and instrumental credit to Beck and DJ Swamp (scratching), this feels like a mashup of Eminem and Berlin-era David Bowie/Brian Eno ('African Night Flight' and 'The Secret Life of Arabia' come to mind). For all that, in a 2000 interview, Beck said this was influenced by Outkast. The title hints at international themes, but the 'word salad' lyrics – which read as if generated by a posturing poetry slam algorithm – harken back to the streets of L.A. Among the more memorable lines are 'Norwegian hockey players passed out in government limos' and '2 PM laser vizzaginal rejuvenation', the latter reflecting L.A. medical alteration ads of the time. It appeared as a bonus track on the Japanese *Midnight Vultures* CD, on some 'Mixed Bizness' configurations, and lead off 2001's limited edition Beck.com B-sides CD.

'Salt in the Wound' 3:24
Featuring a nagging guitar riff, this all-Beck, not-quite-maximum R&B number is a distant relation to 'Sexx Laws', sans horns. It was on the US Best Buy exclusive double-CD edition of *Midnite Vultures*, various configurations of 'Sexx Laws', and B-side/rarities compilations.

'This Is My Crew' 3:55
And just like that, Newcleus shows up for an early 1980s hip-hop jam; well, not really, as Beck is joined here by Manning, Meldal-Johnsen, and DJ Swamp. The song is an old-school step-up challenge rap, with the best dis 'Your brother's a waitress'. The song is on the Best Buy disc and 'Sexx Laws' configurations.

'Sexx Laws (Malibu remix)' 6:52
'Sexx Laws (Malibu Remix Edit)' 3:52
This 1980s electronic dance version is remixed by Tony Hoffer and Malibu, aka Roger Manning Jr. Third song on the Best Buy disc.

Beck ... *On Track*

'Sexx Laws (Acapella)' 3:05
As advertised.

'Saxx Laws (Night Flight to Ojai)' 5:12
The song, reimagined as Kenny G light jazz, laps itself as a joke, although it is more tolerable than most Kenny G songs.

'Sexx Laws (Wizeguyz Remix)' 6:03
This big-beat version pumps up the drums and the soul. The DJ duo Wiseguyz, DJ Touché and DJ Regal, had a UK number two hit in 1999 with 'Ooh La La'.

'Sexx Laws (Wiseguyz Instrumental)' 6:00
Instrumental version of 'Wiseguyz Remix', aka 'Sexx Laws (Instrumental)'.

'Sexx Laws (Wiseguyz Bonus Dub') 3:22
Again, as advertised.

'Mixed Bizness (Dirty Bixin Mixness Remix By Bix Pender)' 3:44
This sticks close to the original, with more guitar and percussion. Icelandic remixer Bix Pender, aka Sjón, was a novelist and frequent Bjork collaborator. On US and UK 12" singles.

'Mixed Bizness (Cornelius Remix)' 4:48
Less mixed, less busyness, the now disgraced Cornelius adds drums and centers his remix around a brief vocal sample from then-partner Takako Minekawa. On US and UK CD singles.

'Mixed Bizness (Cornelius Instrumental)' 4:48
This pulls the vocals from the previous tune.

'Mixed Bizness (DJ Me DJ You Remix #1)' 3:57
This is a bouncy, fun remix that puts one in the mind of Aha. DJ Me DJ You were Craig Borrell and Ross Harris of the electronic band Sukia. Harris was The Wizard on 'Hotwax' and appears on 'Waitin' For A Train' and 'Funky Lil' Song'.

'Mixed Bizness (DJ Me DJ You Remix #2)' 4:12
Borrell and Harris put another spin on Beck's dance-floor intentions

'Mixed Bizness (Nu Wave Dreamix)' 4:19
A repetitive, low-grade, early New Order-wannabe remix by Les Rythmes Digitales aka English producer Stuart Price. The same version as on the UK 12" usually titled 'Alternate Mix'.

'Mixed Bizness (The Latin Mix By Scatter-Shot Theory)' 4:58
Thoughtful, south-of-the-border remix by Beck.com contest winners Scatter-Shot Theory, a sampling trio evidently known for their use of Ensoniq ASR-10 keyboards.

'Mixed Bizness (Hardmixn By Jake Kozel, Aka Socket 7)' 6:16
Also known as 'Hardmixn By Boxtripbox', this grating hard-techno remix by contest runners-up features Beck repeating 'I'm mixing' dozens and dozens of times.

'Mixed Bizness (Transatlantic Rmx)' 4:55
'Mixed Bizness (Transatlantic Rmx Instrumental)' 4:54
'Mixed Bizness (Die Fantastischen Vier Transatlantik Remix)' 4:50
'Mixed Bizness (Die Fantastichen Vier Remix)' 4:50
'Mixed Bizness (Fernando G. Rmx)' 6:34
These five tracks appeared on promo and semi-legal German CD and 12" releases.

'Dirty Dirty' 4:43
This slinky, strangely hypnotic electronica exercise features another frontin' *Midnite Vultures* playa. The character seems to be hitting on a performer at a hotel, as in 'Debra', bragging about them providing real good meals: 'I frequent places that take American Express'. This appeared on 'Mixed Bizness' configurations and B-side compilations.

'Midnite Vultures' 7:18
This long, trippy almost-jazz tune sounds like the song a band pulls together when they all know it's time to go home, but no one wants to go home. Anchored by the legendary session drummer James Gadson and highlighted by David Brown's weaving sax, the song seems to be about a movie set or an Asian metropolis – or both.
    The song was recorded after the *Midnite Vultures* sessions and released in 2000 on the European 'Nicotine & Gravy' single and in 2001 on the B-side compilation.

'Zatyricon' (Beck Hansen, Tony Hoffer) 5:16
Backed by silly electronic music, Tony Hoffer prank calls a doctor to get a fat graft on his recently attached tail. The title is based on the book and Fellini movie *Satyricon*, a film with as much narrative coherence as the previous song. The prank recalls the genius work of early 1990s duo The Jerky Boys. Their 'Egyptian Magician' is a thing of beauty. The song appeared alongside 'Midnight Vultures'.

'Boyz' 2:52
Grand Royal Records (Beastie Boys) and Tannis Root, a music merchandise company named after a *Rosemary's Baby* plot point, sent a Groovebox to multiple musicians in 1999. The Groovebox is a 'band in a box', a collection of classic 1980s bass and drum machine sounds. Beck appears on the resultant essential album along with contemporaneous peers such as Sonic Youth, Cibo Matto, and Buffalo Daughter, as well as electronica godfather Jean-Jacques Perrey. If 'This is my Crew' recalls Newcleus, this track finds Beck and DJ Swamp embracing their inner Whodini.

Beck & Willie Nelson 'Peach Picking Time Down in Georgia'
(Jimmie Rodgers, Clayton McMichen) 3:15
The duo first performed this song on 29 September 1997 on *The Tonight Show*. This version of the Jimmie Rodgers classic was captured on 4 October 1997 at Farm Aid '97 and appears on *Farm Aid: Volume One Live* (2000). Beck lets Nelson shine on lead vocals and guitar, but the star is fiddler Gabe Witcher. The pair also recorded 'Drivin' Nails in My Coffin', released in 1999.

'Computer Girls' 3:50
This features a somewhat comical guitar punctuated by the repeated lyrics 'After school, professor asked if she could see my new computer girls' and occasional synth, guitar, and percussion outbursts. The song appears over the closing credits of *Condo Painting* (2002), a documentary about American artist George Condo, whose work resembles a mash-up of Picasso, Goya, and Botero. It doesn't appear on the soundtrack LP *Condo Painting – Life From A Different Angle*.

Thurston Moore / Beck / Tom Surgal 'Kill Any/All SPIN Personnel' (Beck Hansen, Thurston Moore, Tom Surgal) 36:15
Beck joined Sonic Youth guitarist Thurston Moore and drummer Tom Surgal at New York City's The Cooler on 21 September 1998 for an improvised noise jam. This free-form piece, more Moore-like than Beck-like, ends with Beck dismantling Surgal's drum kit. The performance was a cassette-only release on Minneapolis D.J. Matthew Saint-Germain's underground-friendly Freedom From label. The blood-red spattered tape art featured a list of SPIN magazine editors and e-mails from angry tape purchasers who had to wait while Saint-Germain figured out how to convert Moore's CD-r to cassette.

'Lonesome Whistle' (Hank Williams) 3:04
A Beck live favorite, he delivered a heartfelt rendition of the Hank William country classic for a 3 November 2000 KCRW radio session. It appears on the 2001 compilation *Sounds Eclectic*. Beck also recorded Williams' 'My Bucket's Got a Hole in It' and 'You Win Again' on the demo collection *Beck + Dava*.

'Your Cheatin' Heart' (Hank Williams) 3:42

Beck was scheduled to record the previous song for 2001's *Hank Williams: Timeless* tribute collection, but turned his sights instead to this song. Almost whispered, musically atmospheric and moody, this avoids both the twang of the original and schmaltzy bombast of the Ray Charles hit, offering a surprisingly fresh take on a song that's been recorded almost 300 times. The song also appeared on a Lost Highway Records sampler.

'Put it in Neutral' 2:31

A clip of this song appears on *Don't Get Bent Out of Shape* V2 cassette, but the full-length version showed up in 2000 on Gus Hudson's car-oriented CD *A Hot Wild Drive in the City*.

Bean 'American Car' (Steve Moramarco, David Markowitz) 3:18

Beck contributed vocals to this song, which appeared on Hudson's LP. 'American Car' also showed up on a 2000 flexidisc credited to Steve Bean with Beck & Michael Rivkin, given away with *Glue* magazine.

'Diamond Dogs' (David Bowie) 4:34

Beck's only work with superstar producer Timbaland, this is a curiously unengaging run-through of Bowie's 1974 classic. It appears on 2001's *Moulin Rouge! Music from Baz Luhrmann's Film*. The rocker is modified with a subtle rap/R&B feel, what Beck classed as 'ghetto-tech'. It sounds more like an idea about the original song rather than a cover of the song. Beck's original take on the song appears for a few seconds in the film, a more upbeat version he called 'Al Jolson at the rave tent'.

'Stagolee' (Mississippi John Hurt) 2:46

A legendary fan of the legendary musician, this is surprisingly the only Hurt song Beck has officially recorded. It appears on the 2001 tribute LP *Avalon Blues: A Tribute to the Music of Mississippi John Hurt*. It's stunning, a sensitive guitar picking and vocals interpretation that recalls Dylan's work on *Blood on the Tracks*. The recording is from a March 1994 Sun Studios session that produced the 1997 release 'Devil Got My Woman'. More songs were reportedly recorded but remain unreleased.

Sea Change (2002)

Personnel:
Beck Hansen: vocals, acoustic guitar, synth, glockenspiel, harmonica,
background vocals, keyboards, banjo, percussion, electric guitar, Wurlitzer, piano
Justin Meldal-Johnsen: electric bass, background vocals, electric guitar, upright
bass, glockenspiel, percussion, piano
Roger Joseph Manning Jr.: synth, Wurlitzer, glockenspiel, piano, Clavinet,
background vocals, percussion, harmonium, banjo, Indian banjo
Smokey Hormel: electric guitar, acoustic guitar, percussion, background vocals,
acoustic slide guitar, piano, bamboo saxophone, megamouth, tape recorder
Joey Waronker: drums, percussion, background vocals, beatbox drums
James Gadson: drums
Jason Falkner: electric guitar, background vocals, percussion
Nigel Godrich: keyboards, percussion, synth
Suzie Katayama: cello
David Campbell: conductor, arranger
Produced by: Nigel Godrich
Recorded at: Sounds Way Studios, Record One, 6 March-7 May 2002
Release date: 24 September 2002
Label: Geffen
Highest chart places: UK: 20, US: 8
Running time: 52:24

Sea Change is like Gordon Lightfoot showed up and wanted to make
everyone sad.

Beck churned out breakup songs after his summer 2000 split with longtime
girlfriend Leigh Limon. At first, he found these songs self-indulgent and too
personal, but over time and alteration, he made his peace with the tunes and
decided to record them. He closed shop on *Midnite Vultures* in the summer
of 2001 and was prepared for fall recording, but the 9/11 terrorist attacks
disrupted life and sessions were delayed.

Work in January 2002 with San Francisco-based producer Dan the
Automator (Dan Nakamura) resulted in at least one unreleased song ('Story
of My Life'), but no songs for a follow-up LP. After producing Marianne
Faithfull at Sunset Sound Studios, Beck turned to *Mutations* co-producer
Nigel Godrich, determined to quickly pull together an album. Recording
lasted about three weeks and the whole project, including mixing and
David Campbell's strings, was done in two months.

The album is among the best received in Beck's career. *Spin*'s Will
Hermes called it 'a supremely dainty-assed achievement that jerks real
tears', which, in context, was a major compliment. *Rolling Stone* gave it
five of five stars and named it 2002 Album of the Year, while *NME* (six of
ten) was somewhat less enamored. As was down-on-Beck *Uncut*: 'This is
pretty gloomy going'. Neumu website co-founder Michael Goldberg took

the long view and was on the mark with his assessment: '*Sea Change* is one of those albums that you need to live with for a while. But once it sinks in, you'll have a hard time getting the sound and the melodies out of your head'.

Beck and Smokey Hormel hit the road in late summer for a brief, mostly acoustic, pre-tour. The *Sea Change* tour proper took place in the fall and featured the Flaming Lips as Beck's band. The Flaming Lips would play a set highlighting their songs from their most accessible album, *Yoshimi Battles the Pink Robots* (2002), Beck would play a short acoustic set, and then the Oklahoma City band would back Beck on a full electric set. In 2003, Beck ping-ponged between Europe and the US, with a spring European acoustic tour, an early summer American tour and then a later summer European festival tour. Around this time, he began recording *Guero*, which would be released in the spring of 2005. 2004 was spent mostly out of the spotlight, the most notable events being his April marriage to actress Marissa Ribisi and his second Coachella appearance.

Sea Change went Gold in the US and Silver in the UK. It was nominated for the 2003 Best Alternative Music Album Grammy. There were no commercial singles. As with the two previous LPs, The CD was initially released in HDCD. 2003 further saw the release of a DVD-Audio version, which included surround sound. The 2009 release from Mobile Fidelity Sound Labs found the album mastered from the original tapes and uncompressed. As is not unusual for MFSL (see U2's *War*), this vinyl release includes slightly different edits of some songs (although not different takes), and fans rave about later pressings of the 2016 double-LP vinyl reissues. Many aural decisions for this excellent collection of songs.

'The Golden Age' 4:35

Achingly slow acoustic guitar is soon joined by electric guitar, glockenspiel and some slight drums, later met by understated vocal harmonies, all announcing a song, and an LP, of reflective lament. On the surface, the song is a road song, but the freedom here isn't top-down, wind-in-your-hair, but the kind you don't want because you're suddenly all alone. Despite the disheartened chorus ('These days I barely get by / I don't even try'), the song opens with feigned optimism suggested by title: the glory days are ahead. Of course, in Ancient Greek philosopher Hesiod's telling, the Golden Age was one of peace and harmony...but there were no women – appropriate for Beck (at least temporarily). For all the acoustic/dour press the song gets, the song does open sonically up as it goes along. This was evident live in the fall 2002 tour, when Beck would play the first part acoustic before being joined by the Flaming Lips. It's also evident in Beck's description of the song, 'We wanted it to be a Kraftwerk ending. It starts out on a desert road and you end up on the Autobahn, riding through East Germany'.

'Paper Tiger' 4:36
The almost-optimism of the opening track gives way here to an admission that it's all a front, as the singer is nothing more than a stray dog or a paper tiger. And amid the natural violence – deserts and storms, ruins and weather – he's still driving, one road to the morning (this song is a cousin of 2014's 'Morning'), the truth, and civilization, but 'no road back to you' – gut punch: 'let the tears flow'. Musically James Gadson's drums and Justin Meldal-Johnsen's bass funk up a seductive rhythm, topped by David Campbell's incisive, almost martial string section. The song bears more than a passing resemblance to Serge Gainsbourg's 'Melody', the lead track from his groundbreaking 1971 LP *Histoire De Melody Nelson*, while some detect a sample of the closing track, 'Cargo Culte'. This is the first track longtime guitarist Jason Faulkner recorded with Beck. According to Faulkner, he wasn't making friends that first day: 'I was making some suggestions for arrangements, and he liked them. Other guys in the band were looking at me like, 'you dick', they thought maybe I was getting special treatment in their eyes'.

'Guess I'm Doing Fine' 4:49
This is ostensibly a solo acoustic lament, augmented by a sneaky bed of synthesizers and multiple layers of subtle guitars, keys, harmonica, and background vocals. The lyrics are an unfiltered and not totally processed look at Beck's recent breakup; as *SPIN* wrote in a decade look back at the LP, 'The 'guess' in 'Guess I'm Doing Fine' sums about eleventy-nine kinds of resignation' – peak Sad Beck.

'Lonesome Tears' 5:38
The album's longest song is also its musical centerpiece. Moored by a funereal rhythm section, the song swells to a dizzying conclusion through David Campbell's orchestral maelstrom. Campbell creates this metaphoric sea change by employing a Shepard tone, best known from The Beatles' 'I Am the Walrus'. The tone is a Möbius-like auditory illusion in which sound appears to be ascending or descending the scale but ultimately returns to its starting point, only to start over again. It all starts with a rollercoaster string dive after the second verse. Beck's use of the technique on this song has influenced artists as diverse as musician Amanda Palmer and director Christopher Nolan. Lyrically, the song's sorrow echoes this paradoxical, unresolved feedback loop ('Ever changing / Never change the way I feel'), and the metaphoric sea change is marked by having no more salty tears to cry.

'Lost Cause' 3:47
Opening and closing with backward music (and some studio chatter), like 'Guess I'm Doing Fine', this is another delicate but deceptively robust track.

It's another breakup song, but this time also about the hassles of being seen, especially in L.A., after a breakup. Rumors circulated that this song was in part about stepping out with Winona Ryder, but Beck refused to engage the topic in interviews, saying that 'talking about any of this is weird unless you're a complete exhibitionist'. For whatever the intimacy of the song, it provided a very public non-intimate moment at a 17 January 2005 Indian Ocean Tsunami Benefit concert, when comedian Will Farrell 'came out wearing a red leotard, doing interpretive dancing . . . (and) started humping my pump organ'. Beck's fifth most-performed song, it was released on multiple compilations and as a promo single in UK, Europe and the Far East. A live version (2:13) from 2006 appeared in the UK on the 2007 2-CD set *The Saturday Sessions: The Dermot O'Leary Show*. A re-recorded version (3:15), sounding more *Morning Phase*, showed up on 2022's Amazon Audible *Dear Life* Words + Music.

'End of the Day' 5:03
Beck dips into Gordon Lightfoot vocal territory on this mellow, strolling-pace number that reinforces the album's thematic tendencies. The musical highlights are Manning Jr.'s Clavinet backing and Hormel's inventive acoustic slide guitar. The original title was 'Nothing I Haven't Seen', which would have broken with the LP's generic titles.

'It's All in Your Mind' 3:06
The story goes that Beck was playing around with this 1995 single in the studio, producer Godrich was entranced, and the song was recycled for this album. The tune is accessorized here with synths, Wurlitzers, and cello, transforming the acoustic original into an arm-waving anthem. And cellist Suzie Katayama was an apt choice to help transform this into a plausible power ballad, having played the same instrument on the greatest power ballad of all time: 'Purple Rain'.

'Round the Bend' 5:15
Almost more a feeling than a song, Beck's resigned vocals meet slim acoustic guitar and bass and David Campbell's orchestration to create a tense, otherworldly aural equivalent to a late-night walk past a misty graveyard. The song is perhaps most noted for its similarities to Nick Drake's 'River Man' (1969). A live version (6:03) appeared in 2005 on the double-CD set *The BBC Sessions, Volume 1*, culled from Gilles Peterson's Worldwide program.

'Already Dead' 2:59
Another Lightfoot-like vocal/musical pairing, this compact number is highlighted by Beck and Hormel's acoustic prowess. The chorus' final line sums up the song thematically: "cause it feels like I'm watching something dying'.

'Sunday Sun' 4:44

This tune provides the emotional and spiritual climax for the LP, turns the page on the past, and looks toward a bright tomorrow: 'There's no other ending: Sunday sun / Yesterdays are ending: Sunday sun'. After the angst, second-guessing, and self-flagellation of the first nine songs, the tenth provides some much-needed hope. Musically there's a lot going on, with over 25 credited individual instruments. As guitar.com described it, the 'main riff pairs insistent pedal-note acoustic and piano with eerily discordant results, before willfully vandalizing the whole thing with wild slashes of electric guitar' – translation: this gets crazy and noisy. Although it's not quite the Shepard tone of 'I Am the Walrus', it does share Beatles elements with 'Lonesome Tears', with Beck noting: 'Anything that's descending is Beatles. They have the rights to descending chord structures'. A magnificent achievement.

'Little One' 4:27

Beck follows one anthem with another, this one a swelling semi-lullaby highlighted by Jason Falkner's punctuating electric guitar. The lyrics provide the album's title 'Drown drown / Sailors run aground / In a sea change nothing is safe', although the song feels disconnected from the main narrative, more like a coda. This is not surprising since the song originated in the *Odelay*-era; one gets the impression there are 'puzzles and pagans' lurking in this song's 'snake pit of souls'. And, digging back to the mid-1990s, the Cobain-like bridge is bold rock-and-roll indulgence on an otherwise subdued collection.

'Side of the Road' 3:23

No 'elevator bones and whip-lash tones' by the side of this road, just a touch of optimism and moving on after an album of emotional torment. The blues song is notable for the spacious production of the full band backing Beck's up-front vocals, but there's not much more to recommend it.

Related Tracks
'Ship in the Bottle' 3:11

While there are definite *Sea Changes* tendencies here, from the nautical motif ('the waves getting darker every hour'), to Beck's phrasing on the title line, this song feels adrift from the rest of the collection. While Beck described it as the 'super pop song of the record', it's not upbeat pop, but more like the high school slow dance song in a mid-1980s teen comedy. The song appeared on the original Japanese LP release and on vinyl re-issues.

'I'm So Glad' (Skip James) 3:36

Stunning voice, guitar, and harmonica, Beck tears through this blues classic, best known through Cream's blistering live versions. This song appeared in

The Soul of a Man (sound familiar?), Wim Wenders' entry in Martin Scorsese's documentary series *The Blues* (2003), and on the series soundtrack CD. Beck's version of James' 'Cypress Grove Blues', recorded during the same June 2002 sessions, remains unreleased.

'Everybody's Gotta Learn Sometime' (James Warren) 5:54
Beck adds vocals to Jon Brion's faithful (if long) take on The Korgis' beautiful 1980s UK top-five synth-pop single. An essential element of Michel Gondry's *Eternal Sunshine of the Spotless Mind*, it's a sentimental fan favorite and Beck's most frequently performed cover song. It appeared on the 2004 soundtrack CD.

'Christian Dior Theme' 22:07
Produced by Nigel Godrich, this epic includes snippets and ideas later incorporated into songs on 2006's *The Information*. It was used for the July 2004 Parisian runway preview of Christian Dior's 2005 Men's spring/summer wear and subsequently released through the company's website. The song is mostly electronic, at times veering into ELP-like keyboards, at the closing incorporating acoustic guitar with a melody reminiscent of 'Broken Drum'. It's also known as 'Coming Around Again', one of the few atmospherically repeated phrases. A little-known gem.

'True Love Will Find You in the End' (Daniel Johnston) 3:23
Accompanying himself on acoustic guitar and harmonica, Beck slows down and expands Johnston's achingly optimistic tune. Like Beck, outsider artist Johnston began his musical career creating a series of homemade cassettes. From 1984's *Retired Boxer*, this song has been covered over 30 times, most notably by Wilco and Spiritualized. The song was released as a standalone digital download single on 8 March 2017 after appearing on the 2004 collection *The Late Great Daniel Johnston: Discovered Covered*.

Guero (2005)

Personnel:
Beck: vocals, guitar, bass guitar, additional sounds, slide guitar, intro programming, percussion, tambourines, acoustic guitar, electric guitar, harmonica, vocoder, piano, celesta, drums, beats, keyboards, handclaps, kalimba, 12-string guitar, stomp
The Dust Brothers: beats, handclaps
Paolo Díaz: 'dude'
Charlie Capen: additional sounds
Sean Davis: bass guitar
Roger Joseph Manning Jr.: Clavinet
Money Mark: organ
Justin Meldal-Johnsen: bass, guitar sounds
Joey Waronker: drums
Smokey Hormel: electric guitar
Christina Ricci (as Kurisuti-na): girl
Jack White: bass guitar
Petra Haden: vocals
David Campbell: string arrangements
Produced by: Beck Hansen, The Dust Brothers, Tony Hoffer
Recorded at: The Boat, Madhatter, The Sound Factory, September 2003-August 2004
Release date: 29 March 2005
Label: Interscope
Highest chart places: UK: 15, US: 2
Running time: 49:55

Beck started writing a follow-up to *Sea Change* during his 2002 acoustic tour but lost over three dozen songs when he forgot a demo tape backstage. He didn't start writing again until about a year later. In September 2003, he gathered these new songs and some pre-*Midnight Vultures* songs and once again set to work with The Dust Brothers, now ensconced in their state-of-the-art studio The Boat. The new studio rendered overly crisp audio results, which meant that the trio had to find ways to make the recordings less sterile. One method involved running the songs through an old-time transistor radio. Unlike typical bang-bang Godrich sessions, *Guero* sessions, which included two songs recorded with Tony Hoffer, spread over the better part of a year.

Guero ('Whitey' in East L.A. slang) was scheduled for an October 2004 release, but production delays pushed it back to spring. In the meantime, an alternate, unfinished version of the LP, dubbed *Ubiquitous*, leaked online in January 2005. Beck released the four-track *Gameboy Variations (Hell Yes)* EP on 1 February 2005. The finished album, containing none of the EP mixes, received a late March release and was followed in December by the release of the remix LP *Guerolito*. Around this time, Beck also started to drop unreleased tracks on his website.

The album received strong reviews, with a split between critics apprehensive that The Dust Brothers collaboration would result in *Odelay* 2.0, and those giddy at the prospect. Andy Gill (*The Independent*) was in the latter category, finding the album full of 'judicious blends of beats, riffs, songs and raps spiralling off in a variety of directions, with no noticeable shortfall in coherence'. *The Guardian*, in a very brief review, gave the LP four out of five stars, as did *Rolling Stone*. *MOJO* ('While there are enough inspiring moments on here to suggest Beck hasn't yet run out of ideas, it demonstrates that the best way for him to revisit former triumphs would be to travel somewhere new'.) and *Neumu* ('There is nothing here that thrills with its audacity, beauty, beat or lyrics. Instead, we are given a solid batch of songs that for any other artist would be a crowning achievement, but for Beck is just mediocre.') both trended on the lower side of rankings.

Beck played *Guero* shows in Japan, the UK, and Europe in the spring and early summer of 2005 before embarking on a longer US trek in late summer. He kept up this rigid touring schedule in spite of suffering a spinal injury during the film of the 'E-Pro' video, a mishap only revealed in 2014. It wouldn't be until after the late 2008 *Modern Guilt* tour that Beck accommodated the injury, playing only about 50 dates from 2009-2013 while healing.

Guero debuted at number two on the US charts, his highest position ever. It hit 15 in the UK, bettered by three later albums. It went Gold in the US and Silver in the UK. The album spawned two singles. 'E-Pro' went to number 38 in the UK and 56 in the US, although it topped the Alternative Airplay chart. 'Girl' hit 45 in the UK and scraped the US charts at 100, his last of seven Hot 100 hits. *Guerolito* had its own UK single, 'Ghettochip Malfunction (Hell Yes)', which failed to chart.

The standard and deluxe editions of *Guero* were released simultaneously. In addition to the 13 album tracks, the deluxe edition included seven additional tracks, three new tracks, and four remixes, one of which, 'Still Missing (Röyksopp Remix)', is a commercially released exclusive track. The deluxe edition included a DVD with an essential 5.1 Stereo Surround mix of the standard LP tracks, which are accompanied by videos created by D-Fuse, a London-based visual arts company. The Japan Tour Edition, 21 July 2005, includes a five-track disc that features the exclusive remix 'Girl (Junior Senior Remix)'. The non-exclusive deluxe and tour edition tracks were included on *Guerolito*.

Guerolito was released in the US on 13 December 2005 and in the UK on 23 January 2006. US formats included the 16-track double vinyl LP, listed first here, and a 14-track CD, which dropped the last two songs. The 16-track UK CD included 'Fax Machine Anthem (Dizzee Rascal Remix)' in place of the Dntel 'Broken Drum' remix. Other international releases, such as Canada, Germany, and Japan, dropped the Dntel track in favor of 'Wish Coin (Superthriller Daddy Daddy Remix)', which has not been commercially released in the US or UK, although it appeared on the US promo *Remix EP #2*. The Japan CD also included 'Missing (Remix by Hugo Nicolson)', which shows up on streaming services such as Spotify alongside 'Gucci Bag in Flames [Hell Yes] (Green, Music and Gold)'.

This chapter tries to maintain some chronologic coherence, save the *Hell Yes* EP. It begins with an overview of the core *Guero* tracks, followed by deluxe edition and Japan tracks, *Guerolito*, and then related tracks and Beck. com songs – it was a busy year for a man in pain.

'E-Pro' (Beck Hansen, John King, Michael Simpson, Beastie Boys) 3:22
'E-Pro' is muscular, dumb fun: brain-worm guitar and meaningless 'Na na na' chant chorus meets memorable smooth talk on the verses. The lyrics are an especially caustic indictment of a liar or rumormonger who's 'handing out a confection of venom'. Beck claimed in multiple interviews that the title was just a placeholder that never got replaced. However, considering the Scientology controversies swirling around him at the time, it's difficult not to consider the song in relation to the group's use of the E-Meter (electropsychometer), a key device in the auditing process that clears an individual from negative past occurrences. The song includes a prominent sample of the Beastie Boys' 'So What'cha Want', from 1992's brilliant *Check Your Head*. It was released on multiple various-artist collections, as a UK 7" picture disc, and as a promo radio edit (3:13), with ten seconds of the beginning lopped off. The leaked version is rawer, especially the last 45 seconds, which, as in the video, end abruptly.

'Qué Onda Guero' (Beck Hansen, John King, Michael Simpson) 3:29
Where it's at? How about East L.A.? The bitter opening song is followed by the quasi-title song, an affectionate portrait of Beck's childhood community, one also covered in Cheech Marin's 1985 Springsteen parody 'Born in East L.A.'. The light-Mexican, get-fresh flow of the song's first half finds the singer describing the neighborhood ('Abuelitas with plastic bags / Walking to the church with the Spanish candles' – Abuelitas means Grandmas) and getting called out with the title phrase: 'what's up, white boy?' The second part of the song features street sounds captured by Beck and his 'Guatemalan skater friend'; Paolo Diaz's interjections, mostly in Spanish, eventually devolve into a search for the new Yanni cassette. The leaked version includes an unidentified sample from the name-checked Banda Macho ('Mango ladies vendadoras / At a bus stop sing a Banda Macho chorus' – vendadoras means sellers), a 1970s Mexican band. It also includes a reference to the notorious Mara Salvatrucha gang, aka MS-13, which is obscured on the released version.

'Girl' (Beck Hansen, John King, Michael Simpson) 3:30
This is a vexing song that one critic claimed 'exudes(s) a vaporous disquiet'. It starts off with a disarming chiptune riff and settles into a 1960s surf/girl

group groove, highlighted by Beck's ascending acoustic slide guitar solo. It's all very catchy, but there's a level of sterility in the sonic assemblage, especially in the bass, which is a bit troubling in its cold-hearted directness. This is paralleled in the lyrics, cheerfully delivered, but seemingly about a kidnapping and murder. There is controversy among fans about what is being sung in the chorus: 'sun-eyed girl' or 'cyanide girl' – either way, it's deceptively dark. The song was a few years old by the time it was recorded, going through name changes such as 'Songy' and 'Summer Girl'. The leaked version (3:48) includes a longer opening riff. It's in the top ten of Beck's most-played live songs.

'Missing' (Beck Hansen, John King, Michael Simpson, Vinicius de Moraes, Carlos Lyra) 4:44
This gentle but determined tune sways to the repeated sample of 'Voce E Eu' by Claus Ogerman & His Orchestra, punctuated by Beck and David Campbell's sweeping string arrangement. The lamentable memories ('I can't believe these tears were mine / I'll give them to you to put away in a box') recall the torment of *Sea Change*. And while the second part of the song does seem to be about a woman, there's speculation that the first part and chorus concern departed friend Elliot Smith. Originally titled 'Brazilica', this ends the Brazilian trilogy, following 'Deadweight' and 'Tropicalia'. With the original title, this track opened the leaked version, extending the end by about a dozen seconds (4:57).

'Black Tambourine' (Beck Hansen, John King, Michael Simpson, Eugene Blacknell) 2:47
The core of the track, an off-kilter Bo Diddley beat, is a lift from Serge Gainsbourg's 'Requiem Pour Un Con' (1968), topped by a harsh guitar interlude and tambourine. Lyrically the song is a tick-off from 'Girl', a less violent narrator in another unstable relationship ('I know there's something wrong / Might take a fire to kill it'). Feeding on these sonic and lyric imbalances, the song was used to significant effect in David Lynch's endlessly perplexing *Inland Empire* (2006); the soundtrack album (2007) included a slightly different song mix. A European promo 12" included an instrumental version, and the leaked version added a few seconds in the middle (2:52). The song includes percussion samples from 'We Know We Got to Live Together' (1973) by Eugene Blacknell & The New Breed, and Little Sonny's 'Eli's Pork Chop' (1970). Beck band member Brian LeBarton released two remixes through his website: 'Black Tambourine (Tron Remix)' (3:15) and 'Black Tambourine (The Admirals Remix)' (3:30).

'Earthquake Weather' (Beck Hansen, John King, Michael Simpson, Slave) 4:26
The LP's unheralded gem, this busy *Midnite Vultures*-era retread nods toward the south-of-the-border as it flows and slinks in early 1970s R&B fashion.

The only LP track with a full band, it's hard to choose a highlight among Money Mark's organ, Manning Jr.'s Clavinet, and Hormel's electric stylings: ain't it a groove? Sharing a title with Joe Strummer's post-Clash debut album, the song's about that time before something big happens, the horse latitudes of everyday life. The song includes samples of 'What It Is' (1972) by The Temptations and 'Coming Soon' and 'Just Freak' from Slave's *The Concept* (1978). The leaked version is almost imperceptibly longer (4:33).

'Hell Yes' (Beck Hansen, John King, Michael Simpson) 3:18

The dutchie is once again passed from coast to coast, as Beck returns to funky hip-hop/rap mode in this commentary on the shallowness of consumer and celebrity culture ('Perfunctory idols rewriting their bibles'). There's a kitchen sink quality that works – vocoder vocals, a harmonica, and Christina Ricci as 'Kurisuti-na', a sushi waitress. The Dust Brothers had auditioned waitresses to hollowly say 'Please enjoy', but had no satisfaction. Ricci turned up in the studio, was recruited for the part, and nailed it with encouragement from Beck. The leaked version (3:28) has an alternate fade. The song includes samples from Ohio Players' 'Far East Mississippi' (1976), one of the slinkiest songs ever, and 'Under the Influence of Love' (1973) by Barry White's Love Unlimited.

'Broken Drum' 4:30

One of two tracks co-produced by Tony Hoffer, this song both stands apart from the more clinical beats-vibe that constitutes the bulk of the LP and serves as its spiritual center. A hymn to fallen comrade Elliot Smith ('Fare thee well / my only friend'), the pensive solo track features a metronomic pulse that echoes the dull, constant pain of loss, augmented by bursts and waves of sonic memories. The song was originally titled 'Outerspace'.

'Scarecrow' (Beck Hansen, John King, Michael Simpson) 4:16

Anchored by a determined bass, this electro-blues number with some distorted vocals and atmospheric guitar flourishes wouldn't sound out of place on U2's *Zooropa* (1993), co-produced by Brian Eno. While I don't think Beck ever directly acknowledged Eno in print, his approach embodies that discussed in Eno's seminal lecture 'The Recording Studio as a Compositional Tool' (1979), and the producer's 1977 collaboration with German band Cluster, 'Ho Renomo', led off Beck's 2013 Spotify playlist. Here's Beck embracing an Eno-like studio approach: 'there's a haunting, high-pitched sound that goes through the whole thing – that's me singing through the echo effect. All the percussive-type stuff on there is just me yelling through the delay pedal'. Lyrically the song seems to be about being tricked, losing control of the self ('Sometimes the jail can't chain the cell') and spiritual self-doubt ('I wanted hope from a grave / I wanted strength from a slave'). Beck uses the figure of a scarecrow in the album closer 'Emergency Exit' and

'Fuckin with My Head', and also puts the similarly slim skeletons in jail in 'Lord Only Knows'. Hard not to think of them as Beck proxies. The leaked version (6:56) is the most distinct from the released version, smoking and expansive – more guitar, more harmonica, more blues. It's a better version but would have stuck out on the finished LP.

'Go It Alone' (Beck Hansen, John King, Michael Simpson, Jack White) 4:09

This blues shuffle was co-written by, and features bass from then-White Stripes head honcho and Beck pal, Jack White. The duo reportedly worked on another song at the sessions and would collaborate in the future. The song seems to be about a guy who's deciding to hightail it out of town and not pop the question, although some lines ('Strike a match on a bathroom wall where my number is written') might indicate the song is from a woman's point of view. The song's end marks the return of Beck's Wurlitzer, the first since 'Where It's At'; he was unsure whether to use the instrument, saying, 'It would have been too obvious to use it, so I kept myself from doing that for a while'. The leaked version (4:16) features a longer fadeout. The song includes a sample of 'Outside Love' (1970) by Brethren, a band that featured David Bowie's longest-tenured sideman, keyboardist Mike Garson.

'Farewell Ride' 4:19

The second Hoffer co-production is a bluesy funeral march that finds Beck reconnecting on record with his folk music roots. A solo tune featuring harmonica and some fine slide guitar, the song is about a man – an outlaw? A scarecrow in a cell? – envisioning his final trip to the cemetery. The song is an adaptation of the traditional song 'Two White Horses in A Line', first recorded in 1931 by The Two Poor Boys. It's also adjacent to 'See That My Grave is Kept Clean', recorded by Blind Lemon Jefferson and Bob Dylan, among others, and 'One Kind Favor', recorded by Peter, Paul and Mary and Canned Heat. The Subtle remix incorporates more of the source material lyrics.

'Rental Car' (Beck Hansen, John King, Michael Simpson) 3:06

Attention people: we are about to both rock and roll! And 'Rock' was an early title of this heart-pumping, fist-shaking *Midnite Vultures* leftover. Beck, joined here by Meldal-Johnsen on 'guitar sound' and Manning Jr. on Clavinet, has the top down and he's letting it all hang out – in-your-face bass, summer-groove handclaps, and crunching guitar. Beck downplayed the song's meaning, saying: 'It went through a lot of different stages lyrically, but ultimately the chorus is 'Yeah yeah yeah'. It doesn't mean anything else'. Fair enough, but while the song is about 'kicking the dust' in a rental car, it's also a reminder that we're all just inhabiting rentals, as 'At the end of the night there's a road we'll be on', a place 'where the reaper is walking alone'. For all this, the most memorable aspect of the song is Petra Haden's bridge vocals, countered halfway through by a furious guitar burst. The producers wanted to sample some 'yodeling', but couldn't find the sample owners, so instead, they brought in Haden to sing the opening of the Barry Sisters' version of the traditional Yiddish song 'Chiribim Chiribom'. After the 'la la la' portion, Haden sings 'Lomir zingen', which means 'let's sing'. While not out of place here on an album that touches on religious/spiritual renewal, thematically, this would have been a better fit on the Jewish-trending *Midnite Vultures*.

'Emergency Exit' (Beck Hansen, John King, Michael Simpson) 4:03
This slow gospel-blues anthem closes both the album proper and the album's more personal, spiritual song cycle that began with 'Broken Drum'. Beck shines on 12-string and slide guitar, backed by his dad's orchestration. The plantation musical rhythm is reinforced by sharecropper lyrics: 'Now hold your hand onto the plow / Work the dirt till the sun goes down'. Like other song cycle tunes, this one's about letting go, this time of earthly things, and ending up where 'kindness will find you'. While not an endorsement, per se, the song has a religious bent ('What's left of death is more than fear / Let dust be dust and the good Lord near'), and it ran through the Christian titles 'Gospel' and 'Nazarene' (either Jesus Christ or one of His followers) before settling on its more secular, less direct title. Addressing the song's soundscape, The Dust Brothers recall some issues with their digital sample library playing at half speed for this song, a problem that provided its own solution: 'The average person would say 'That sounds horrible, they need to improve their stretching algorithms', but Beck was like 'Wow, that sounds amazing''.

Deluxe and Japan tracks
'Send a Message to Her' (Beck Hansen, John King, Michael Simpson) 4:30
This stripped-down, angular pop/new wave song sounds like a late 1970s/ early 1980s Bowie song minus the wild Fripp or Belew guitar solo. It's fun to hear Beck jam a bit, even if it's only with himself. With some edits and maybe some literal bells and whistles, it could have been a single.

'Chain Reaction' (Beck Hansen, John King, Michael Simpson) 3:28
A 'Novacane'-like loud punch of a song that wavers between the yelling title chorus and the grim rap verses, with lyrics such as 'They spit pig iron, tell you nothing is wrong / Put a heart on a pike sing a resurrection song'. The song contains samples from the 'Wasp/Behind the Wall of Sleep/Bassically/ N.I.B.' suite that ends the US first side of Black Sabbath's 1970 eponymous debut LP. Definitely a bonus track, it was also on the leaked *Ubiquitous*. Not to be confused with the 2022 Joy Downer single featuring Beck.

'Clap Hands' (Beck Hansen, John King, Michael Simpson) 3:21
This vaguely Middle-Eastern electronic dance number could serve as an
overture to 2005-2006 Beck, a clear bridge to '1000BPM'. It became a
mainstay of his live show around this time and was performed on *Saturday
Night Live* on 28 October 2006 alongside 'Nausea'.

'Still Missing (Röyksopp Remix)' (Beck Hansen, John King, Michael
Simpson) 4:59
Beck's vocals are here, but otherwise, the Norwegian duo pick up the pace,
go heavy on the rhythm, and move this out of the somber zone and onto the
dancefloor.

'Girl (Junior Senior Remix)' (Beck Hansen, John King, Michael
Simpson) 4:13
The first part of this features a bright guitar riff and female background
vocals, reminiscent of major-label period Dandy Warhols, while the second
part sounds like an off-kilter electro-line dance. The Danish duo Junior Senior
had a number one UK dance hit in 2002 with 'Move Your Feet'.

Guerolito

'Ghost Range' (E-Pro Remix by Homelife) (Beck Hansen, John King,
Michael Simpson, Beastie Boys) 4:24
This creditable ghost/hauntology remix by UK group Homelife thrives on the
eccentricities of the legendary multi-instrumentalist Paddy Steer.

'Qué Onda Guero' (Islands Remix) (Beck Hansen, John King, Michael
Simpson) 2:29
A French horn, clarinet, and bass clarinet act as a warped Mariachi band on
this remix by Islands, a group formed by ex-members of The Unicorns.

'Girl' (Octet Remix) (Beck Hansen, John King, Michael Simpson) 3:54
This pounding remix highlights the piano, guitar, and drums before slipping
into electronic dub. The song was mixed by Krikor, a producer who was
part of the French Touch scene that also spawned Daft Punk, and remixed/
produced by French duo Octet. Also known as 'Recluse Street Remix'.

'Heaven Hammer [Missing]' (AIR Remix) (Beck Hansen, John King,
Michael Simpson) 4:54
Heavy on gated drums and clipped synths, this cold remix by Air would be at
home in the climax of a late 1980s TV crime drama.

'Shake Shake Tambourine [Black Tambourine]' (Smallstars remix by
Adrock) (Beck Hansen, John King, Michael Simpson) 3:37

The Beastie Boy Adam Horowitz (aka Ad Rock aka 41 Small Stars) adds some vocals and successfully reimagines the guitar line as an infectious keyboard riff.

'Terremoto Tempo [Earthquake Weather]' (Remix by Mario C.) (Beck Hansen, John King, Michael Simpson) 3:47
Producer/collaborator Mario Caldato Jr. strips away most of the track and adds enticing Tropicalia backing from Brazilian +2 members (Alexandre) Kassin (bass, keyboards) and Domenico (Lancellotti), each of whom released superb LPs on David Byrne's Luaka Bop label in 2018.

'Ghettochip Malfunction [Hell Yes]' (remixed by 8-Bit) (Beck Hansen, John King, Michael Simpson) 2:42
Counterintuitive to describe a video-game version as 'warm', but 8-Bit funk-up the groove and create a more intimate vibe. Also on *GameBoy Variations* 'Hell Yes' EP.

'Broken Drum' (Boards of Canada Remix) 5:40
Trippy and melancholic, Beck said in a 2005 interview that this was 'his favourite remix he ever had done'. It's referenced as 'Blank Space', as Boards of Canada had remixed the song when it was called 'Outerspace'. Includes a reverse sample of BoC's 'Forest Moon'.

'Scarecrow' (Remixed by El-P) (Beck Hansen, John King, Michael Simpson) 4:37
Brooklyn producer El-P (Jaime Meline) remixes with an upfront fake-drum rhythm and some Eno-like textures circa *Achtung Baby* by U2.

'Wish Coin [Go It Alone]' (Remixed by Diplo) (Beck Hansen, John King, Michael Simpson, Jack White) 3:46
An early remix by three-time Grammy winner Diplo, this amusing version samples, but pulls up short of a straight mash-up with The (English) Beat's 'Twist and Crawl'.

'Farewell Ride' (Remixed by Subtle) (Beck Hansen, Doseone) 4:51
This remix by the Oakland hip hop group Subtle is anything but what their name suggests. The first 1:30 pumps up the volume, at which point rapper Adam 'Doseone' Drucker adds some nasally takes on parts of 'See That My Grave is Kept Clean'.

'Rental Car' (Remixed by John King) (Beck Hansen, John King, Michael Simpson) 2:59
This low-key remix by Dust Brother John King features banks of synths and sounds from TV composer and co-producer Brad Breeck, a bigger vocal part

for Petra Haden, and live Tenacious D. member John Spiker running his guitar through a Maestro Ring Modulator.

'Emergency Exit' (Th' Corn Gangg Remix) (Beck Hansen, John King, Michael Simpson) 3:18
Remixed by The Unicorns/Island side project Th' Corn Gangg, this electro-old-time mashup reminds one of a slower 'Cotton Eye Joe' by Rednex.

'Clap Hands' (Beck Hansen, John King, Michael Simpson) 3:21
Same as the deluxe edition but listed in places as 'The Dust Brothers Remix'.

'Qué Onda Guero' (Nortec Collective Remix) (Beck Hansen, John King, Michael Simpson) 4:44
Nobody walks in LA, but this punchy synth-horn punctuated remix will have you strutting through the barrio. Nortec's name is a mashup of norteño, a Mexican regional music most associated with Los Tigres Del Norte, and techno. Beck would later turn to fellow Mexican electronica act Mexican Institute of Sound for a 'Wow' remix.

'Broken Drum' (Remixed by Dntel) 4:18
This sweeping, textured remix by The Postal Service's Jimmy Tamborello, aka Dntel, is gentle but moody, like a lost Badalamenti *Twin Peaks* song.

'Fax Machine Anthem' (Dizzee Rascal Remix) (Beck Hansen, John King, Michael Simpson) 3:07
Grime pioneer, 2012 Olympics performer, and 2020 MBE appointee Dizzee Rascal offers a minimal, electronic reading of the already angular tune.

'Wish Coin' (Superthriller Daddy Daddy Remix) (Beck Hansen, John King, Michael Simpson, Jack White) 3:26
English band and 2005 Beck tour-opener Superthriller foreground the vocals and turn the song into electronic modified reggae.

'Missing' (Hugo Nicolson Remix) (Beck Hansen, John King, Michael Simpson) 4:27
This almost-a-ukulele version hits the near side of too precious. Nicholson is a producer/engineer best known for working with Julian Cope, Primal Scream, and Bjork.

'Gucci Bag in Flames (Hell Yes)' (Green, Music and Gold) (Beck Hansen, John King, Michael Simpson) 2:41
Green, Music and Gold reimagine the song at some point in the early 1980s when Dad is grooving to an R&B beat at the same time Junior's doing a breakdance head-spin on a cardboard refrigerator box.

Related Tracks

'Venom Confection' (E-Pro Remix by Green, Music & Gold) (Beck Hansen, John King, Michael Simpson, Beastie Boys) 3:05
This keyboard-heavy, light-dance version puts one in the mind of Röyksopp. On 'E-Pro' remix CD.

'Gameboy/Homeboy' (Qué Onda Guero Remix) (Beck Hansen, John King, Michael Simpson) 2:38
A busy, percussive remix by 8-Bit, a self-proclaimed 'robotic old school Nintendo rap crew'. *GameBoy Variations* EP.

'Bad Cartridge' (E-Pro Remix) (Beck Hansen, John King, Michael Simpson, Beastie Boys) 2:55
Chiptune remix by Swedish artist Paza (Rahm) of the X-Dump collective. The mid-2000s saw an 8-bit music revival, but the biggest hit in the genre was one of the earliest, Buckner and Garcia's 1982 US top-ten single 'Pac-Man Fever'. *GameBoy Variations* EP.

'Bit Rate Variations in B-Flat' (Girl Remix) (Beck Hansen, John King, Michael Simpson) 2:44
Alternately titled, 'Paza Remix', this sounds the most like a video game soundtrack of the four *GameBoy Variations* tracks.

'Black Tambourine' (Remix by South Rakkas Crew) (Beck Hansen, John King, Michael Simpson) 3:34
An 8-bit, Dancehall remix from the Canadian DJs that wouldn't be out of place on *Midnite Vultures*. On the North American promo *Remix EP #1*.

'Qué Onda Guero' (Money Mark Remix) (Beck Hansen, John King, Michael Simpson) 1:03
This snippet, with a clean guitar sample and a more emphatic rhythm, is part of the 19-song Beck soundtrack to Brian Lotti's skate film *1st & Hope* (2006). This is the only exclusive track on the DVD.

'Funky Lil' Song' (Bruce Haack) 5:16
Beck embraces the loose kids vibe and has a lot of fun with the vocals, including a wonderful falsetto. He's accompanied by Ross Harris (The Wizard on 'Hotwax') and Erik Richards, both of DJ Me DJ. Recorded in 2001, it's a tribute to Bruce Haack, who along with Esther 'Miss' Nelson, released a decade's worth of trippy electronic kids music from 1963-1972. The song appeared on 2005's *Dimension Mix: A Tribute to Dimension 5 Records*.

'E-Pro (CapeLion V2 Remix)' (Beck Hansen, John King, Michael Simpson, Beastie Boys) 2:04
A hard-riff, chorus-chant remix by Swedish pop duo Cape Lion that showed up online in 2019. Beck probably fell in love with their 'Oh Girl' (2015), as anyone would.

Beck.com Tracks

The following appeared on Beck.com after a November 2005 website redesign.

'Untitled Song 2' 4:42
Brian Wilson fronting the Travelling Wilburys, this is an extremely catchy song that somehow fell through the cracks. I have no evidence, but the vocal timber and phrasing, such as on the 'When we wake up to ourselves / What's left of ourselves' couplet, seem to indicate this is one of the Nashville songs recorded in 2005 that eventually led to *Morning Phase*.

'Day for Night' 3:52
A very slow song that almost feels like a muddy remix of 'Lonesome Tears'.

'Sorrow' 3:44
An enticing, percussion-heavy song with a slight Middle Eastern feel. The lyrics read like being stuck in a foreign hotel with someone you no longer want to spend time with.

'Premonition' 3:25
This instrumental alternates George Winston-like New Age piano passages with Neil Young *Arc*-like guitar outbursts.

'Which Will' (Nick Drake) 2:53
'Pink Moon' (Nick Drake) 2:54
'Parasite' (Nick Drake) 4:22
These three tracks showed up on Beck.com on 27 December 2005. Beck offers mostly faithful versions of the pensive songs, all from Drake's 1972 acoustic LP *Pink Moon*. Not totally a dry run for the acoustic sincerity of *Morning Phase*, but not far off the mark. 'Parasite' includes LeBarton on drums and keyboards. Oddly, the song showed up in 2012 on the double-CD US promo *BMG's Got You Covered*.

'Acropolis Now' 4:50
Popped on Beck.com on 2 July 2006, this is a gentle piano instrumental that's periodically interrupted by screaming. This is an outtake from the *Nacho Libre* sessions.

The Information (2006)

Personnel:

Beck: vocals, acoustic guitar, electric guitar, melodica, piano, organ, keyboards, programming, effects, scratching, sitar, bass guitar, harmonica, kalimba, percussion, drums, drum effects, glockenspiel, Game Boy

Nigel Godrich: keyboards, programming, effects, scratching, tambourine, percussion, background vocals, Speak 'n Spell, whistle, Tote-A-Tune, kalimba, drums, Game Boy

Jason Falkner: bass guitar, electric guitar, acoustic guitar, African bass, Moog bass, background vocals, percussion, drums

James Gadson: drums, percussion, background vocals

Joey Waronker: drums, percussion, background vocals

Alejandro 'Alex' Acuna: percussion, background vocals

Brian LeBarton: Speak 'n Spell

Justin Stanley: electric guitar, acoustic guitar, background vocals, percussion, flute

Greg Kurstin: keyboards, berimbau, piano, bass keyboard, synthesizer, background vocals, acoustic guitar

DJ Z-Trip: scratching

Stevie Black: cello, percussion, background vocals

Lucia Ribisi: girl on 'Cellphone's Dead'

Cosimo Hansen: talking

David Campbell: arranger, conductor

Harvey Mason: drums

Sean Davis: bass guitar

Rachel Shelley: shipping forecast

Spike Jonze: talking on 'Exoskeleton'

Dave Eggers: talking on 'Exoskeleton'

Produced by: Nigel Godrich

Recorded at: Ocean Way, Conway, Sound Isadore, Beck's garage, 2003-2006

Release date: 3 October 2006

Label: Interscope

Highest chart places: UK: ineligible for charts, US: 7

Running time: 61:33

Official recording for the sprawling *The Information* began in 2003, before The Dust Brothers' *Guero* sessions. Beck and third-time producer Nigel Godrich laid down tracks at that time for their 'hip-hop' record and periodically returned to the material over the course of four years, building it up and tearing it down, a process that Beck termed 'painful'. The sporadic nature of the sessions is noticeable in the expansive personnel lineup and, to be honest, the uneven quality of the material. And the length: It's the first time Beck stretched an LP over an hour.

The album generally received warm reviews on release, although critics (especially in the UK) were beginning to discuss Beck in the past tense.

Entertainment Weekly called it a 'sonic tour de force', while Jon Pareles, (*New York Times*) said: 'His musical allusions once sounded like amused memories, something to toy with for fun. Now, on this darkly intelligent album, they sound like something to hold on to as everything else crumbles'. *MOJO* gave it three out of five stars, as did Caroline Sullivan in *The Guardian*, tempering a bit with: 'Taken on its own kaleidoscopic terms, however, *The Information* is a bracing reminder that Beck's musical imagination has survived his fall from fashion'.

The initial release featured a generic front cover and one of four sticker sheets for fans to create their own cover, and the UK release featured two bonus tracks. All these enticements disqualified the album from the UK charts. The initial limited edition of the LP also included a DVD with low-production videos for every song. The 27 February 2007 deluxe edition included all four sticker sets, a re-sequenced original LP plus three bonus tracks, the DVD, as well as a six-track remix disc. And 2008 saw a double-LP limited edition vinyl release. In addition to the 18-track album and six remix tracks, the vinyl set includes 'ten sticker sheets which have been re-sized exclusively for this release, two coloring books, and a 20-color fine art pen set'. As of this writing, unopened LPs sell for over £800/$1,000.

Beck toured UK/Europe in the late summer of 2006 prior to the LP's release and briefly toured the US in the fall. He offered a handful of dates in Australia and Japan in April 2007 before playing three South American shows in December, opening for The Police.

The Information went Gold in the US but didn't receive UK certification. There were three singles, none of which charted on either country's main chart.

'Elevator Music' 3:38

After a count-off opening, the LP starts at a smooth and funky pace propelled by bass and drums that disappear on occasion, leaving Beck's vocals alone. A toolbox of sounds is sprinkled on top, including some guitar and synth, and most notably, a phased melodica during the choruses. The song, rapped on the verses, is generally about the joy of music and sound, but seems more specifically about growing older and more domestic, along with the difficulties of transitioning from nights on the dance floor ('Tell me what's wrong with a little grind and bump') to the home and office where the elevator music plays. Most sources indicate 'na na na' fadeout vocals, but it sounds like distorted words, with another conversation going on lower in the mix.

'Think I'm in Love' 3:19

The album's third single is a catchy, bass-looped pop song. It's notable for piano crashes during the chorus and bongo riffs that run up to an infectious, questioning David Campbell-orchestrated bridge (one of Beck's best). Lyrically it's a love song about a guy who's unsure about being in love. The single was US promo only, and studio live versions appeared on

2007's *Live at The World Cafe: Vol. 24* (2:52) and 2012's *This Is BBC Radio 6 Music Live* (2:40).

'Cellphone's Dead' 4:45
The LP's second single – perhaps the most unlikely in Beck's career – is not something that the kids would be singing on the schoolyard. Unlike many assembled songs that hold together, such as 'Diamond Bollocks', this feels a bit more abruptly segmented, with the rapping verses coming up unexpectedly against the infectious bass-synth riff in the choruses and then against the festive intro/bridge that evolves into the two-minute outro of modified scratching, regular and monkey drums, cello, and a chorus of Becks. It feels a bit clever for the sake of being clever, but it also feels like the unusual structure would be at home on, say, David Bowie's *Low*. Building on a theme, the singer here is in search of meaningful music in an empty age ('Been a long time since the federal dime / Made a jukebox sound like a mirror in my mind').

The song features Beck's son Cosimo saying 'Hi!' and his niece Lucia Ribisi contributing on the 'one by one I'll knock you out' chorus and other background vocals. The Michel Gondry video version fades out at 3:45 and the single at 3:53. A studio live version (4:52) appears on the 2008 DVD *From the Basement*, alongside 'Motorcade'. *From the Basement* was producer Godrich's web-based musical variety show. This version of 'Cellphone's Dead', with live transitions between the parts, works better than the LP version and points toward 2013's expansive, suite-like version of *Low*'s 'Sound and Vision'.

'Strange Apparition' 3:48
This anthem of soaring harmonies, piano riffs, and falling-apart rhythms (and beats) feels like a 19th track for The Rolling Stones' *Exile on Main Street* (1972), although Beck claimed he 'wanted it to sound like when The Beatles get out all their percussion and go bananas'. The song opens with a reference to Psalm 22 ('Lord, please don't forsake me'), which is about being unworthy except with redemption through the Lord, and moves on to Matthew 19:24, which discusses how hard it is for the rich man to enter the Kingdom of God ('All the riches and the ruins / Now we all know how that story ends'). The slowed-down last 90 seconds are a letting go of earthly cares ('Anything should make you happy / Nothing could make you scared'). It's one of Beck's most underappreciated songs (although *The Guardian* did have it in their top ten in 2015).

'Soldier Jane' (Beck Hansen, Nigel Godrich) 3:58
Forward bass and James Gadson's drumming highlight this light dance song. The song reads like a simple pep talk ('Don't be afraid / Take your heart out of the shell') to someone who's hesitant to explore life.

'Nausea' 2:55

A slightly Latin acoustic rhythm is joined by all manner of percussion, beats, keyboards, and unidentified samples on this busy first US single. Sources report that Beck wanted the song 'to sound like The Stooges in South America'. While live versions were closer in sound to Iggy's band, the song's tongue-in-cheek bravado ('I'm a dead generator / In a cloud of exhaust') seems to parody 1973's 'Search and Destroy' ('I'm a street-walking cheetah with a heart full of napalm'). A live studio version (2:46) appeared on 2007's *Live From SNL*, recorded on 28 October 2006, on the US late-night TV program. The song was nominated in the now-discontinued best solo rock vocal performance, losing out to Dylan's 'Someday Baby'.

'New Round' 3:25

This quiet Dad song lands somewhere between a lullaby and a benediction, both comforting in the moment and an acknowledgment of an eventual sending out into the world. The music starts similarly to 'Sunday Sun' and the tune shares guitar elements with 'Dior Theme'. When discussing the album, Beck said: 'There are tracks where you can hear sprinklers and air-conditioning units – there's all kinds of atmosphere like that for a lot of it' – this is one of those tracks. This was dropped from seventh to fourteenth in the deluxe edition running order.

'Dark Star' 3:45

With a slinky bass-keyboard riff and a blast of harmonica, this haunting rap tune owes more than a nod to Stevie Wonder's 'Have A Talk with God' (1976). While Stevie's song is straightforward lyrically, this laidback rap is opaque and bleak; something bad is happening, but it's unclear what that something is ('Robots teach you all the rules to delete you / Backspace my brain / My equilibrium goes'). Beck says that both this and 'We Dance Alone' work against hip-hop's 'built-in masculinity', as he tried to introduce more 'vulnerability' to the genre. David Campbell's string arrangements augment the sound. The song ends with the 'One two' opening from 'Elevator Music'. This song moved up to track seven on the deluxe edition.

'We Dance Alone' 3:56

With a light funk groove and almost-whispered vocals, this song is a lament for a relationship that's passed ('Afraid of what pain might do to the pleasure we knew / Before we had to move on I did my best for you'). Minus the dark overtones and with a few tweaks, this would be at home on late 2010 LPs.

'No Complaints' 3:00

A brief, well-crafted pop song, it runs on clicky acoustic guitar, with a riff borrowed from The Toadies' 'Possum Kingdom' (1994), and a less-than-shredding Speak 'n Spell solo. The song is about enjoying domestic life enough that you don't acknowledge all the crap that's going on around you.

'1000 BPM' 2:29
Loud, frantic, and ominous, Beck serves up a techno-nightmare funk rap that sounds like The Bomb Squad meets *There's a Riot Goin' On*-era Sly Stone. Like a lot of earlier word assaults, the lyrics, such as 'Categorize the Antichrist / With credentials and a backstage pass', are intriguing and could be very specific whilst holding a lot of meaning...or could just sound good.

'Motorcade' (Beck Hansen, Nigel Godrich) 4:15
An experimental partner to the lullaby 'New Round', which it samples, this features a disarming acoustic guitar track, a memorable chorus, African percussion, precision synth-beats that eventually break free from the song, and an EQ-fried-wire solo outro (for lack of a better descriptor). The lyrics are geographically schizophrenic (desert, tundra, jungle, mountaintop, Moon, galaxy) and, taken with the melodic but inhuman vocal delivery, bring to mind the pre-surrealist landscape visions of Italian artist Giorgio de Chirico (and maybe some Dali). A live version (3:13) appears on the 2008 DVD *From the Basement*. While appreciating the diversity of musical approaches on *The Information*, this mannered version makes me wish that this LP had been less electronic and more studied as a band project.

'The Information' 3:46
Beck's first title track is a thrusting drums-and-bass-centered song that pulsates with haunting, slightly distorted lead vocals and (more) synthetic cowbell. The song finds an ill reckoning of our technological pursuit of information (as opposed to knowledge or wisdom?), bemoaning 'a heaven that we left behind'. The concept moves from the abstract ('transmission') to the embodied ('mannequin') to an active, poisoned, personified 'she' ('the sister of avarice') – ominous stuff.

'Movie Theme' (Beck Hansen, Nigel Godrich) 3:53
Ground control to Marissa Ribisi: 'Somebody needs you / Somebody who's far away'. Beck goes Bowie-quiet-synthy-spacey on this chorus-free 'remember I love you while I'm on the road' song. Beck says the song came about when 'we just messed . . . one afternoon before we started work'. He thought they 'strayed off the path', but he kept it on the LP because 'that's what makes an album diverse'. On the deluxe edition, 'Movie Theme' moved from track 14 to eight (between 'Dark Star' and 'We Dance Alone').

'The Horrible Fanfare / Landslide / Exoskeleton' (Beck Hansen, Nigel Godrich) 10:36
This joins three different songs into one extended, thematically connected track. The first two minutes are a rumbling, atmospheric rap. As noted in online sources, the title comes from the opening verse of French poet Arthur Rimbaud's 'Morning of Drunkenness', written in the mid-1870s and appearing

in print in 1886 in *Les Illuminations*. Rimbaud's free-flowing verse was a huge influence on Surrealism as well as rock stars from Jim Morrison to Patti Smith to Van Morrison. Beck's 'Horrible Fanfare' is another apocalyptic vision, in which the self must be removed from contagion to be saved: 'When the poison's coming from the person you're next to / Let the voltage of thought pull the plug from the wound'. Yes, much like getting Clear in Scientology. This first passage transitions to 'Landslide' through a backwards unreeling of a shipping forecast for Scotland's Northwestern Islands, read by *Lagaan* (2001) star Rachel Shelley – it appears forwards at the song's end. The second part is a traditional song, the only portion Beck attempted live. The song, under three minutes, is anchored by a fat bass sound and features an oh-so brief electric guitar solo. The lyrics are, again, cryptic and somewhat apocalyptic, but there's 'she' and 'poison' and 'eyes', and Himalayan (the 'tin-can mountaintop' of 'Motorcade' and the 'high-rise eyes' of 'The Information'?) and it's all coming down in a landslide. It's all either really important or, as the *NME* wrote, a 'slightly embarrassing *Battlefield Earth* moment'. The final movement, 'Exoskeleton' begins with another bass riff, this one sounding a bit exhausted. Then that fades away and we enter a Kubrickian echo chamber of ambient hums and drones. I expected a Monolith to appear in my bedroom; instead, I was greeted by writer Dave Eggers and director Spike Jonze talking about illuminated manuscripts. That is their answer to Beck's question: 'What would the ultimate record that ever could possibly be made sound like?' Beck says he originally wanted the conversation to run throughout the entire album, like a *Mystery Science Theater* commentary. Thankfully, it doesn't.

Deluxe Edition
'Inside Out' 3:44
The funky rhythm for this tune is born of UK new wave, sounding like a hybrid of A Certain Ratio's 'Do the Du' (1979) and Simple Minds' 'Theme for Great Cities' (1981). Beyond the dense instrumentation, Beck's vocals are the highlight. The song is a backwards or opposite song ('Take your voice back from the ventriloquist' 'Dead sun rays giving me shivers'), with the effect that the movement up the (spiritual) ladder of 'Movie Theme' is reversed: 'Down another rung / We're slipping down now' (which would also be the case in 'Heaven's Ladder'). Also known as 'Remain in the Dark', as it was performed live in early 2005. US Target retail store free download.

'This Girl That I Know' 2:44
This is a lackadaisical funk-rap number reminiscent of Sly and the Family Stone's looser 1970s jams, with some sharp ear-slicing percussion strewn on top. While the verses are in keeping with the falling-apart technological vision of *The Information* ('Cities in shambles / Untangling tangles / People get together to uncover the ruins'), the choruses, about meeting hip girls (she

works at a literary journal, likes French movies) at hip shows (minutemen, Sonic Youth), are a bit jokey for the body of the LP. The video version (3:24) adds a 25-second instrumental intro before the CD's opening laser blast and a brief coda after a few seconds of silence at the end of the CD version.

'O Menina' 2:09
The fourth quarter of the Brazilian Trilogy? Beck has fun with this brief Brazilian dance song which is the title/chorus ('the girl') wrapped around a verse about a nightmare hippy goth who's 'throwing daggers with her eyes' and terrorizing Rio de Janeiro. Was known as 'The Girl from R.I.P.-anema' when Beck discussed it in a *Rolling Stone* preview article.

'Cellphone's Dead: Ellen Allien Remix' 5:37
Drums/dance-oriented sub-techno version from the German remixer that blends in the chorus and the 'eye of the sun' chant.

'Nausea Pirates Mix: Bumblebeez Remix' 2:28
Produced by Invisibl aka the Australian band The Bumblebeez, siblings Christopher and Pia Colonna, this strips the driving bite from the song and adds some loose guitar that gives the song a 'teenager playing guitar in front of a mirror' feel.

'Dark Star: David Andrew Sitek Remix' 4:08
TV on the Radio producer Sitek turns in a gem. The first half is a more percussive take on the original, but the second half opens the song up, building on the song's orchestral riff with King Crimson-like cacophony of flutes, saxes, synths, and more percussion. Also known as the 'TV on the Radio' Mix.

'Nausea: The Chap Remix' 3:55
The London band sticks close to the structure and goes full-up Kraftwerk for the first two minutes before experimenting electronically with different phases of the track for the second half. Also appeared on the Atlanta radio station compilation CD *99x Live X 11: Strange Apparition* (2006), featuring cover artwork by Beck.

'Cellphone's Dead: Jamie Lidell Limited Minutes Remix' 4:32
Not far from the original, with some blips and beeps and beats added by the multi-instrumentalist who opened for Beck and would soon collaborate on solo and Record Club recordings.

'Cellphone's Dead Villalobos Entlebuch Rmx: Ricardo Villalobos Remix' 14:38
This minimalist, click-track percussion remix gets love from fans of the

German DJ Ricardo Villalobos, but there's not enough dynamism as only reshuffled vocal lines vary much over the extreme length. Entlebuch is a city in Switzerland, for what it's worth.

Related Tracks
'There is No Place for Me in This World' 1:42
A sweet acoustic instrumental featuring harmonica and humming, it recalls *Pat Garrett / Self Portrait*-era Bob Dylan. This and the next two tracks were released on the *Nacho Libre* soundtrack CD, in the US on 24 October 2006 and the UK on 7 May 2007.

'10,000 Pesos' 1:54
Guitarist Justin Stanley and future Crowded House drummer Matt Sherrod round out Beck's humming and whistling for a sentimental instrumental on the verge of Lynyrd Skynyrd's 'Tuesday's Gone'.

'Tender Beasts of the Spangled Night' 1:51
The most fully formed song, this heroic instrumental features acoustic guitar, various shakers, and glockenspiel.

'Holy Man' 4:02
Backed by LeBarton and Stanley, Beck's inflected vocals highlight a slower, sing-along adaptation of Mr. Loco's 'Hombre Religioso (Religious Man)'. The Mr. Loco version leads off the *Nacho Libre* soundtrack release; a portion of Beck's version is in the film and the full version circulates online. Beck sampled Mr. Loco's 'Bubble Gum' on 'Hotwax'. The unreleased tracks 'My Heart is with the Children' and 'Return of the Luchador' also feature in the film.

'Last Fair Deal Gone Down' (Robert Johnson) 3:34
Accompanied by a Smokey Hormel's mean slide, and channeling some combination of Bono, Jack White, and Robert Plant, Beck teases out a different, deeper voice in this boisterous take on a lesser-known Robert Johnson track. The song, the only Johnson track Beck has recorded, was captured on 26 August 2001 during a two-day celebration of recordist Harry Smith and his *Anthology of American Folk Music*, his three-LP Folkways collection of the late 1920s and early 1930s American roots 78s. The song appears in the video *The Harry Smith Project – Live* and on the double-CD collection, *The Harry Smith Project: Anthology of American Folk Music Revisited*, both released in 2006.

'Forget Marie' (Lee Hazelwood) (2:36)
Beck recorded this country track in late 2006 in Nashville. The original is from Lee Hazlewood's 1968 LP *Love and Other Crimes*. It was streamed

on Beck.com in August 2007. In a 2015 interview, Beck recalled trips to Nashville that ultimately ended in never released albums: 'I recorded a lot of material, and most of it was traditional country music, using a lot of local musicians, and I had a great time doing it. And then, when I went home, I was not sure if I quite nailed it'.

'Timebomb' 2:50

This frantic, one-off, dumb-fun single is a pulsing electro-dance track about, well, having a timebomb. As a press release announced, it is 'a song for bonfires, blackouts, and the last hurrah of summer' (released 21 August 2007). Brian LeBarton does yeoman's work here, as do the five female backing vocalists. Anyone familiar with Toni Basil's video smash 'Mickey' (1981) will have their memory jogged. The song was released online before its release as a US vinyl 12", which featured an instrumental version B-side. It snagged a Grammy Award nomination for Best Solo Rock Vocal Performance, losing to Bruce Springsteen's 'Radio Nowhere'.

Modern Guilt (2008)

Beck: vocals, guitars, flute, percussion, electric piano, bass guitar, marimba, tambourine, slide guitar
Brian LeBarton: synthesizer
Jason Falkner: bass guitar, guitar
Chan Marshall: vocals
Danger Mouse: beats, keyboard bass, synthesizer, programming, sounds
Greg Kurstin: organ, piano, synthesizer
Joey Waronker: drums
Matt Mahaffey: bass guitar
Larry Corbett: cello
Drew Brown: beat
David Campbell: string arrangements, conductor
Produced by: Beck Hansen, Danger Mouse
Recorded at: Anonyme Studios, 2008
Release date: 8 July 2008
Label: DGC (US) / XL (UK)
Highest chart places: US: 4, UK: 9
Running time: 33:33

Beck contacted Danger Mouse (Brian Joseph Burton), co-founder of Gnarls Barkley and producer of multiple hit artists, including Gorillaz, Black Keys, and Adele, in late 2007. Early the next year, the two spent a week talking about their influences and built an easy-flowing working relationship that led to a tight ten-song LP plus a few outtakes.

Just as critics complained about *The Information* being too long, the main complaint about *Modern Guilt* is that it's too short. They'd have to wait for *Morning Phase* for the baby bear album length. The reviews for *Modern Guilt* weren't poor as much as unenthusiastic. Among the more positive, Joan Anderman (*Boston Globe*) said 'with ten songs clocking in at just 33 minutes, *Modern Guilt* feels fleeting, even temporal, and that seems to be the point. It's destined to be an artifact of an age that's rocketing, Beck suspects, toward oblivion'. *Q* and *The Sun* both gave four out of five stars. *Uncut* paid a backhanded compliment: 'So Beck is finally fun again, and you suspect the person most surprised by how well *Modern Guilt* turned out is the guy who made it'.

Among the glummer assessments, Rob Fitzpatrick (*The Guardian*) offered two out of five stars, opining, 'there is no attempt to reach out, none of the classic pop singles Beck has been revered for, just ten inward-looking, unlovable tracks'.

Unlike the two previous releases, *Modern Guilt*'s marketing was free of bells, whistles, stickers, and remixes. It was also the last LP of Beck's Geffen/ Interscope contract, and it failed to achieve any sales certifications. Three singles failed to bother the charts.

Beck played about ten UK/European shows in early summer 2008 before a more extensive early fall US/Canada tour. This would be his last extensive touring until 2014, at which time he revealed that the 'E-Pro' back injury almost made him give up touring entirely.

In March 2009, Beck, backed by Brian LeBarton, Jessica Dobson, Bram Inscore, and Joey Waronker, recorded and filmed an acoustic version of the album. Videos were released on Beck.com weekly starting in July 2009. Beck's official follow-up album to *Modern Guilt* wouldn't be released until February 2014, a gap of five and a half years. But the time wasn't unproductive: some was spent with his growing family, some on healing his back, and some on less Beck-central projects. The last category included production work, the Record Club recordings, and the *Song Reader* project (see Chapter 17). He also reworked the music of legends Phillip Glass and David Bowie and released three of his most adventuresome singles. It's a rich period that ultimately fueled his commercial revival in the mid-2010s.

'Orphans' 3:16

This acoustic-based psychedelic opener is one of a few LP tracks that pulls from 1960s pop a la Belle and Sebastian. Beck, here on flute(?!), amongst other instruments, is joined on vocals by a feather-in-the-mix Chan Marshall, aka Cat Power. The song is about being disposed and overwhelmed by larger, elemental forces ('And the rain it comes and floods our lungs / We're just orphans in a tidal wave's wake'). The song was the first Beck worked on with Danger Mouse. It was completed in a day ('he only had one day available, because he was finishing the [second] Gnarls Barkley record') and convinced the duo to complete an album together. The acoustic version (3:34) stays close to the original, with Jessica Dobson picking up the Marshall's vocals.

'Gamma Ray' 2:57

The second song recorded, it's a tight surf-rock song most notable for the precise staccato mix separation for the lead instruments, Danger Mouse's keyboard bass, and Beck's guitars. As with the opening song, there's a feeling of helplessness in the face of larger natural obstacles ('ice caps melting down'), although here, the urgent helplessness is juxtaposed with a girl apparently bored by it all ('With a dot dot dot on her brow'). According to Beck, quoted on whiskeyclone.net: 'I wanted this one to have the feeling of one of those Chuck Berry songs that straddles the line of being a song about cars, but then resonates with something else you can't put your finger on'. Further, Beck wanted to avoid being 'too heavy-handed and meaningful'. In addition to invoking Berry, the song references 'smokestack lightning' (sparks from a train's smokestack), best known from Howlin' Wolf's 1956 classic song of the same name, and a 'Chevrolet Terraplane'. A Terraplane was a mid-1930s American car made by Hudson Motor Car Company that was popular enough to inspire Robert Johnson's 'Terraplane Blues' (1936). The second single, 'Gamma Ray', offered two different B-sides: Beck's 'Bonfire Blondes' or the late Jay Reatard's cover version. It was featured in Guitar Hero 5. The acoustic version (3:36) gives Jessica Dobson a larger vocal presence and removes some of the song's driving urgency.

'Chemtrails' 4:40
Howlin' Wolf watched smokestack lighting from trains, Beck watched chemtrails from planes. The album's disheartening, inconvenient truth about environmental dangers continues as Beck uses, but doesn't necessarily endorse, the conspiracy theory that airplane condensation trails are really poisonous assaults on an unknowing public. The first single, it's the only song without Danger Mouse's beats/sounds, Beck's falsetto being the highlight here. Musically, this is a full-scale heavy/prog rock anthem down to the final half-minute guitar ejaculation. Thematically, structurally, and sonically, it bears a strong resemblance to 'The Four Horseman' (1972) by Aphrodite's Child, a group formed by electronic-music godfather Vangelis. The song winds up on many top-ten Beck song lists and it's hard to argue the inclusion. The acoustic version (4:35), again featuring Dobson, replaces the fist-pounding anthemics with a solemn, hymnal quality, beautiful in its own right.

'Modern Guilt' 3:14
This is a bouncy song that sounds like post-Beatles British power pop written for a soft-shoe stage show. As with the opening song, which has two different choruses, the structure here is unusual: two verses and a twice-repeated chorus that only repeats the title phrase, and then the final third/minute of the song, a melodic, repeated 'Da da da' fadeout – an odd pop song. The vocals, with slight distortion that's also in the drums, internalize the environmental calamities of the first three songs: 'Don't know what I've done / But I feel ashamed'. Beck recounted in an interview that about a dozen songs into the sessions, the album coalesced around this song. The acoustic version (3:36) slows the tempo to a 'Go It Alone' blues pace. There's some nice guitar interplay between Dobson and Beck and the fadeout has more of a vocal duet between the two.

'Youthless' 2:59
A bit deeper in Danger's Mouse's beats than other LP tracks and moved along by taut rhythm from Matt Mahaffey's bass, this track is most notable for the vaguely Middle Eastern cello played by Larry Corbett. Corbett, who died soon after the LP's release, had previously played on 'Nobody's Fault but My Own' and 'Nicotine & Gravy'. The song seems to be about the difficulties of maturing as an artist, of trying to dig yourself out of and move beyond your past, while the past is what your followers most value about you: 'You're treading water in the past / Trying to re-animate something

that you can't understand'. Beck and his brother Channing named their mid-1980s art and poetry zine *Youthless*. A 16-year-old Beck can be seen discussing the zine in a 2015 DVD that accompanied scholar Sophie Rachmuhl's book *A Higher Form of Politics: The Rise of a Poetry Scene, Los Angeles, 1950-1990*. He also adopted the title as the name of his new music publishing company in 2008. A UK 7" single was released, backed by 'Half & Half'; a digital download, 'Youthless (Mix K)', was actually the same mix. The acoustic version (2:59) seems to be an exercise in precise instrument execution.

'Walls' (Beck Hansen, Danger Mouse, Paul Guiot and Paul Piot) 2:22
Danger Mouse brings the beats on this remarkably brief earworm that's powered by a violin sample from Paul Guiot and Paul Piot's 'Amour, Vacances et Baroque' (1968) and Cat Power's altered, high-pitched background vocals. On an album with a dim vision of contemporary life, this song seems especially indicting. Although typically lacking specifics, it seems generally about the nerve-wracking up-and-down nature of US involvement in unending wars ('Some days we get a thrill in our brains / Some days it turns to malaise') and, perhaps more specifically, about US President Texan George W. Bush ('With a rattlesnake step in your rhythm'). The third verse ominously cuts off with the line, 'But your words ring out just like murder'. The acoustic version (2:33) adds melodica and turns the song into street-corner R&B, more at odds with the lyrics than on the original.

'Replica' 3:25
This Danger Mouse adventure sounds more like a remix of a song than an original: a replica. The core song is difficult to pin down amongst a fuzz dub-bass rhythm, descending string and piano riffs, and periodic drum outbursts. What's the song about? Parents with a newborn might identify with some of the sleep deprivation and contradictory doubts of dealing with a new version of yourself ('I'm so tired don't know where to begin / It's so unreal / It's all I need'), but the song seems similar to 'Youthless' and its concerns about dealing with new versions of yourself that you may or may not (wish to) recognize. The acoustic version (3:16) is calmer and richer vocally, with more emphasis on the cello riff.

'Soul of a Man' 2:36
This song has always put me in the mind of The Cars and 'You Might Think' circa *Heartbeat City*, with Danger Mouse's Gorillaz-to-Adele production breadth paralleling producer Mutt Lange's Cars-to-Celine Dion trajectory. A musical anomaly here, this new wave/rock stomp excels in the instrumentation, from some fine acoustic guitar to extended call-and-response between electric piano and guitar around the one-line chorus, 'What makes the soul a soul of a man' (which could be a twice-repeated

bridge if you conceive of the song differently). Lyrically, we're again not in a good place, with the singer struggling with another existential crisis. The song appeared on the *I Love You Man* soundtrack CD (2009). The acoustic version (2:36) reconfigures the song as atmospheric blues, with the predictably unpredictable addition of Bram Inscore's cello and Dobson's stringed instruments, the Hindustani sarangi and the Chinese guzheng.

'Profanity Prayers' 3:43
As with *Guero*'s 'Rental Car', Beck's again on the road with an unexpected rocker on an LP's penultimate song. Here he's left waiting at a light and 'watch(ing) for a sign that you're breathing'. The song (shades of Supergrass) opens with a synth sample that's quickly absorbed into a bassy/handclappy rhythm that sets the stage for a fat staccato lead guitar that pauses for a clean George Harrison interlude before a long, surfy outro. The vocals are unusually buried in the mix, not so much under the instrumentation as much as tunneling thorough it. The song seems to be about persistently being in the wrong place at the wrong time, resulting in a profane invocation asked not of a deity, but of the self. The gorgeous acoustic version (4:16) slows it down and emphasizes the Brian Wilson vocal elements, adding cello and slide guitar. If Beck were rearranging his songs for a choral performance, this would top my wish list. Good Shoes' 'The Way My Heart Beats' (2010) borrows liberally from the guitar riff.

'Volcano' 4:29
Although Beck didn't go through the Primal Scream therapy as John Lennon did, his similar journey into the soul of a man ends as on *Plastic Ono Band*, with a return to the warmth of the womb and a repudiation of a false past – perhaps it's the story of Beck going Clear. This ballad gently roams forward to David Campbell's swelling strings, saved from a turn toward easy listening by beats and abrasions. As in other LP songs, the singer is sick of the superficial pressures of the world and the past and, seemingly, the demands of stardom. Whereas Lennon repudiates Hitler, Elvis, and The Beatles, realizing 'I just believe in me / Yoko and me', Beck reaches similar conclusions, singing 'I'm tired of people who only want to be pleased / But I still want to please you'. There is a further epiphany in the song's title, recounted in the story of a Japanese girl who jumped into a volcano; Beck wonders, 'Was she trying to make it back / Back into the womb of the world?' before concluding that he'll visit the volcano, but won't jump in, as he 'Just want(s) to warm my bones / On that fire a while' – the dream is over. The acoustic version (4:28) sticks close to the original and appeared on *Hear to Help – A Compilation Benefiting the Haiti Recovery Effort* (2010). The Haitian CD also included a Beck-produced acoustic version of the Beck-written Charlotte Gainsbourg song 'Dandelion'.

Related Tracks
'Vampire Voltage No. 6' 2:16
This 'Chemtrails' B-side is two songs packed into one 136-second track, embracing Beck's *Modern Guilt* ethos: 'I wanted everything to be really concise, over before you're done with it'. The song equates the concept of 'vampire voltage', the fact that many household appliances drain electricity even when they're not turned on, to a 'fear (that) is creeping under my bones': Beck's got soul problems. The first/verse part of the song is an echoey ballad that points toward *Morning Phase*. With 45 seconds left, the lid comes off and an early 1980s punk song breaks out. There's no indication why it's No. 6.

'Bonfire Blondes' 2:25
The 'Gamma Ray' B-side, this is a catchy electro-rockabilly song pushed along by a clap-track drum rhythm, Beck's acoustic guitar, and Brian LeBarton's wonderful synth riff on the choruses. The rhymes are a bit weak (pace/race, earth/worth), the song is abstract but doesn't create a mood, and, after three albums with busy co-producers, the Beck solo production feels a bit hollow. Seems like, with a few tweaks, it could have been a single.

'Brandon Nevins' (Beck Hansen, Brian LeBarton) 12:10
Seattle radio station 107.7 The End ran a contest to have Beck write a song about the winner. Brandon Nevins won with this biographical entry:

> Inventor of the rocket ship, designer of planet Earth, editor for the Holy Bible, coolest guy since the Abominable Snowman. I'm a realistic person, I never tell a lie, met up with Superman and spit him in the eye. Funny, loud, and all-around amazing.

Beck presented the song to Nevins at Bumbershoot, an annual Seattle festival, in September 2008. In a 2017 reddit, Nevins said that Beck 'pondered my omnipotence' when he wrote the song'. Further, Nevins says he got to listen to the original 25-minute version of the song, which was soon cut in half. The song itself is an outrageous, extended goof on Nevins and an excuse to swear. Musically it leaves 'eclectic' in the dust. I hear seven major movements that I'd classify as: 'Eleanor Rigby' / Violent Femmes / Someone practicing for Yanni *Live at the Acropolis* / 'Frere Jacques' / Heroic folk / Groovy funk-synth (with some 'Let's Hear It for The Boy' for good measure) / guitar outro. The song was available through The End's website.

'Sarah Bassarab' (Beck Hansen, Brian LeBarton) 2:53
Bassarab was a radio contest winner on the October 2008 Toronto stop of the *Modern Guilt* tour. This song is much more compact than the previous entry, mainly Beck and LeBarton talking about Bassarab over an electronic beat, offering observations such as: 'Man, she's like three-hundred spider men'.

'Half & Half' (Beck Hansen, Danger Mouse) 2:21

All buzzing synths, tapping piano, and guitar flourishes, this pining, slow-dance collaboration with Danger Mouse is the trippiest Lesley Gore tune ever. It was the 'Youthless' B-side.

'Necessary Evil' 3:36

Beck takes another drink of the early 1970s Rolling Stones-loving cup with some acoustic swamp blues layered over Danger Mouse's crackling vinyl sample. It was a bonus track on UK iTunes in February 2009 and part of a Japanese limited edition of the LP housed in a Zucca bag, released in March.

'Sunday Morning' (Lou Reed) 3:12

Featuring Giovanni Ribisi on glockenspiel, this beautiful song is culled from the Record Club's cover of *The Velvet Underground & Nico* (1967). The one-sided 7" was included in the 28 May 2009 vinyl release of *One Foot in the Grave* expanded edition.

'The Way It Seems' 2:45

People who ordered the expanded *One Foot* from Beck.com were e-mailed this track as a thank you in 2009. It's an acoustic folk song along the Nick Drake, Donovan, Elliot Smith continuum. It was recorded in 1994 for a never-completed follow-up to *One Foot*.

'Leopard-Skin Pill-Box Hat' (Bob Dylan) 3:03

The War Child organization provides support for children in conflict zones. This song appears on the organization's 2009 collections *War Child Heroes* (UK) and *War Child Presents Heroes* (US). Bob Dylan picked this song from his 1966 masterpiece *Blonde on Blonde* for Beck to record. Joined by Brian LeBarton, this version eschews the always-falling-apart ethos of the original, opting for a quicker blues-rock version that would be at home on 1974's live collaboration with The Band, *Before the Flood*. Beck performed the song live in the summer of 2008, when this was likely recorded, and also at a 6 February 2015 MusiCares Person of the Year Dylan tribute.

'Green Light' (Kim Gordon, Lee Ranaldo, Steve Shelley, Thurston Moore) 3:43

A US April 2009 Record Store Day double-A-side with Sonic Youth's cover of 'Pay No Mind', this was pressed on 2,500 black and 100 green vinyl singles. Sonic Youth was assembling a (still unreleased) box set and asked Beck to contribute a cassette. He recorded the entire *EVOL* album, but only this has been released. Beck transforms the standard issue early SY rock song into an acoustic tribute that uses the band's famous repeating guitar-note percussion technique to interpolate 'Sunday Sun' – brilliant. The song was also released on CD on *The* Mojo *Anthology* (2018) and on cassette on the five-track UK compilation *I Hear Moore* (2018).

'Harry Partch' 10:30
Not sure which is more out there: this song or the story behind it. On 5 August 2009, Radiohead released 'Harry Patch (In Memory Of)' online to commemorate the death of the last British soldier from World War I and raise money for the Royal British Legion. Matthew Friedberger of the US band The Fiery Furnaces responded to the release with a multi-paragraph missive attacking Radiohead for, among other things, 'brazenly and arbitrarily associating yourself with things that you know people consider cool', asking: 'Is it 48 notes to the octave?' Friedberger evidently confused Patch with Harry Partch, a music composer and performer who created several new instruments and is best known for using a 43-note microtonal scale. Friedberger responded to the ensuing confusion by issuing a statement claiming he knew the difference between the two men and attacking Beck: 'Matt would have much preferred to insult Beck but he is too afraid of Scientologists'. Not long after, Beck responded with 'Harry Partch' on Beck.com, claiming that it 'employs Partch's 43-tone scale, which expands conventional tonality into a broader variation of frequencies and resonances'. It's less a song than a sound collage, an extended version of the inter-song tape snippets found on the early independent LPs. Beck claimed that it was similar to the comparatively tame 'Inferno'. When asked if he recorded any new material for the song, he said: 'I don't know – I'd actually have to ask somebody. That song was maybe a bit more hyper'. Even unprovoked, a Beck tribute to Partch wouldn't have been out of the musical question. Needle-drop on something like Partch's 'And on the Seventh Day Petals Fell in Petaluma' and you might think you're in a Beck song.

Tobacco Manic Meat
'Fresh Hex' (featuring Beck) (Beck Hansen, Tom Fec) 1:35
'Grape Aerosmith' (featuring Beck) (Beck Hansen, Tom Fec) 1:51
Tobacco, aka Tom Fec of Black Moth Super Rainbow, heard Beck on these tracks in his head and reached out to Beck through Brian LeBarton. As Fec described it: 'I would send MP3s of the finished instrumental and he just went to town. On 'Fresh Hex', he did the vocals and the chopping and editing himself'. The 2010 result of this long-distance collaboration is Beck singing on these two manic, noisy songs. 'Fresh Hex (Instrumental)' (1:39) was available as a download. 'Grape Aerosmith (Original Mix)' (1:54), featuring 'Beck's original vocal mix that was edited and rearranged for *Manic Meat*', was released in 2017 on *Ripe & Majestic*.

'Bad Blood' 3:28
Beck sounds a bit like Mick Jagger and channels some rockin' blues, a la Jack White or Black Keys, for this mostly forgettable song found on

the *True Blood: Music from The HBO Original Series Volume 2* (2010) soundtrack CD.

'Let's Get Lost' Beck & Bat for Lashes (Beck Hansen/Natasha Khan) (4:10)

Not the Chet Baker classic, this atmospheric duet with UK top-ten artist Bat for Lashes (Natasha Khan) banks on Khan's Kate-Bush-like romantic/gothic vocals for Beck's second creepy creature tune of 2010. The song appears on *The Twilight Saga: Eclipse*. Beck produced and wrote the mostly synth music while Khan wrote the lyrics. It was released in the UK as a limited edition 7" on Record Store Day, 16 April 2011, backed by a Bats for Lashes B-side.

'Summertime' 2:09

Not the Gershwin classic. Available as an iTunes download prior to the *Scott Pilgrim vs. the World* film/soundtrack release, Beck's version eventually appeared on deluxe versions of the soundtrack. The song sounds like a rocking mashup of the Pixies and Modern Lovers, although Beck discussing the song's creation, namechecked Pussy Galore and Sonic Youth. The song is performed in the film by the fictious Sex Bob-Omb band. Their version appears on the 2010 soundtrack, alongside their versions of the Beck-penned tunes 'We Are SEX BOB-OMB', 'Garbage Truck', and 'Threshold'. The band's version of Beck's 'No Fun' and 'Indefatigable' appear on the 2021 vinyl edition, while Beck's versions of the two songs remain unreleased.

'Ramona (Acoustic)' 1:00

Scott Pilgrim director Edgar Wright picked this from among 'like seven versions of the 'Ramona' acoustic song'. It's 'what you hear Beck singing at a later moment in the movie where you hear a sad version'. The 2021 deluxe *Scott Pilgrim vs. the World Soundtrack* includes three of these earlier versions, 'Acoustic Demo Idea' 1 (0:53), 2 (1:12), and 3 (1:07).

'Ramona' 4:21

Beck travels back in time and imagines himself as a conventional pop-rock songwriter in his early 20s, which he never was, or, as producer Nigel Godrich said: 'He gets to just do something that's a guilty pleasure in a way'. The result is a convincing acoustic-based power ballad with a long title fadeout. The 2021 deluxe edition includes 'Ramona (Mellotron)' (4:23), which replaces the already minimal vocal verses with said instrument.

'Garbage Truck' 1:48

Beck unofficially rewrites Iggy Pop's shotgun-riding tune 'The Passenger' (1977) as perhaps the most unromantic song ever: 'I'll take you to the dump / Cos you're my queen'. On *Scott Pilgrim* deluxe edition.

'Threshold' 1:43
Another fast, convincing Pixies-like punk rocker. Brian LeBarton plays bass and drums and contributed an '8-bit Version' to the soundtrack. A remix/mashup, 'Katayanagi Twins vs Sex Bob-Omb' (3:10), credited to Cornelius and Beck, appears on Nigel Godrich's *Scott Pilgrim vs the World* original score, released as a download in 2010 and on vinyl in 2021. The score releases also included two clips credited to Nigel Godrich and Beck: 'We are SEX BOB-OMB (Fast)' (0:59) and 'Death to all Hipsters' (0:41), neither much more than frantic count-offs.

'Curfew' 4:05
A snippet of this hard-rocking, guitars-a-blazin' tune showed up in the 2011 film *I Am Number Four,* before being leaked a few years later. A hard fit in the Beck catalog – elements of 'Profanity Prayers' and 'Rental Car', maybe.

'Attracted to Us' The Lonely Island (feat. Beck) (Akiva Schaffer, Andy Samberg, Beck Hansen, Cole Marsden Grief-Neill, Jorma Taccone) 1:52 by The Lonely Island
Beck joins the comedic trio on a goof about geeky guys. Chicks dig Beck. On the group's 2011 CD *Turtleneck & Chain.*

'Stormbringer' 4:26
Beck and his band contributed a respectful version of the pastoral folk tune to *Johnny Boy Would Love This ... A Tribute to John Martyn* (2011). The song was originally released on John and Beverly Martyn's *Stormbringer!* (1970). Martyn's musical trajectory, from traditional folkie to later genre and technology exploration, is a rough parallel to Beck's musical evolution and the direct influence of songs such as this are especially apparent on *Sea Change*.

'Iron Horse' 4:17
Beck models a tough-guy persona for this slow, heavy piano, drums, synth, and harmonica delight. The lyrics invoke standard blues/country/folk phrases, including the 16 coaches of another train: Elvis' 'Mystery Train'. A portion of the song debuted in a 2011 episode of the TV series *Sons of Anarchy* and also cropped up in 2012 in *Hell on Wheels* before leaking online.

'Looking for a Sign' 3:39
This gentle love song featuring harmonica and banjo is a midway point between the slow folk of *Sea Changes* and the dreamy vocals of *Morning Phases*. The song was released as a digital download a few days after the US theatrical release of *Jeff Who Lives at Home* (2012). In November, the song featured as an A-side of the Australian tour 7", backed by 'Corrina Corrina'.

The single, the first release on Beck's Fonograf Records, came in a tote bag and with a copy of the Thurston + Beck limited edition (270 copies) cassette *Mind Wars*.

'Corrina, Corrina' (Armenter Chatmon aka Bo Carter) 2:42

A sensitive version of the oft-covered tune, originally recorded in 1928 by writer Carter and Charlie McCoy in a much more light-hearted manner. Beck's acoustic guitar and vocal version is a more serious take on Bob Dylan's 1963 version. Also appeared on the US Starbucks CD *Every Mother Counts 2012*.

'I Only Have Eyes for You' (Al Dubin, Harry Warren) 4:02

Multimedia artist Doug Aitken's SONG 1 was installed at the Smithsonian's Hirshhorn Museum in Washington, D.C., from 22 March to 10 May 2012. The outdoor exhibit ran from dawn until midnight and 'allowed visitors to the National Mall a chance to witness the first-ever work of 360-degree convex-screen cinema'. Beck was among dozens of contemporary artists who contributed material to the project. The classic song first appeared in the 1934 film *Dames* and has been interpreted at least 500 times. Beck's take is slow, atmospheric, and echoey – more menacing than reassuring as on, say, Art Garfunkel's 1975 UK number one single. Beck's version appeared on the Pitchfork website.

'I Just Started Hating Some People Today' 5:08

Label free-agent Beck recorded this country A-side in 2011 in Nashville with Third Man Records owner/producer Jack White while in town recording a still unreleased follow-up to *Modern Guilt*. The 7" was released in 2012 on TMR on black and limited edition tri-color vinyl, backed by 'Blue Randy'. It's a humorous revenge fantasy about people 'talking trash behind your back all day / Saying things that a garbage man would not say' – it's a hoot. Beck is in fine drawl before being replaced about four minutes in, first by White's punk-rock outburst and then by Karen Elson, White's wife at the time, who offers a jazz interpretation. Beck backed Elson on her cover of Fleetwood Mac's 'Gold Dust Woman' (2012). With White on multiple instruments, the song also features Dean Fertita, White's bandmate in The Raconteurs and The Dead Weather, on bass and synth, and Fats Kaplin, longtime session man and a practicing magician, on fiddle and pedal steel. The song got no chart satisfaction in the US or UK but was the first of Beck's nine top 50 songs on *Billboard*'s Mexico English-language countdown.

'Blue Randy' 3:52

Randy shows up in the latter verses of the A-side, threatened with death by White and Elson. Here, the poor man has met his demise as 'there's a police chalk outline where you last been seen'. Beck, with an unusually throaty gravitas (Johnny Cash meets Leonard Cohen), has fun with rhymes ('With your syntax in repose / And a clothespin on your nose') that aren't burdened with the weight of the world. The same band features as on the A-side.

'Silk Pillow' Childish Gambino (featuring Beck) (Beck Hansen, Donald Glover) 4:10
Beck gets his Eminem on in this smooth rap from the 2012 *Royalty* mixtape. Beck co-produced this with multimedia star Glover and produced the LP's 'Bronchitis' (3:02).

'I Ain't Got No Home' (Woody Guthrie) 2:24
Beck recorded this for Rage Against the Machine's 20 January 1997 Radio Free LA program, broadcast the day of US President Bill Clinton's second inauguration. This humble acoustic version sticks close to home but is severely truncated, Beck admitting: 'Well, it's got a hell of a lot more verses, but I can't remember them right now'. The program was streamed through radiofreela.com. Beck also performed 'Pay No Mind (Snoozer)' and an otherwise unreleased Son House song: 'Grinnin' in Your Face'. The broadcast was sold as a Sony cassette for $3.00, with a j-card that credits Beck, but it's unclear if any of his three songs are on the 1997 cassette. The Guthrie song was released on Beck.com on 12 July 2012 to commemorate Guthrie's 100th birthday.

'Michelangelo Antonioni' (Caetano Veloso) 4:12
A beautiful, dreamy full-band cover of a track from the Tropicalia legend Caetano Veloso's 2000 LP *Noites Do Norte*. Lyrically the song offers a nod toward the genius of the titular Italian director, who later used Veloso's song in the 2004 anthology film *Eros*. The song has some melodic similarities to 'Ramona'. Beck has played with Veloso a few times, including on 13 November 2010 when he and Devendra Banhart joined on Veloso's 'Maria Bethania' at the Los Angeles Museum of Contemporary Art. On *A Tribute to Caetano Veloso* (2012)

'Cities' 5:33
'Touch the People' 6:01
'Spiral Staircase' 5:12
August 2012 saw the release of the downloadable PlayStation Three video game Sound Shapes. Beck contributed three tunes, each of which generated a complete song once a player completed a game level. This means there are no definitive versions of these songs, but many versions circulate. The times here are from the most compelling online versions. The minimal lyrics are mostly about playing the game, with 'Cities', aka 'Happy Africa', repeating the phrase 'Move a little / Turn a little / Break a little'. Musically and vocally, the songs point toward *Hyperspace*. The game was also released on disc, *Best of Playstation Network Vol. 1* (2012).

'NYC: 73 – 78' (Philip Glass, Leonard Cohen, Beck Hansen) 20:51
Part original composition, part interpellation, part sample, part remix, Beck creates a soundscape that both reconfigures and reflects the essence of Philip Glass. The stunning piece, which appears on the collection *REWORK_Philip Glass Remixed* (2012), pulls from more than a dozen Glass works, including 'Puppet Time', the Leonard Cohen collaboration from 2007's *Book of Longing*. The title comes from an interview in which Glass discussed the years he worked as an NYC cab driver; among the original creation here, Beck repeats the lines '73 / 78' at the song's end. In an e-mail with NPR, Beck alluded to the song's unusual composition, say that 'When listening to pieces from all the different eras of Philip Glass' work it felt like there was a continuum – an accretion of harmonic ideas that built over time into a larger, less definable work'. And, when asked if he had any stories about Glass, Beck recounted, 'Well, there was the time the boat capsized and we had to row to shore and there were Somalian pirates. But I'll save that one'.

Thurston + Beck *Mind Wars*
'Mind Wars **Side A'** (Beck Hansen, Thurston Moore) 24:00
'Mind Wars **Side B'** (Beck Hansen, Thurston Moore) 21:00
This instrumental (or at least non-vocal) sound collage was on a limited edition (270 copies) cassette included in a tote bag with the 'Looking for a Sign' single at 2012 Australia shows. Unlike the 'hyper' 'Harry Partch', this is more settled as the duo stick with ideas and allow concepts – melodies and other sounds – to develop and grow. Worth listening to out of more than just curiosity.

'Sound and Vision' (David Bowie) 9:00
Beck recorded the 1977 Bowie classic on 5 February 2013, accompanied by a 157-person group of musicians wrangled by his father. The result is a precise, dynamic, expansive, and inventive exploration of the original three-minute song. As Beck said at the time: 'I attempted to conjure some scenario that could only exist in this kind of space for a one-time performance' and 'I was thinking a lot about Busby Berkeley films and multiples of musicians and dancers'. The event was filmed for a Lincoln car commercial. The video/ad debuted on the carmaker's website as both a conventional clip and a navigable, interactive, 360-degree immersive experience. A grand and successful attempt at Art with a capital 'A'.

'Defriended' 3:46
'Defriended (Extended Version)' 14:01
Started in 2008 and finished in 2012, Beck dropped the single version online in April 2013 as a standalone song around the same time he announced he was working on an acoustic album and a proper follow-up to *Modern Guilt*. Two weeks later, he released the 12" vinyl version, which included the

single and extended track, plus a digital download. Neither this song nor the following two singles were released on an LP. When asked about the free-floating singles, Beck said: 'For ten years, I've been talking about putting out a series of 12-inch singles one at a time. But I was holding them back cos I wasn't sure what I was doing with them. And I just wanted people to hear them'. The song is a trippy drums-as-lead-instrument dub with immensely reverbed vocals, which is probably the closest Beck has come to reggae. With a repeated 'cheating', the song seems to be about an imagined and/or failed affair, or at least a tryst. The single sleeve is taken from a diptych (hence the horizontal line across the sleeve image) by Swedish artist Karin 'Mamma' Andersson, 'About a Girl' (2005). The song appears to be addressed to a Karin, who is at turns unfaithful, unavailable, and ungrateful. Andersson's work would grace the front of all three 2013 singles.

'I Won't be Long' 5:05
'I Won't be Long (Extended Version)' 14:49
The second 2013 standalone single, this July 2013 release is a breezy keyboard-pop track that sounds like what would have happened if the Alan Parsons Project decided to hang out with Cornelius (especially around the 11:00 mark of the extended track). The breezy, much-repeated title chorus is single-worthy catchy, the verses provide their own memorable melody, and Sonic Youth's Kim Gordon contributes some background vocals. It's unclear what the song is about, but it clearly doesn't come from a happy place: 'No one has a clue where we are'. But one place we might be is The Beatles' 'Blue Jay Way' with its 'Please don't be long' chorus, similar to this song's title/chorus (which is also similar to the group's 'It Won't Be Long'.). And The Beatles feature on the single sleeve, another Mamma Andersson work, this one titled 'Master's Voice' (2003).

'Gimme' (Original Mix) 2:25
'Gimme' (Instrumental) 2:25
'Gimme' (Georgic Mix) 10:28
'Gimme' (Extended Version, Part 1) 14:53
'Gimme' (Extended Version, Part 2) 10:15
The original version of the final summer single (September 2013), a mere whisper compared to the extended version, is a percussion-heavy world-music track that recalls early 1980s material from Peter Gabriel's fourth LP and the David Byrne-Brian Eno collaboration *My Life in the Bush of Ghosts*. Lyrically the song is more atmospheric than thematic, with much of the song featuring pitch-altered versions of the lines 'Off we go / Yes, I'm dreaming / I've no idea' and the 'Gimme gimme gimme' refrain. The song is notable for its three drummers (a greatest hits collection of James Gadson, Joey Waronker, and Cole Marsden Greif Neill) and Bram Inscore and Brian LeBarton on gamelan, which includes any number of Indonesia-based

percussion instruments. Especially on the extended version, the gamelan offers an expansive crispness that recalls the orchestration of Beck's 'Sound and Vision' cover – precise yet never sterile. Although, at 25 minutes, there's a lot of other stuff going on, too, from guitar blasts to a rhythmic affinity with 'Modern Guilt'. The Georgic (which means pastoral) mix pulls out most of the drums, leaving a not-quite acoustic version. The song was released as a double 12" record, with the single mixes on the A-side of the first disc, backed by the 'Georgic Mix', and the two parts of the 'Extended Version' on the two sides of the second disc. Mamma Andersson once again provides the cover image: 'Funny Lesson' (2000). Of the 2013 singles, the extended 'Gimme' is the least like anything else in Beck's catalog and the one I most often revisit.

'Back to You' 3:07
A clip of this song first showed up on 20 November 2012 in the 'Skin Deep' episode of *NCIS: Los Angeles*, weeks before the full version was included in the Sony PlayStation game Gran Turismo 6 and, in 2014, as an instrumental in Luc Besson's film *Lucy*. It's another blues-rocker a la the Black Keys, very similar to 'Bad Blood'. With its opening 'Look out your red red eyes', it seems possible it was a werewolf song rejected by *True Blood* in favor of the vampire song, or the song referenced in this 2010 quote: 'I sent them something for the last [*Twilight*] movie that they didn't use'.

Morning Phase (2014)

Personnel:
Beck Hansen: vocals, acoustic guitar, keyboards, electric guitar, piano, sound collage, tambourine, electric bass, ukulele, charango, celeste, dulcimer, harmonica, synthesizers, glockenspiel, organ
Joey Waronker: drums, percussion
Roger Joseph Manning Jr.: piano, synthesizers, background vocals, Rhodes, Clavinet, B3 organ, electric piano
Justin Meldal-Johnsen: bass guitar
Stanley Clarke: upright bass, electric bass
Bram Inscore: electric bass
Cody Kilby: guitar
James Gadson: drums
Fats Kaplin: banjo
Smokey Hormel: acoustic guitar, EBow, electric guitar
Stephanie Bennett: harp
Roger Waronker: piano
Steve Richards: cello
Greg Leisz: pedal steel guitar
Jason Falkner: electric guitar
Matt Mahaffey: organ
Matt Sherrod: drums
David Campbell: conductor, orchestrations
Produced by: Beck Hansen
Recorded at: Ocean Way, Blackbird, Gang, RAK, Capitol, Sunset Sound, The Library, 2012-2013
Release date: 21 February 2014
Label: Capitol / Fonograf
Highest chart places: US: 3, UK: 4
Running time: 47:08

Beck quickly recorded a batch of songs in Nashville in 2005 with the intent of releasing a 'country' album. He again recorded in Nashville in 2011 and revisited some of the earlier songs in the Tennessee city in 2012, but couldn't make them work. In early 2013, he returned to Los Angeles and decided to record with his *Sea Change* band, feeling enough time had passed since that quieter collaboration. Unlike the earlier LP, Beck flew solo as the *Morning Phase* producer, although there's more collaboration with his father, David Campbell, than on other albums.

The critical praise for *Morning Phase* was overwhelming. Tim Jonze (*The Guardian*) gave the LP four out of five stars, saying: 'Despite the lyrical themes, the record's sun-dappled shimmer suggests Beck sees a way out of his emotional hole. The bad news for him is that being in it seems to make for some of his best music.' *Rolling Stone* (four and a half out of five stars) called it 'an instant folk-rock classic'. *NME* also played the folk card, saying: 'It couples a moody sort of glamour with a concrete feeling of loneliness, and it makes for some of the most affecting comedown folk you're likely to hear all year'. There was little dissent from major outlets, with many, such as *The Guardian* and *Time Out*, putting it in their top LPs of 2014 and *MOJO* placing it at number one.

Beck spent the spring and summer of 2014 touring, typically including a handful of songs from *Morning Phase*. With health needs still a consideration, from 2015 through 2017, he played a light schedule of over 20 dates per year before gearing up for a longer *Colors* tour.

The album was nominated for five Grammy Awards and won three: Album of the Year, Best Rock Album, and Best Engineered Album, Non-Classical. The latter included ten winners, but not Beck, who subsequently made sure he was included as an engineer (winning a 2019 Grammy). Despite the praise and accolades, *Morning Phase*, his first Capitol LP, only went Gold in the US and Silver in the UK. There were no special editions, but the vinyl version is coveted for its rich audio reproduction. The LP produced four singles; none of the four were released commercially in a physical format, but 'Blue Moon' was the first of Beck's four US Adult Alternative Airplay number one singles. 'Waking Light' did a respectable 43 on the US Rock Songs chart.

'Cycle' 0:40
This mood-setting instrumental features orchestral string instruments that reappear throughout the LP. Beck spoke at this time of breaking cycles, such as the album and supporting tour grind, and being out of phase, such as being naïve about some things at age 40, while simultaneously embracing some habits of a 60-year-old.

'Morning' 5:20
The expanse of the golden age returns as a sliver of corroded dawn. As on the *Sea Change* opener, things are falling apart. Here it's a relationship, as the morning after reveals 'the roses full of thorns' and an appeal, evidently unheeded, to 'start it all over again' – sad Beck is back. This slow, slow sweeping acoustic song, improvised in the studio, features a robust chorus, memorable acoustic guitar from Beck, and piano/synth from Roger Manning Jr., who also contributes some sweet background vocals. The big reveal is the upright bass from jazz wizard Stanley Clarke. Clarke, *Downbeat* Magazine's Critics Poll winner for Best Electric Bass Player in 2014, is uncharacteristically subdued here. Clarke had long admired Beck, saying: 'Yea he's really talented that guy. I think that he's always been on the cutting edge of whatever he's doing and that's what I've always liked about him'.

'Heart Is a Drum' 4:31
Buoyed by Clarke on electric bass, this is an upbeat song with roots in late 1960s folk, with nods to Nick Drake (some suggest 1971's 'One of These

Things First'), Van Morrison, and The Band – especially pianist Richard Manuel. But the focus is more on Beck's gorgeous, soaring vocals than the music, although there's a lot going on sonically deep in the mix, especially in the long coda. As in many Beck songs, the pronouns present a somewhat intractable puzzle: me is probably 'me', but is you 'you' or 'me' or 'everyone'? Whatever the pronoun, the heart drumbeat has taken a toll on the singer ('Going beat beat beat, it's beating me down'), although there is some hope, as he just 'Need(s) to find someone to show me how to play it slow'. The song was the fourth single, released as an edited (3:39) digital download on 28 July 2014. It's also the last song in Cameron Crowe's forgettable *Aloha* (2015), appearing on the soundtrack CD. Coldplay's Chris Martin appeared with Beck performing this song on *The 57th Annual Grammy Awards* telecast on 8 February 2015. The 'RDM Remix' appeared in 2018 on the Afro-Latin music collective Rhythms Del Mundo's downloadable remix collection *Plastic Oceans*. The 2022 *Dear Life* version (3:49) plays up the rhythms at the expense of the vocals.

'Say Goodbye' 3:29
The first of two countryish songs, this is grounded in James Gadson's ever-intriguing drumming, Cody Kilby's finger-pickin' guitar, and Fats Kaplin's modest banjo. Kilby is a bluegrass musician, also proficient on banjo and mandolin, best known for working with Ricky Scaggs, while Kaplin is a fiddler by trade and a frequent Jack White collaborator, including on mandolin on White's 2014 take on the *Song Reader* tune 'I'm Down'. With these players, it's not surprising that this is one of three album songs originally recorded in Nashville, along with 'Blackbird Chain' and 'Waking Light', although the songs did not survive unscathed, as Beck said: 'I did take some of those Nashville songs and we re-recorded parts of them and I kept certain parts, so there's sort of a Frankenstein recording'. For all that, the song, which never really finds a second gear, is a platform for Beck's intense vocals, especially the chorus. The song is a look at a breakup from another point in the morning prism. Several critics compare this to Neil Young's work on *Harvest Moon*, another album sequel, but a more apt comparison for this, and much of Beck's pastoral work, might be Paul Weller, especially *Wild Wood* (1993). The track was released as a UK promo CD.

'Blue Moon' 4:02
The first single, 'Blue Moon' is a soaring pop ballad, finding Beck at his most earnest and exposed, with the timber of his heartbreaking vocals reaching far beyond the isolation framed in the lyrics. And those lyrics were influenced by Elvis Presley's 1956 version of Lorenz Hart and Richard Rodgers's 'Blue Moon' (1934). Beck connected with the song after reading Peter Guralnick's second Elvis biography, *Careless Love: The Unmaking of Elvis Presley* (2000). Beck thought Elvis' version of 'Blue Moon' 'encapsulates him at the beginning

– this sort of purity', a time when he was 'accessible'. Channeling The King's pain, Beck offers one of his most devastating opening lines: 'I'm so tired of being alone'. And Elvis' legendary performing bravado echoes in what might be Beck's most epic vocal performance, the 'See the turncoat on his knees / The vagabond that no one sees' bridge which, followed by warm, pulsing background vocals, also owes more than a nod to U2. Below the vocals, Beck weaves a charming bed of ukulele and charango, a small Andean stringed instrument in the lute family that Europeans might have heard in a town-square panpipe (siku) band, and Roger Manning Jr. dazzles with an unanticipated Clavinet solo.

The song was nominated for the 2015 Grammys for Best Rock Performance, losing to Jack White's 'Lazaretto', and Best Rock Song, losing to Paramore's 'Ain't It Fun' (produced by longtime collaborator Justin Meldal-Johnsen). The song appeared in the TV show *Girls* and the accompanying soundtrack, *Girls Volume 2: All Adventurous Women Do...*, on the *Grammy 2105 Nominees* CD, and was released on 20 January 2014 as a US promo single, featuring a radio edit (3:47). Beck performed the song on a few American TV shows, including *Saturday Night Live*, and on a stunning KCRW performance (4:22) that was part of the four-track France-only digital download *Live from KCRW / 2014*, recorded on 16 April and released on 28 August 2014. 'Blue Moon (Instrumental)' appeared in 2014 on the Universal Music promo CD *Strictly Background 14*.

'Unforgiven' 4:34

This is the final song on vinyl side one and the first of the two 1970s Pink Floyd-ish songs on the LP – you can start singing 'Comfortably Numb' at points. The song's slow, spacey pace is nudged along by Gadson's determined drumming that backs Beck's piano, Stephanie Bennet's plucked harp, and Smokey Hormel's atmospheric EBow, a device best known from Blue Öyster Cult's '(Don't Fear) The Reaper' and songs from Big Country. The song also shares affinities with *Sea Changes*' equally unhappy 'Lonesome Tears', both songs dealing in weakened sunlight, driving as release, and waiting in an undetermined distant place, in this case, the chorus' 'somewhere unforgiven'.

'Wave' 3:40

If 'Cellphone's Dead' structurally recalls the first side of David Bowie's *Low*, this elegiac tone poem recalls the mostly instrumental, contemplative second side or even projects to the Thin White Duke's unnerving impending-death meditation *Blackstar* (2016). The song features Beck on chilling, mannered vocals, backed by double bass player David Stone, three violinists, three cellists, and ten violinists (many of whom would reappear on *Colors*), all led by concertmaster Joel Derouin and conducted by Beck's dad. The song, Beck's favorite on the LP, is about being alone and carried away, sufficiently summarized in the closing incantation: 'Wave / Wave / Isolation / Isolation / Isolation / Isolation'. Although Beck covered John Lennon's 'Love' around this time, another track from Lennon's solo debut, *John Lennon/Plastic Ono Band*, the negative-BPM 'Isolation' and its takes on failed relationships, fame, and loneliness, would not be out of place on *Morning Phase*.

'Wave' was the first song recorded for *Morning Phase* in 2009, taking advantage of the lush Capital Studios that once hosted Nelson Riddle for classic Frank Sinatra orchestrations. Beck tried to get other artists interested in the song, but the reaction he received led him to build around the song, so much so that the song was 'always the center of the record'. As in the song itself, Beck was carried away by the orchestral recording process: 'As we recorded it, it began to become its own thing. I didn't want to get in the way of what was happening'. Beck debuted the song on 24 November 2013 at a *Song Reader* concert at L.A.'s Walt Disney Concert Hall, backed by the L.A. Philharmonic Orchestra, and performed it on *Saturday Night Live* on 1 March 2014 with a pared-down string backing. A song unlike any other in Beck's catalog.

'Don't Let It Go' 3:09
And after 20 years releasing LPs, Beck includes his first filler track. Ok, that might be a bit dramatic (and forgiving of a few songs from *Midnite Vultures* and *The Information*), but there's nothing Beck-clever musically or lyrically in this generic folk song. Of course, maybe that's part of the point of the *Song Reader* phase of his career, that he can easily produce well-structured, non-quirky songs that anyone could play and/or enjoy. Beck admitted that he didn't spend a lot of time writing this song, unlike many rejected for the record, saying: 'I just did [it] as a demo then I re-recorded it with the band.' A rare misstep.

'Blackbird Chain' 4:27
This broad, more hopeful folk-rock song is the second recouped from the Nashville sessions. Beck discussed being influenced in the Nashville sessions by 'Hank Williams, George Jones, (and) Conway Twitty', and about going to the city 'just to sort of fulfill some kind of 18 to 19-year-old daydream'. At some point, Beck found all the Nashville songs sounding the same and tried something different here, deciding to 'break up the structure and take the idea of a country song and break up the tempos and the time signatures and have these really separate sections and these moments'. The result, as evidenced in this laidback, California, Byrds-adjacent groove, is a song that's 'kind of early 1970s folk, late 1960s folk rock'. Unlike other LP songs, here a relationship seems to be on the mend, or at least on a truce level. Musically the song is most interesting in its musical bridge, featuring Beck's celeste, Manning Jr.'s keys, string orchestration, and Greg Leisz's pedal steel guitar.

'Phase' 1:07

'Phase' is an instrumental companion to the opening 'Cycle'. Beck explained how the tracks came about: 'We did all these instrumental fragments with the orchestra after we were done doing a day of tracking all the orchestral parts'. He originally included a handful of these snippets before settling on two, concerned that the album was getting too long. The orchestral nature of the songs explicitly link back to the album's centerpiece, 'Wave', and help bring 'about the record as one piece, as opposed to a collection of just a bunch of songs on a CD'.

'Turn Away' 3:06

After 'Phase' marks one conclusion to the album, this song pushes forward toward the coda, the final three songs that have, if not a bit more optimism, then at least some problem-solving to get past the loneliness of the first part of the album. With that, the singer seems to be urging himself not to listen to himself and all the troubles he's discussed: 'Turn turn away / From the sound of your own voice' and 'From the weight of your own words'. Musically the core of the song is Beck's vocals and acoustic guitar, augmented by his turn on the dulcimer and Stephanie Bennett's harp. Taken all together, it sounds like a Simon and Garfunkel outtake.

'Country Down' 4:01

Beck banks the corner and hits the redemption straightaway, continuing to 'turn away' from the past that's 'all behind you now' because 'You just found what you're looking for'; an uneasy compromise with the unsettled self of the earlier songs has been reached. The second of two straightforward country songs on the LP, it's another Nashville retread that got re-recorded in California. The song features some fine pedal steel and a 'Cold Brains'-like harmonica solo that recalls Neil Young.

'Waking Light' 5:01

The second song with Pink Floyd overtones, this album closer doesn't so much conclude as reframe and resolve the album's thematic and musical issues. Lyrically, as with the previous two songs, this continues to shake off the album's earlier concerns about isolation, which perhaps all took place in the confused, non-intentional thought time between when you stop sleeping and when you actually wake up and greet the new day – although this might be overthinking it. Beck wrote this quickly in Nashville on a Steinway grand piano, but when he had to work with the orchestra, he couldn't get the lyrics right and he 'ended up just doing a kind of improvisation where I spent a few hours just improvising lyrics'. He claims the issue was that he was trying to incorporate the personal when he just needed 'one of those simple sentiments'. Musically the song shakes off the country/folk vibe. The song starts with synthesizer and obviously modified vocals, building towards a collision of brass and orchestra and an electric guitar solo (shades of Hendrix's 'Little Wing'). Beck claimed that he had tried for years not to make this a type of 'sonic, grand statement, because that's usually the point where the bands you love trip up and fail miserably.' Maybe, but it works here, and you can debate if he hadn't already entered this 'treacherous territory' on songs such as 'Little One' and 'Chemtrails'. Beck performed a powerful version of the song on *The Tonight Show with Jimmy Fallon* soon after the LP's release, backed by his band and Father John Misty on vocals and tambourine.

Related Tracks
'Love' (John Lennon) 3:14
'Love' is a *Sea Change*-y sounding Beck-as-band cover of the track from *John Lennon/Plastic Ono Band*, recorded for the US Starbucks Valentine's Day LP *Sweetheart 2014*. Beck was supposed to perform the song in late September 2001 but had to cancel because of the 9/11 terrorist attacks. Beck posted a piano version on Instagram on 9 October 2020, the 80th anniversary of Lennon's birth.

'Wah Wah' (George Harrison) 2:35
Beck and the *Morning Phase* touring band played this *All Things Must Pass* classic on the US late-night show *Conan* on 24 September 2014 as part of 'George Harrison Week'. Quick, tight, and no-nonsense.

'Moonquake Lake' Sia & Beck (Greg Kurstin, Sia Furler, Will Gluck) 2:53
After surviving *Morning Phase*, this song is like flying in February from a cold climate to Orlando: the burst of heat and energy is almost too much to handle. It's billed as a duet, but Beck just gets two verses in the Caribbean-tinged song about a fictional film in the remake of *Annie*. The song is on the soundtrack release. The music and production here are by Greg Kurstin, who worked with Beck as far back as *Modern Guilt* and would loom large on *Colors*. Beck collaborated with Sia a few other times and famously performed live duets of 'You're the One That I Want' from *Grease* a handful of times in the mid-2000s.

'Heaven's Ladder' 3:17
Beck's contribution to *Song Reader: Twenty Songs by Beck* (2014) when no one else would record the song. A bit more Pink Floyd, although here, early Syd Barret psychedelia meets The Beatles – it's wonderfully trippy. The one-time backing band here is Benji Lysaght (guitar), Nate Walcott (piano), Jake Blanton (keyboards), Josh Adams (drums), and Gus Seyffert (bass), who have variously worked with artists including Ryan Adam, Father John Misty, and the legendary Zander Schloss. This Heaven isn't a happy one, as

occupants are descending the ladder: 'Down below / Down Below / Where there's nowhere else to go / Just as far as nowhere and then you're on your own'. Makes sense: Lucifer was an angel who came down from Heaven. Beck performed the song for the web version of *The Colbert Report* on the day of the CD's release along with the TV-broadcast 'Heart is a Drum'.

The Chemical Brothers
'Wide Open' (feat. Beck) (Tom Rowlands, Ed Simons, Beck Hansen) 5:54
'Wide Open' (Kölsch Remix) (Tom Rowlands, Ed Simons, Beck Hansen) 8:33
'Wide Open' (Joe Goddard Remix) (Tom Rowlands, Ed Simons, Beck Hansen) 10:24
'Wide Open' (By the Light of the Moon Mix) (Tom Rowlands, Ed Simons, Beck Hansen) 5:30
Beck sings lead on this memorable, if lightweight, closing track from the techno legends' eighth album, *Born in the Echoes* (2015). The latter three tracks appear on the digital download EP *Wide Open (The Remixes)*. The first two remixes are more club-friendly, while the latter opens up on the mellow and Beck's vocals. The remixes also appear on the Japan deluxe edition of the album. An edit of the original single (4:13) was made available on 12 February 2016.

'What This World Is Coming To' Nate Ruess Feat. Beck(Nate Ruess, Jeff Bhasker, Beck Hansen, Emile Haynie) 4:00
The fourth single from the fun. singer's debut solo album, *Grand Romantic,* is a country-tinged adult alternative song with some tweaked lead vocals that are tough on the ears. Beck sings background and plays guitar, letting loose on a cheesy electric solo. Ruess sang lead on *Song Reader*'s 'Please Leave a Light on When You Go'.

'I Love You All the Time' Fabrizio Moretti, Nick Valensi, & Beck (Jesse Hughes, Josh Homme, Mark Ramos Nishita) 2:54
Beck joined The Strokes' rhythm section of Moretti (drums) and Valensi (bass) on this 2016 cover of The Eagles of Death Metal's third single from 2015's *Zipper Down*. The trio were among five dozen artists who met the call to record the song to raise money to help victims of terrorism, including survivors and the families of those killed in the 13 November 2015 Paris attacks, which included a murderous assault on an Eagles of Death Metal concert. The is an electronics-heavy take on the simple love song.

Flume 'Tiny Cities (feat. Beck)' (Harley Streten, Beck Hansen) 3:56
Beck sings lead on this slowish electronic anthem from Australian electronic musician Flume (Harley Streten). From the LP *Skin* (2016).

Flume 'Tiny Cities (Lindstrøm & Prins Thomas Remix) [feat. Beck]' (Harley Streten, Beck Hansen) 10:26
The Norwegian remixers pick up the pace and send the song into a more spacey direction on this long reimagining from *Skin: The Remixes* (2017).

'Can't Help Falling in Love' (George David Weiss, Hugo Peretti, Luigi Creatore) 3:15
Beck contributes vocals to a Danger Mouse/Sam Cohen production of this 'Blue Moon' adjacent cover of Presley's 1961 *Blue Hawaii* UK number one hit. Beck's approach is less bright and on-the-nose than The King's version and much less goofy than UB40's reggae-lite UK number one from 1993. The song appears on *Resistance Radio: The Man in the High Castle Album* (2017) and is meant to be a rebel song in the adaptation of the dystopian book that imagines the US losing World War II.

Colors (2017)

Personnel:
Beck Hansen: vocals, guitar, piano, Rhodes, organ, synthesizers, bass guitar, glockenspiel, percussion
Greg Kurstin: guitar, bass guitar, drums, piano, synthesizers, Clavinet, Rhodes, mellotron, marimba, organ, percussion
Roger Joseph Manning Jr.: background vocals
Dwayne Moore: additional bass
Ilan Rubin: drums
Feist: background vocals
Charlie Bisharat: violin (concert master)
Andrew Duckles: principal viola
Steve Richards: principal cello
Nico Abondolom: double bass
Geoff Osika: double bass
David Campbell: string arrangements, conductor
Produced by: Greg Kurstin, Beck Hansen, Cole M.G.N.
Recorded at: Greg Kurstin's studio, 2013-2017
Release date: 13 October 2017
Label: Capitol
Highest chart places: US: 3, UK: 5
Running time: 39:39

Beck started recording his Grammy coronation follow-up in 2013, working with producer Greg Kurstin in Los Angeles off and on through early 2017. Kurstin previously appeared as a musician on four *Modern Guilt* tracks. Beck began releasing session tracks periodically, beginning with the 15 June 2015 release of 'Dreams', which found its way into his setlist a few weeks later. Three other tracks would surface before the October 2017 album release.

The album received mixed reviews, with the praise not as loud as before, and the critical murmurs just a bit louder than usual. Terence Cawley (*Boston Globe*) had the most on-target analogy for the LP: 'If Beck is Generation X's answer to David Bowie, then *Colors* is his *Let's Dance*: an intentionally lightweight, enjoyable mid-career effort with one eye on the dance floor and one on radio playlists'. *Rolling Stone* offered four out of five stars, saying 'The result is his most straight-ahead fun album since the Nineties', while *The Guardian*, at three out of five countered, writing '*Colors* is depressingly short of real surprises, its energy a poor substitute for drama or ideas'. Jillian Mapes writing for the often-caustic website Pitchfork, echoed the 'ideas' angle, saying, 'Beck . . . spent a lot of time trying to get the balance of 'not retro and not modern' just so. He more or less nailed that bit, but what's lacking from his Big Happy Pop Record is some kind of strong emotion that could elevate these songs above the 'well crafted but innocuous' camp – something more than an idea'.

Beck played tracks live from 2015 onward but toured *Colors* in earnest for most of 2018, playing North America twice and shows in the UK, Europe, and East Asia. He continued touring North America in 2019, including with Cage the Elephant and Spoon, with a greatest hits rather than *Colors*-centric setlist.

Colors was released digitally with a bonus track, the single version of 'Dreams', and the physical release offered at least five different cover variants. There were five singles: 'Dreams' hit number one on the US Adult Alternative Songs charts, staying there for 12 weeks in 2015; 'Wow' followed in June 2016, hitting number five; 'Dear Life' failed to chart, but 'Colors' hit number three and 'Up All Night' also hit the top of the charts.

The album hit number one on the US Top Alternative Albums and Top Rock Albums charts and was number 30 on NME's 2017 Albums of the Year. Beck won his third Grammy Award for Best Alternative Music Album (from a total of eight nominations) and his second of three Grammys for Best Engineered Album, Non-Classical.

'Colors' (Beck Hansen, Greg Kurstin) 4:21
The album opener and fourth US single, 'Colors' is an over-the-top celebration that's 'so much larger than life', to reference the similarly exuberant 'Big Time' (1986) by Peter Gabriel. The song is about promise and hope, about embracing the present, as in the pre-chorus: 'Found our way through the lost years / Now the day brings it all here'. Aurally the frenetic dance song is an assault on the ears, a 15-piece David Campbell string section, including cellist Suzie Katayama from the 2002 'It's All in Your Mind', Beck and Kurstin on a dozen instruments, including mellotron, marimbas, and glockenspiel, and chopped-up, modulated background 'oh-ah' chorus vocals from Roger Manning Jr.. The song was included as a demo track in Apple's Logic Pro 10.4, released on 25 January 2018. This allowed mixers full access to the song's 135 tracks, revealing layers of sound and instrumentation that you can hear on the track but don't notice until they've been isolated, such as 'funk guitar'. 'Colors (Picard Brothers Remix)' was released on Spotify on 3 August 2018. The Ibiza-friendly mix from French brothers Clément and Maxine drops the pre-chorus for a hypnotic repetition of the bridge-opening 'I got all the love you need' and the 'do you feel alive' refrain. Beck performed the song, along with 'Wow', on the *Late Show with Stephen Colbert* on 18 July 2018, with the host mentioning that the artist used to sleep on his couch.

'Seventh Heaven' (Beck Hansen, Greg Kurstin) 5:00
Powered by a light funk bass, shimmering guitars, and quasi-celestial sounds, one critic called this a song Hall and Oates never wrote. The assessment is apt – the song is throwaway but not quite forgettable pop. The verses offer a nod toward more intricate Beck wordplay ('I want to see you / With the pharaoh's curse / The apple flower doggerel / The batteries burst'), but the

bridge, chorus, and coda head toward disappointingly trite optimism. It's got a major chorus but it's a minor entry in the Beck canon.

'I'm So Free' (Beck Hansen, Greg Kurstin) 4:07
This song opens with an angular guitar and piano, joined soon by the rhythm section and Beck's almost spoken verse vocals. The two verses engage in some fun phraseology (e.g. 'I'm on a tangent/textbook ephemeral' and 'I see the silhouette of everything I thought I ever knew / Turning into voodoo') and return to the title phrase every fourth line. The verses slide into a rap pre-chorus before heading into the fist-pumping title chorus. The song turns over about halfway through the second chorus, as Beck is joined by Feist on vocals. Feist gets the 'Nobody's going to keep me down' muscular guitar bridge to herself, taking the song to another level as Petra Haden did on the equally muscular 'Rental Car'. From here, the song returns to the opening riff and then a celebratory fadeout. Nine Inch Nails' Ilan Rubin features on drums. What's the song about? Beck is so free now, as far as I can tell.

'Dear Life' (Beck Hansen, Greg Kurstin) 3:44
There's no getting around the fact that this is a (McCartney) Beatles song, from the melodic bass, to the sweet vocals, to David Campbell's whirling string section, to the irresistible 'Martha My Dear' piano line. Or at least a World Party song. Beck had some inclination to mold the entire LP in this 'simple, classic, Beatles-esque kind of thing', but decided to move in a different direction. He admits the song sticks out on *Colors* but kept it because it has sentimental value as the first track recorded for the LP. Beck told iheartRadio what the song is about: 'I know things have been hard and things are difficult, and we've seen a lot, but I just want life to show me what it's about again' – fair enough. The song was an August 2017 pre-LP download and was shipped physically to UK radio. Beck re-recorded the song for the 2022 *Dear Life* Words + Music Amazon Audible. The song appeared in the 'Opening Credits' (1:04) and as a distinct, although incomplete, track (2:56).

'No Distraction' (Beck Hansen, Greg Kurstin) 4:32
The contemporaneous critical reception of this song was not kind. Many reviews noted the lite-reggae, adult-alternative sounds of latter-day Police, complete with Sting-like vocals, and piled on after that. One noted that it's 'the sort of song that a TV-show music supervisor might option if the Cars were too expensive', while another was more dire, hearing the beginning of Beck's relevant end in a song that 'feels constructed not channeled, the bridge is burnt'. Others were disappointed in the directness and ordinariness of the lyrics. For his part, Beck talked about the song's theme as 'Anybody who has a phone or computer lives with the distractions pulling you this way and that. We haven't figured out how to have access to everybody and

everything all the time and how it affects us psychically and neurologically'. 'No Distraction (Khruangbin Remix)' (3:18) was released online on 8 July 2020 and on 7" as a Record Store Day B-side to 'Uneventful Days (St. Vincent Remix)'. The slow, lounge-dub version from the Texas band improves on the original. 'No Distraction' was used in the trailer for the second season of HBO's *Divorce*. Maybe 'You Might Think' cost too much.

'Dreams' (*Colors* mix) (Beck Hansen, Greg Kurstin, Andrew Wyatt) 4:57
This dance/rock number features a funky bassline, slinky/jangly guitar, and multi-layered vocals buried somewhat deep in the mix. And that all makes sense, as Beck said that the song 'started out kind of like a heavy garage rock thing and then it became much more of a kind of dance or, some other kind of hybrid'. With this combination, the song recalls Niles Rodger's work with David Bowie, which makes sense, as Beck had been listening to and hanging out with Daft Punk, who won a Grammy with Rodgers (and future-Beck producer Pharrell Williams). Thematically, the song seems almost like a parody of an uplifting pop song: 'When nothing's right, just close your eyes / Just close your eyes and you're gone'. This reconfigured album version features touring band bassist Dwayne Moore, recorded on 3 November 2016, if his Instagram is accurate. The song is co-written with *Colors* collaborator Kurstin and indie band Mike Snow leader Andrew Wyatt.

Beck released 'Dreams' online in early June 2015, followed by a four-track US promo CD on 15 June 2015. The CD includes 'Radio Edit' (4:21), 'Explicit Album Version' (5:14), 'Edited Album Version' (5:14), and 'Instrumental' (5:14). Confusingly 'Album Version' is not the album version, although it is included in streaming versions of *Colors*, and 'Edited Album Version' is not edited for length, but for language. The latter three versions appeared on US and UK 12" releases in August. 'Album Version' is rawer, with the guitar and vocals higher in the mix and the interlude more rude: 'Ahhh, stop fucking with my dreams, dreams yeah'. It's also the version that hit the top of the US Adult Alternative Airplay charts for 12 weeks. 'Dreams' didn't make the UK singles chart but hit 16 on the UK Physical Singles Chart.

Beck said this song was made to be played live and it quickly jumped into his top 25 most-played songs. He and St. Vincent joined Taylor Swift on stage to perform the song at Swift's 25 August 2015 L.A. Staples Center show.

'Wow' (Beck Hansen, Cole M.G.N.) 3:40
'Wow' is the steady-drone frown of earlier work like 'Movie Theme' turned upside down with intimations of trap drums and pan flutes. The 'live every day to the fullest' song was co-written and co-produced by Cole M.G.N., aka Cole Marsden Greif-Neill. The two worked together primarily in 2012-13, so it's possible the song originated then. Whenever it was created, Beck didn't plan it:

I didn't go in the studio to make that. I just freestyled it, and then I put it away for a year. Then my kids overheard it one day and they were like, 'You have to put this on the record'! They were emphatic.

The song was released as a digital download on 2 June 2016, the second pre-album single, nearly a year after 'Dreams'. It hit number five on the Adult Alternative Airplay charts. Released on 2 August 2016, the 'Wow (GUAU! Mexican Institute of Sound Remix)' (3:44) features Mexican percussion and a great opening focusing on the song's most Beck line: 'girl in a bikini with a Lamborghini shih tzu'. MIS is a project fronted by DJ/producer Camile Lara. Mü, Muelas De Gallo, from Mexican hip hop group La Banda Bastón, adds a rap verse in Spanish. 'Wow (TOKiMONSTA Remix)' (3:14) was released on 14 October 2016. TOKiMONSTA, the stage name for DJ/mixer Jennifer Lee, clears out a lot of the atmospheric sound and opens up the song, highlighting the piano.

'Up All Night' (Beck Hansen, Greg Kurstin) 3:10
Beck dropped the fourth worldwide single about a month before the LP's release. It's an upbeat dance-pop track, probably Beck's breeziest single, one that emotionally recalls Pharrell Williams' 'Happy'. Beck recounts telling his manager when prepping *Colors* that he didn't have plans, but 'All I know is I want to do something that's really happy'. Moments later, he entered a studio with Williams, who proceeded to play him 'Happy', which proceeded to go to number one in 24 countries.

Beck said, 'It was one of those moments where you laugh to yourself and think, 'O.K., so maybe we'll do something else because I think you kinda nailed this one''.

Beck played the song on three US and UK talk/music shows and the song went to number one on the US Rock Airplay and Alternative Airplay charts. A 30-second clip of the song featured in a US TV commercial for Fossil Q Smartwatches. 'Up All Night (FIFA version)' (2:49), a bit heavier on the strings and 'Get Lucky' vibes, was released on 27 September in the US, although the song was leaked earlier. 'Up All Night (Oliver Remix)' (4:26), according to a press release 'infused with an epic coat of twisted yacht rock smoothness, sure to keep the good vibes rolling', was released on 15 March 2018 as a digital download. It sounds like Quincy Jones and Al Jarreau snuck into the mixing booth, but Oliver, the now defunct L.A.-based production/DJ crew Vaughn Oliver and Oliver Goldstein, were behind the board. 'Up All Night x Daoko' appeared on 25 August 2018 on the Japan deluxe edition of *Colors*. Daoko is a Tokyo-born singer/rapper who added her own Japanese verse to the track. She joined Beck onstage to sing the song on 19 August 2018 at ZOZO Marine Stadium in Chiba, Japan. Live versions appeared on the aforementioned Japanese DVD and the *Paisley Park Sessions* (3:04), released on 11 November 2019 as a digital download.

'Square One' (Beck Hansen, Greg Kurstin) 2:55
Bathing in catchy piano riffs and falsettos, this approximates nothing so much as an outtake from The Apples in Stereo, especially 2010's *Travellers in Space and Time* (it would take Beck another album to catch up with their space motif). As with a few other tracks on *Colors*, this is part love song (the second part) and part pep talk: 'You'll be fine if you try / To keep your eyes on the consolation prize'. If he had just taken the leap and substituted 'constellation prize'.

'Fix Me' 3:13
As with other Beck album closers, 'Fix Me', a piano ballad with beats, is out-of-step musically with the rest of the album, a seeming point backwards toward the folk of *Morning Phase*. Or we can even bring this back to the *Modern Guilt* closer 'Volcano', with which this track shares some musical tendencies and wave imagery. The 'Fix Me' video also picks up on the Japanese vibes of 'Volcano', featuring a girl and her three poodles in the mountains of Yamagata. All told, a Beck-like ending to Beck's least Beck-like album.

Related Tracks
'Here Comes the Sun' (George Harrison) 0:40
Beck posted a 40-second clip of The Beatles classic on social media, backed by Roger Manning Jr., Jason Faulkner, and Ilan Rubin, the *Roma* band. The full version remains unreleased.

'I'm Waiting for the Man' (Lou Reed) 3:15
Beck recorded a version for the 2009 Record Club release *The Velvet Underground & Nico*. This 2018 version was recorded in New York City December 2017, with Kevin Faulkner on guitar for Spotify's *Music Happens Here* podcast series. As with most of his solo covers, Beck sticks pretty close to the original, although this is less tense and the more angular guitar line recalls Bowie's 'TVC-15'.

'Tarantula' (Ian Robbins, Martin Young) 3:48
'Tarantula' was the B-side of 4AD artists Colourbox's debut single 'Breakdown' (1982). The song was subsequently covered by labelmates This Mortal Coil on their second LP, 1986's *Filigree & Shadow*. Beck's somber orchestral version, arranged with his father, is more a cover of the latter than the former. The lead vocals are at the center of the mix, supported by Feist and Alex Lilly, who was part of Beck's touring band, and backed by NIN drummer Ilan Rubin. The song appeared on *Music Inspired by The Film Roma* (2019) but did not appear in Alfonso Cuarón's neorealist masterpiece. Inspired how? Not entirely clear, but Beck was further inspired as he composed other songs for the film, as revealed in a 2019 *New Yorker* article

in which engineer David Robertson shows up with hard drives containing 'alternate tracks from *Hyperspace*, even more songs inspired by *Roma*, old demos, (and) a series of heavy, spiraling, Kraftwerk-esque songs for an unfinished record that he had thought of titling *Rococo*'. Beck performed a beautiful version on 4 February 2019 on *The Late Late Show with James Corden*, backed by the L.A. Philharmonic and Feist, Lilly, The Bird & The Bee's Inara George, and Bat for Lashes' Natasha Khan.

'Super Cool' (feat. Robyn & The Lonely Island) (Beck Hansen, The Lonely Island, David Greenbaum) 3:24
'Super Cool' is a self-referential dance track that plays over the end credits of *The Lego Movie 2: The Second Part* (2019). The funky-smooth chorus pretty much sums up the song's ethos: 'Unbelievable super cool outrageous and amazing / Phenomenal fantastic so incredible woo hoo'! The song was available online on 6 February 2019, prior to the LP/CD physical soundtrack release. Beck is joined by Swedish singer Robyn, who enjoyed a UK number one in 2007 with Kleerup, 'With Every Heartbeat', and The Lonely Island – Beck appeared on The Lonely Island's 'Attracted to Us' in 2011.

'Night Running' (Bred Shultz, Daniel Tichenor, Jared Champion, Matt Shultz, Matthan Minster, Nick Bockrath, Beck Hansen, Natalie Belle Bergman) 3:28 by Cage the Elephant feat Beck
Beck swaps leads with Cage the Elephant vocalist Matt Schultz on this hazy, neo-Two-Tone jam. The band had the song hanging around for a while and couldn't finish the verses. They were working with David Campbell, which inspired guitarist Brad Shultz to think of Beck as a verse solution. They sent it off to Beck and two days later had a completed song, which appears on the band's *Social Cues* (2019). The two acts performed the song regularly on their summer 2019 tour.

'The Bells of Rhymney' (Idris Davies, Pete Seeger) 3:33 by Jakob Dylan and Beck
Music producer Andrew Slater (Warren Zevon, Fiona Apple) directed *Echo in the Canyon* (2019), a celebration of the fertile, folky Laurel Canyon music scene of the mid-1960s. Slater also produced the soundtrack LP that featured Jakob Dylan teaming up with artists to cover songs associated with the Hollywood Hills neighborhood. Beck swaps vocals with the younger Dylan on a version that's faithful to The Byrd's sweet track from their 1965 debut *Mr. Tambourine Man*. Old friend Greg Leisz ('Sissyneck') features on banjo.

'Goin' Back' Jakob Dylan and Beck (Gerry Goffin, Carole King) 4:09
Dylan and Beck offer another Byrds-version take on the Goffin and King tune, perhaps best known as a Dusty Springfield UK top ten hit in 1966. Beck performed alongside Dylan at two concerts on 12 October 2015 that were

recorded for the film. This song, a take on the Byrds-arranged 'Wild Mountain Thyme' with Cat Power and Regina Spektor, and a run-through of the Mamas and the Papas' 'Monday Monday', all appeared in the film and DVD, which was released on 10 September 2019 in the US.

'Hypocrite' (Cage the Elephant) 3:55

Beck covers this tune from Cage the Elephants' second LP, *Melophobia*, as the A-side of a 7" that hit the merch table in 2019 near the end of the summer tour. The band's version is more upbeat musically and includes a small horn section. Beck's version is...atmospheric? He slows the song down and offers plaintive vocals over drums and strings. From the ambience, it sounds like Beck sang over a backing track during a soundcheck.

'I Turn My Camera On' (Britt Daniel) 3:09

The B-side of the tour single, Beck covers the Prince-wannabe's first single from Spoon's 2005 LP *Gimme Fiction*, albeit in much less Princely style. Once again, it sounds like Beck was recorded live singing to a pre-recorded backing track, aggressively lo-fi – gotta keep the street cred.

Hyperspace (2019)

Personnel:
Beck Hansen: vocals, keyboards, guitar, slide guitar, piano, harmonica, bass
Pharrell Williams: keyboards, drums, mumbles
Roger Manning Jr.: keyboards, background vocals
Cole M.G.N.: bass, guitar, drums, keyboards
Sky Ferreira: vocals
Alex Lilly: background vocals
Brent Paschke: guitar
Greg Kurstin: drums, bass, synthesizers, keyboards
Terrell Hines: vocals
Chris Martin: vocals
Jason Falkner: guitar
Smokey Hormel: guitar
Produced by: Pharrell Williams, Beck Hansen, Cole M.G.N., Greg Kurstin, Paul Epworth
Release date: 22 November 2019
Label: Capitol
Highest chart places: UK: 33, US: 40
Running time: 39:16

Beck wanted to work with the legendary Pharrell Williams around the time of *Midnight Vultures*, but the two didn't connect until 2012. They met up off and on for a few years before working in earnest together soon after the December 2018 end of the *Colors* tour. Beck's marriage to Marissa Ribisi would end in 2019, making this, in part, another breakup album.

Hyperspace received mostly positive reviews. David Fricke in *Rolling Stone* gave the album four stars, saying 'For all of his vigor for partnership, (Beck) is a solitary classicist, a singer-songwriter wrestling with the dynamics of desire and emotional commitment'. Elizabeth Aubrey (*NME*) gave the same star rating, noting that 'There are a few early misfires here, but they are rescued by a stunning second half on which Beck's trademark sound is stripped back and drenched in a glistening synth-filled air that takes him into a daring new era'.

On the less enthusiastic side, a pair of writers for UK's *The Independent* echoed critiques of the previous LP: 'While these are enjoyable enough tracks to soundtrack your day, there's little of the lasting emotion or progression for which we know Beck'.

Beck played three *Hyperspace* songs at 2019 shows ('Saw Lightning', 'Uneventful Days, 'Dark Places'), but was never able to mount a tour due to the COVID-19 global pandemic, which shut down the world in late winter 2020. In May 2020, he cancelled a 14-date UK/Europe summer tour and didn't play a public live show until a spectacular 27 July 2021 show at the Newport Folk Festival. In June 2022, he played a 14-date UK/Europe tour, followed by

July dates opening for the Red Hot Chili Peppers and a fall 2022 acoustic tour opening for Arcade Fire.

Beck spent some of his pandemic time tinkering with *Hyperspace*, releasing *Hyperspace 2020* on 12 August 2020. The deluxe edition (with a black cover of Beck and a Celica replacing the red of the original) claimed in total to offer 'only' four new mixes, two new songs, and two remixes, but many of the original tracks seem to have been altered. Some 2020 versions also included *Hyperspace: A.I. Exploration*, a 13-track video collaboration with footage from NASA's California-based Jet Propulsion Lab.

The album spawned three singles, although only 'Uneventful Days', which spent five weeks at number one on the Adult Alternative Airplay charts, had a physical release. 'Saw Lightning' hit number three on the same charts in June 2019, while 'Dark Places' failed to chart.

In a touch of career summary, Beck released an Amazon Audible autobiography, *Dear Life* (Words + Music | Vol. 28), on 1 July 2022. The one-hour and 48-minute audio book featured Beck recounting incidents from his life and reworking nine songs.

'Hyperlife' (Beck Hansen, Pharrell Williams) 1:36

A teaser for the title track, 'Hyperlife' is a thematic and musical introduction. Thematically, as with many other Beck projects, there are concerns about how people (mis)use technology, in this case, social media. For Beck, 'incredible photos on Instagram' create an unfulfillable hunger that shows up in the lyrics: 'I just want more and more / Beauty, light and crushing life'. Musically the song leans on downbeat, atmospheric keyboards and altered Beck backing vocals, heavy on modulation and in-line key changes, the latter a hallmark of the album.

'Uneventful Days' (Beck Hansen, Pharrell Williams) 3:17

At its core, this is a simple Beck folk song with a light-rap interlude, awash in inoffensive synths and almost literal bells and whistles. There's no dig-in hook one would hope for from a single and the whole song feels a bit sleepy, with the lyrics 'Living in the dark / I'm waiting for the light' recalling *Morning Phase* dawn malaise. Beck said the song reflects those times at a precipice: 'It's like those moments in the aftermath of a period of time. Like a new job in a new town'. A 3" record was released on 29 November 2019 for Record Store Day Black Friday, part of about a dozen 2019 RSD 3"/33 1/3 vinyl single releases. 'Uneventful Days (St. Vincent Remix)' (3:00) was a digital release on 10 January 2020 before winding up on an RSD 24 October 2020, A-side 7", backed by 'No Distraction (Khruangbin Remix)'. St. Vincent, aka Annie Clark, adds funky guitar, bass, and keys, backed by session drummer Sam KS (Kauffman-Skloff). Clarke said she had been 'listening to a lot of 1970s Herbie and War' and it's there in the grooves that better the original track. Beck performed a stagey version on a 3 December 2019 broadcast of *Jimmy Kimmel Live!*

'Saw Lightning' (Beck Hansen, Pharrell Williams) 4:01
The first single from *Hyperspace* and one of the first songs created with
Williams back in 2013, it was also the last man standing among the more
forceful tunes prepared for the LP. As Beck said: 'There were a lot more
aggressive songs on the records, and upbeat/up-tempo songs, but we took
them all off at the last minute'. Some versions of this song would not be
out of place among Beck's earliest work, but Beck said that Williams 'was
also excited to explore songs that had a blues sound', and this version, with
synthed-up production, is as much Williams (who contributed the 'there was
a day' lick) as Beck, slide guitar notwithstanding. It's not just the slide guitar
that puts this in the blues/gospel idiom, but also the apocalyptic visions,
lyrical extremes ('dead of night', 'longest day', and 'hardest day'), and the
sycamore tree, which is associated with Biblical clarity and seeing Jesus.
Beck brought the song back to its roots on the 8 July 2019 video release
of 'Saw Lightning (Freestyle)' (2:16). Sans rap, it's just vocals, harmonica,
and footstompin', both feet out of the grave. This version appeared as a
Hyperspace 2020 digital deluxe bonus track.

'Die Waiting' (with Sky Ferreira) (Beck Hansen, Cole M.G.N., Kossisko
Konan) 4:04
No Pharrell on this track, co-written, co-produced, and programmed by Cole
Marsden Greif-Neill, who also plays the bulk of the instruments. This all
points toward this track originating in 2013 when Greif-Neill was heavily
involved in three stand-alone singles. The song features Sky Ferreira vocals,
but not very forward in the mix, as well as rapper Kossisko Konan as co-
writer. His contribution is unclear, but one can only hope that he wrote all
the lyrics, which go nowhere one wouldn't expect in a love song with this
title. The 2020 remix is cleaner and brighter, with more separation and less
of a haze over the whole song, so much so that it feels faster, although the
length remains the same.

'Chemical' (Beck Hansen, Pharrell Williams) 4:18
Beck uses 'anodyne' here as a noun meaning 'painkiller' ('They say that love
is a chemical / Anodyne to the soul'), but its adjectival meaning, 'purposefully
inoffensive', is an apt description of this song, if not the first half of the
LP. As Beck explains of this and other songs on the album: 'It's a mixture,
like life. There's something beautiful and transcendent in small moments,
and there's just complete boredom and hopelessness at the same time. It's
all mixed together.' Musically the song is minimal and hazy, Pharrell on
keyboards and drums, joined by his guitarist Brent Paschke. Although not
a formal remix, the 2020 version brings the guitar forward and tweaks the
vocals, especially the last 40 seconds. 'Chemical' (Chloé Caillet Remix) (4:34)
was released as a digital download on 11 June 2021. The French DJ's dance
mix foregrounds the synths and pumps up the house rhythms.

'See Through' (Beck Hansen, Greg Kurstin) 3:38
The only song co-written and co-produced by Greg Kurstin, this opens like funeral-home organ before a slight island synth vibe takes over. Beck's voice is heavily modulated and most interesting when he's swapping vocals with Manning Jr. on background. The song is about the edge of a breakup – do you see through the rest of the relationship or simply see through the other person? Ultimately, it's a song about shame and a tinge of regret: 'I feel so ugly when you see through me'. The synths are further up in the mix and the vocals cleaner on the 2020 remix.

'Hyperspace' (with Terrell Hines) (Beck Hansen, Pharrell Williams, Terrell Hines) 2:45
Set the controls for the heart of Instagram: the title song starts off the LP's second side, which trends toward more majestic Pink Floyd rock/pop, both Syd Barrett and post-Syd incarnations. The song is a longer take on the opening track, with synths deeper in mix, replaced by a propulsive mix-center percussive drumbeat. The song picks up on the opener and the album's major theme of needing to move beyond technology to real human contact. The song features a rap from co-writer Terrell Hines, a singer/activist from Georgia. Hines had just signed to Capital when he ran into Beck at a label party. Beck asked him if he wanted to work on a track, so 'he sent the track, I did my verse and him and Pharrell fucked with it'. And then Beck went back and fucked it up again on the 2020 mix, dropping down the song's unique drumbeat in favor of more atmospheric sounds and new/altered vocals, creating a more spacey but less compelling mix.

'Stratosphere' 3:56
Beck written and produced, this is a touching, acoustic-guitar-based folk-rock ballad. As with the rest of the *Hyperspace*, it lacks the dynamics or histrionic solo that would get an arena crowd waving their power-ballad-loving arms in unison, but compensates with some mid-1970s Fender Rhodes sounds and tender backing vocals from Coldplay's Chris Martin. The song is at once about living in the out there, the stratosphere, a place 'where it kind of feels suddenly like we are in the future', but also about a friend who died of a heroin overdose almost two decades prior. The 2019 vinyl version adds a 12-second acoustic guitar intro that sets up the song well, but sounds out of place on such a slick album. The 2020 mix, which isn't advertised as a different from the original, sweetens and centers the vocals, taking off about two minutes in with a heavy bass and drums power ballad ploy. The original version is the best song on the album.

'Dark Places' (Beck Hansen, Pharrell Williams) 3:45
When Beck and Pharrell started working together, the latter encouraged the former to explore 'singer-songwriter type of songs'. The album's third single is

that type of song; a dreamy, floaty meditation about admitting that it's ok to feel sad sometimes. What's most striking about the song is the childlike freedom of the lyrics and sentiment ('Some days I go dark places on my own'). While he has many times declared his freedom, this time he sounds free and, unusual for this LP, human, aided by some drop-dead simple drums by Williams and some of Beck's most direct vocals. While the previous song is emotionally engaging, this one seems emotionally honest. Musically the song has the strolling psychedelia of 1967 Beatles, filtered through the space-time continuum of *Dark Side*-era Pink Floyd and various Beatles and Floyd admirers such Alan Parsons Project, World Party, and Oasis. 'Dark Spaces (Soundscape)' (1:30) appeared in 2020. It features a glee-club dreamy Beck(?) alternating 'do do do' with 'come see me' vocals backed by a version of the original song's spacey keyboard part.

'Star' (Beck Hansen, Paul Epworth) 2:50

This tight soul/funk groove couldn't find a home on *Colors* and doesn't exactly fit here, but the album's better for its presence. It's co-written and produced by Adele collaborator Paul Epworth. Beck laid down a demo at Epworth's The Church Studios in London, along with six or seven other still unreleased tracks, and 'essentially redid it' for *Hyperspace*. The album song grooves on Beck's falsetto, Epworth's bass, and the Casio melody. The go-to reference for the vibe is Prince, but predecessor Sly and the Family Stone's *Fresh* and, once again, Karl Wallinger's World Party, are cogent comparisons. Lyrically the song is in line with much earlier character portraits. The 2020 remix isolates the main instruments in the mix, bringing up the reverb and volume on the bass, and more emphatically injecting the guitar eruptions a la 'Sign 'O' The Times'.

'Everlasting Nothing' (Beck Hansen, Pharrell Williams) 5:00

When he began working with Pharrell, Beck said he was 'just curious to see where working with him could go' – this is where it went. It's the first song the duo worked on together, the last song on the LP, and the fourth and final single, a song that has, according to Beck, an 'elegiac, hymn-like quality, but with 808 beats'. Anchored by an initial left-channel acoustic guitar, the folk song swirls upwards, part break-up, part up-lift, reminding one of Blur's 'Tender', with a touch of Pink Floyd's 'Great Gig in the Sky' bursting out of the nine-person choir, and reminding us of our connection with the great beyond referenced in the title. The album's most striking line is 'Like a standing ovation for the funeral of the sun'. Supposedly, Flaming Lips' Wayne Coyne had suggested 'standing ovation for the funeral of the sun' as a title for Beck's previous breakup LP, *Sea Change*. A grand note to end a classic LP side.

Related Tracks
'I Am The Cosmos (42420)' (Chris Bell) 1:33

Beck shared this solo acoustic song on 24 April 2020 on his Instagram, about a month into the COVID-19 lockdown. It's a sincere version of former Big

Star member Chris Bell's 1978 single, most notably revived by This Mortal Coil in 1991. This appears on the *Hyperspace* deluxe edition.

'The Paisley Experience' (Prince) 5:24
The three-track *Paisley Park Sessions* EP was released about a week before *Hyperspace*. Beck was the first artist to record at Paisley Park's Studio A after Prince's death in April 2016. 'The Paisley Experience' is a respectful, if somewhat tame, medley of hits: 'Raspberry Beret', 'When Doves Cry', 'Kiss', and '1999'. Beck performed 'Raspberry Beret' live on 28 January 2020 at *Let's Go Crazy: The GRAMMY Salute to Prince 2020*, broadcast on 21 April 2020 in the US 'The Paisley Experience' was augmented by Paisley Park versions of 'Where It's At' and 'Up All Night'. The tracks were available through Amazon Prime before being released to other streaming services and were on the Japan *Hyperspace* deluxe edition, released on 4 December 2020.

'Don't Come Around Here No More' (Tom Petty, David A. Stewart)
Beck played acoustic guitar and sang on this incomplete version of the 1985 Tom Petty and the Heartbreakers' experimental classic. Streamed on *tompetty.com* as part of Tom Petty's 70th Birthday Bash (23 October 2020), Father John Misty bassist Jeffertitti Moon joined on harmony vocals. Petty covered Beck's 'Asshole' in 1996.

'The Valley of the Pagans' Gorillaz featuring Beck(Damon Albarn, Remi Kabaka Jr., Beck Hansen) 2:44
This was the ninth and final single from the Gorillaz's seventh studio LP, *Song Machine, Season One: Strange Timez*, the songs released as a periodic web series that consumed most of 2020. A Beck collaboration with the theoretical, animated collective, mostly Blur front-man Damon Albarn and artist Jamie Hewlett, had long been rumored and made all the sense in the world. Beck adds co-vocals to this catchy, bouncy, synth-pop song that could be mistaken for another Lego movie entry, minus the curse words. Leaked earlier in 2020 as 'West Hollywood', Beck's observations about his hometown meet up with Albarn's even more cynical vision of L.A., where there are '100 million Viagra tablets stored in a warehouse'. An official karaoke instrumental version was released simultaneously. Beck started playing the song live during his summer 2022 European tour and joined Gorillaz on stage on 11 June 2022 at the Primavera Sound festival in Porto, where he had headlined the previous night.

'Find My Way' Paul McCartney (feat. Beck) (Paul McCartney) 4:53
Paul McCartney released his critically acclaimed COVID-19 lockdown solo work *McCartney III* in December 2020, garnering his first UK number one LP in over 30 years. *McCartney III Imagined* soon followed, with versions and remixes from a dozen artists. On the original LP, 'Find My Way' is the type of upbeat, cheery pop song that numbers in the hundreds in the Macca catalog.

Beck, who first met Sir Paul through producer Nigel Godrich in the early 2000s, reworked the song as a darker, funk/disco number. As Beck says: 'I actually changed it from major to minor, so I had to do a little bit of altering, but I think it served the groove a bit'. This new version, which also features Beck somewhere in the high-range vocal mix, is one that would be at home among the experimental synth explorations on the future-looking but at-the-time dismissed *McCartney II* (1980).

'You've Got a Woman' Natalie Bergman Ft. Beck (Peter de Leeuwe) 3:25

Beck provides vocals on Natalie Bergman's cover of Lion's 1975 track, a B-side to the band's only single 'But I Do'. It's a faithful, inoffensive cover, hitting that 'who knew?' sweet spot where Dutch psychedelia meets lite reggae. Bergman's group Wild Belle opened shows for Beck and Cage the Elephant in the summer of 2019 and she typically joined Beck onstage. Her father and stepmother were killed in an accident in 2019, which led to a period of withdrawal that resulted in her first solo album, *Mercy*, released on 7 May 2021. In addition to co-vocals on this non-LP single, released in July 2021, Beck appeared in the video for the *Mercy* track 'Home at Last' and remixed the single's B-side, 'Paint the Rain' (3:59), turning the mostly acoustic track into something more sinister a la the Pixies' 'Wave of Mutilation'. 'You've Got a Woman' was released on CD on 8 April 2022 on a Third Man Records Mix in a limited edition of Jack White's *Fear of the Dawn* LP – and that's a mouthful.

'Ladies Night' (Robert Bell, Ronald Bell, George Brown), Meekaaeel Muhammed, Claydes Smith, James Taylor, Dennis Thomas, Earl Toon Jr.) 2:00

Beck appears as a for-hire rock-star version of himself in Judd Apatow's pandemic-era Hollywood satire *The Bubble*. Beck's tongue-in-cheek version of Kool & The Gang's 1979 smash hits home, but little else does in this squandering of so much talent.

'Chain Reaction' Joy Downer Feat. Beck (Joy Downer, Jeffrey Downer, and Beck) 4:04

Beck gets a breathless co-vocal verse and some background vocals on this sweet, drum-heavy pop single from Joy Downer. The song, released on 22 April 2022, also features Pearl Jam's Mike McCready on guitar. Beck previously performed with LA indie-scene mainstay Downer on *The Late Late Show with James Corden* on 22 March 2021, playing bass on 'Over & Out' from her 2020 LP *Paper Moon*.

'Archangel' 3:22

This is a gentle, atmospheric interlude with acoustic guitar and wispy background vocals, released on 20 May 2022. It's Beck's contribution to the

US National Audubon Society's project *For the Birds: The Birdsong Project Vol. 1*, featuring '220 music artists, actors, literary figures, and visual artists, all coming together to celebrate the joy birds bring to our lives.' An archangel is a fancy, domesticated pigeon.

'Eye in the Sky' Awolnation Featuring Beck (Alan Parsons, Eric Woolfson) 4:03

This cover of The Alan Parsons Project's 1982 number three US hit appears on *My Echo, My Shadow, My Covers & Me*, Aaron Bruno's Awolnation's sixth LP. Beck is on background vocals, and he might take lead on one verse, but there are no credits as of this writing.

'take it back' JAWNY Feat. Beck 2:25

Beck and early Beck wannabe Jawny (formerly Johnny Utah) swap lines on this 2022 melodic kick-in-the-pants indie-rocker remake of the 2021 EP *The Story of Hugo* track. Jawny opened for Beck at his June 2022 UK shows.

'Old Man' (Neil Young) 3:28

Beck's affectionate and at times almost choral version of the Neil Young acoustic classic accompanied a September 2022 U.S. commercial for a National Football League match. The game featured the 45-year 'old man' Tom Brady against the 27-year-old Patrick Mahomes. It remains to be seen if the two-time Super Bowl winner Mahomes is a lot like the seven-time Super Bowl winner Brady, but the elder Young was displeased with the younger Beck using his song in a commercial. The full version streamed a few days later. Beck has covered a handful of Young songs, most notably 'Pocahontas', accompanied by Young at his 2011 Bridge Benefits shows.

'Thinking About You' 3:38

Beck followed his gentle Young cover with his own reflective ballad, backed by Blake Mills on guitar and mandolin, Roger Manning on keyboards, and Justin Meldal-Johnsen on bass, the latter reappearing after a stint with St. Vincent. The song is the tale of a lost lover ('and she's gone, she's gone'), its mournful, resigned tone recalling earlier breakup lamentations. Beck unveiled the song live in December 2021, two months after his divorce from Marissa Ribisi, streamed it in February 2023, and performed it on *Jimmy Kimmel Live!*, backed by Mills and bass legend Pino Palladino.

'Possession Island' Gorillaz featuring Beck (Damon Albarn, Beck Hansen, Greg Kurstin) 3:26

Beck's in the mix, but Albarn dominates the vocals on this misty hymn. The hummable track, more Blur than Gorillaz, closed out 2023's *Cracker Island*. Beck joined Gorillaz on stage for this song and 'The Valley of the Pagans' at a pair of Los Angeles shows in September 2022.

Early Recordings

Like any aspiring musician in the late 1980s, Beck created a series of self-distributed cassettes to share with friends and fans. These recordings were never released by record labels, so in some sense, they're not official releases, but since they come from Beck, they're also not bootlegs (at least originally, since most fans have come to know them through bootlegs). As such, while these early recordings are part of the Beck release story, they tend toward apocrypha; texts 'kept secret because they were the vehicles of esoteric knowledge considered too profound or too sacred to be disclosed to anyone other than the initiated' (thanks, Wikipedia!). These recordings aren't too profound or too sacred, but are esoteric and mainly for the initiated. If you're reading this, you're probably one of the initiated. If not, then consider this a nudge to learn the secret handshake.

Banjo Story (1988)

This is Beck's first DIY cassette of all-original material. Recorded in New York City, it's Beck solo on acoustic guitar, harmonica, some percussion and, yes, banjo. None of the 12 songs appear on official releases (and three are more recordings than songs).

Beck and Dava (1990)

Over 39 tracks, Beck and the otherwise unidentified singer Dava, fill a cassette with tunes from an all-star assemblage of American roots giants (Hank Williams, Bob Dylan, Woody Guthrie), with eight slight Beck originals sprinkled in.

Beck, Like the Beer (1992)

This leaked cassette contains three unique songs, tentatively titled 'Hotdogs', 'Watchtower Magazine', and 'Bonus Beer Noise'. It's mainly Beck on guitar until the 'Beer' noise jam. The songs were untitled on the original cassette.

Don't Get Bent Out of Shape (1992)

Beck self-released two versions of this cassette with the same packaging and notes. The insert, 'copywrit 19-9-2', reads: 'Songs herein writ and played off Beck's guitar. Thanks to Steve for lending banjo and squeezebox and to Rev. Mike for hosting the proceedings'. Eight songs are effectively demos for official releases, six appear in some form on other demo collections, a dozen are unique to these collections, and 'Special People' was officially released unscathed.

1992 Tape (1992)

This was a Beck-assembled cassette that was shared in his private circles before being leaked on CDr. The first side includes three contemporary covers, three unique originals, seven songs that appear on other demo collections, and two songs with Hanft vocals. The B-side, released online in 2006, is by Loser, a band Beck and Steve Hanft started around the time the latter was filming *Kill the Moonlight*. Hanft sings lead, Beck sings some and contributes electric guitar; two songs appeared in different versions in the Hanft film.

Fresh Meat + Old Slabs (1993)
Released after Beck's official label debut with *Golden Feelings*, he made this compilation for his mother, Bibbe Hansen, so she could play it in her café. It includes four exclusive songs (three of which are under a minute) and acts more like a greatest hits collection for the transition from self-releasing music to working with labels – a kid showing off some of his best work to his mom.

Feel The Bunny (2008)
These five tracks of early 1990s folk-Beck wackiness, including a cover of the 'Theme from Dukes of Hazzard', total less than 5 minutes of music. They're pulled from Steve Hanft's *Feel the Bunny* video, which the director popped online in 2008.

Bogusflow (1993)
In 2017, Steve Hanft put a December 1993 audio recording of him and Beck on YouTube. The duo was joined on tracks by Lisa Dembling (drums, backup vocals), Clare Crespo (bass), Martha Atwell (bass, backup vocals), and Leo LeBlanc (pedal steel). The ten original songs are co-composed by Beck and Hanft, and two songs from Hanft and Dembling's Liquor Cabinet were also included.

141

Compilations and Live Collections

Unusual among major artists, Beck has never released a commercially available greatest hits or live album in the US or the UK, although he has released both types of collections as promotional items and in other markets. This section covers these promo and global releases.

Beck Geffen Records Promo Cassette France (1994)
This 21-track collection mixes early independent tracks with a few *Mellow Gold* hits. Most interesting for the misspelled titles 'Powboat' ('Rowboat') and 'Spetial People' ('Special People'). I have not heard this tape, but if the 2:58 time for 'Gettin' Home' is correct, it would appear to be the version from the 1992 cassette *Don't Get Bent Out of Shape* Version 1.

The History of Beck – A Selection of His Non-DGC Work DGC Promo CD US (1994)
The first side is from a 23 July 1993 KCRW *Morning Becomes Eclectic* broadcast. The opening track is a clip of Woody Guthrie discussing writing 'I Ain't Got No Home'. This is the only official release of 'Death is Coming to Get Me' and 'Whimsical Actress', discussed in the *Mellow Gold* chapter. The last five songs on indie-release side B are from *Stereopathetic Soulmanure*, listed as *Telepathic Astro Manure* on the cassettes.

Live On KCRW'S 'Morning Becomes Eclectic' With Chris Douridas DGC Promo Cassette US (1994)
A 4 March 1994 radio performance with Chris Ballew features four otherwise unreleased songs, plus the rarely performed 'Bogusflow' and the single version of 'It's All in Your Mind'. The unique songs are discussed in the *Mellow Gold* chapter.

Thurston/Beck KXLU 3/8/94 DGC Promo Cassette US (1994)
Joined by guitarist Chris Ballew on 'noise', this three-song, half-hour in-studio collaboration with the Sonic Youth frontman can generously be called abrasive. It would be a mind-blowing experience for anyone who's intro to Beck was, say, *Colors*. Songs are discussed in the *Mellow Gold* chapter.

The Mix – 138 BBC Radio International UK (1996)
A half-dozen mostly mistitled songs (e.g., Millius' for 'Jack Ass') were included on a 22-song compilation distributed by the BBC World Service. I have not heard the songs, but they seem to come from a 3 September 1995 show at BBC Studios and a 31 March 1996 show at King's College in London, which wouldn't explain where 'Waiting for A Train' (which might actually be Son House's 'Grinnin' in Your Face') was sourced.

In Concert – 706 BBC Radio International UK (1997)
Another BBC World Service offering, recorded live at the Brixton Academy, London, 10 December 1996. No surprises in the 13-song, 56-minute set that omitted 'Derelict' and the yet-to-be-released 'Debra'.

Sonic Net All Access Jones Radio Network US (2000)
Six songs from an unidentified *Midnite Vultures* show, plus five additional live tracks from Vertical Horizon, including their 1999 US number one 'Everything You Want'.

In Concert – 820 BBC Radio International UK (2000)
Another BBC World Service CD, this one from a 25 March 2000 show at Clyde Auditorium in Glasgow, Scotland. A dozen songs are included.

Stray Cat Blues: A Collection of B-Sides Geffen Records Japan (2000)
A fan-favorite Japan-only CD that brings together an eclectic mix of eight non-LP tracks.

Beck DGC (2001)
Also known as *Beck.com B-sides*, this limited edition, website-only CD collects *Midnight Vultures* additional tracks and includes two exclusive 'Mixed Bizness' remixes from contest winners, both discussed in the *Midnite Vultures* chapter.

Live In San Francisco Geffen Records France (2002)
A France-only CD-ROM with three videos ('Lost Cause', 'Guess I'm Doing Fine', and 'The Golden Age') from San Francisco's Palace of the Fine Arts Theatre, either 28 or 29 September 2002. They're pulled from a half-hour video about the pre-*Sea Change* tour concert stop that's worth searching out.

Absolutely Live in The Zone Westwood One Radio Networks (2003)
One of about 30 releases in the title series, these half-dozen songs come from an unidentified concert. The second CD is from the heavy metal band Disturbed, who were enjoying the first of five consecutive US number one LPs at the time.

A Brief Overview (2005)
An eccentric promo disc featuring material from indie days to *Guero* that DGC released to remind retailers and radio that Beck existed. The UK version includes 'Girl', and both UK and US editions include the latest single, 'E-Pro', twice.

Remix EP #1 Interscope US (2005)
This six-track promo-only CD includes the only legal release of the South Rakkas Crew's 'Black Tambourine' remix. Unusually, on Apple Music at the time of this writing.

Remix EP #2 Interscope US (2005)
This six-track promo CD includes the only legal release of the Superthriller 'Go It Alone' remix.

Live De L'été Canal + Canal + France (2005)
Beck's eight-song *Guero* set, recorded on 23 March 2005 at Canal + Studios Rive Gauche in Paris, aired on the TV channel on 20 August 2005. The broadcast was also released as a promo DVDr that also included a half-hour Foo Fighters set recorded in May 2005.

Live from KCRW / 2014 Download (2014)
Four songs culled from an intimate 15-song, 14 April 2014 show at Apogee Studio in Santa Monica. 'The Golden Age', 'Soldier Jane', 'Don't Let It Go', and 'Country Down' were briefly available through the KCRW website.

Live At Shinkiba Studio Coast Hostess Entertainment Unlimited Japan (2018)
This Tokyo show, recorded on 24 October 2017, was included as a 17-song DVD in the *Colors* Japan deluxe edition. The video omits the live debut of *Colors* songs 'Seventh Heaven', 'Fix Me', 'Dear Life', and 'I'm So Free', plus 'Timebomb' and 'Where It's At', although the entire show can be found online.

Dear Life (Words + Music | Vol. 28) Amazon Audible (2022)
This one-hour and 48-minute audiobook features Beck recounting incidents from his life and reworking nine songs.

Collaborations

This chapter covers Beck's work with other artists, those times when he's working with or for other artists and his name isn't the one selling the product. The chapter starts with Beck's work in the *Modern Guilt / Morning Phase* interregnum – Record Club, production gigs, and *Song Reader* – before heading back to a chronological overview of his work as a sideman, writer, producer, and remixer.

Record Club

Beck's Record Club started in the spring of 2009 and continued through the late summer of 2010. The idea was to assemble a group of friends and cover a complete LP in one day. All tracks were released as videos through Beck. com, one new video each week. Five LPs were recorded. A ten-track *Record Club Songs* collection, with favorites voted by fans, was planned, but never completed. While there are straight versions of songs, most tracks interpret rather than adhere to the original, especially on the Yanni disc.

The Velvet Underground & Nico – The Velvet Underground & Nico (1967) 18 June 2009

Beck and frequent collaborators Nigel Godrich, Brian LeBarton, Bram Inscore, and Joey Waronker were joined by Thórunn Antonía Magnúsdóttir, singer of the short-lived English/Icelandic band Fields, Smashing Pumpkins sideman Chris Holmes, and brother-in-law Giovanni Ribisi. The VU album choice won out in a unanimous group vote over Digital Underground's *Sex Packets*. The versions are respectful but inventive, breathing new life into well-known tunes. Beck sings lead on all but two of the dozen tracks (two versions of 'Heroin'), and variously contributes guitar, erhu and piano.

Leonard Cohen – Songs of Leonard Cohen (1967) 3 September 2009.

Beck was joined by alt-indie singer-songwriter Devendra Banhart, MGMT's Will Berman, Ben Goldwasser, and Andrew VanWyngarden, Binki Shapiro from Little Joy, and Andrew Stockdale from Wolfmother, in addition to holdovers Bram Inscore and Brian LeBarton. The group covered another 1967 debut LP, this from Canadian poet/musician Leonard Cohen. A note on Beck. com accompanying the ragged version of 'Suzanne' announced:

> There is no intention to 'add to' the original work or attempt to recreate the power of the original recording. Only to play music and document what happens. And those who aren't familiar with the albums in question will hopefully look for the songs in their definitive versions.

Cohen was chosen instead of Ace of Base's *The Sign*. Beck sings lead on 'Hey, That's No Way to Say Goodbye' and has co-lead vocals on seven of the other nine songs. He doesn't appear on 'Teachers', but variously plays guitar, kalimba, and keyboards on other tracks.

Alexander Spence – Oar (1969) 12 November 2009

Oar was the only solo album from the Jefferson Airplane drummer and Moby Grape guitarist Alexander 'Skip' Spence. Spence played all the instruments on *Oar*, a Nashville-recorded DIY-type affair reputed to be Columbia Records' worst-selling LP to that time. Beck is joined here by an all-star collection including Leslie Feist, James Gadson, Jamie Lidell, Brian LeBarton, and Wilco (Jeff Tweedy, John Stirratt, Glenn Kotche, Mikael Jorgensen, Nels Cline, Pat Sansone). Beck has a less prominent role in this project, only taking solo lead vocals on three tracks while contributing musically to all other tracks.

INXS – Kick (1987) 25 March 2010

Beck was joined by Annie Clarke and her then St. Vincent collaborator Daniel Hart, Sergio Dias of Os Mutantes, The Liars' Angus Andrew and Julian Gross and, once again, Brian LeBarton. Beck said of the effort on his website:

It was recorded in a little over 12 hours on March 3rd, 2010. It was an intense, hilarious, daunting and completely fun undertaking. Many classic moments, inspired performances and occasional anarchy.

Beck sings lead on 'Devil Inside' and 'Loved One', which is essentially a solo effort, and co-lead on the title track. He contributes guitar, keyboards, percussion, and background vocals on 11 of the dozen tracks but doesn't appear on 'Mediate'.

Yanni – Live at the Acropolis (1994) 1 July 2010

Greek musical wizard Yanni performed in September 1993 at the Herodes Atticus Theatre, located on the southwest slope of Athens' Acropolis. The performance was released on CD and as a video, subsequently broadcast on America's PBS at least one million times in the mid-1990s. Possessed by repeated broadcasts, Beck settled on this unusual choice as the final Record Club recording. Beck teams with Sonic Youth's Thurston Moore, with the duo sharing vocal duties and adding lyrics to six of the album's ten instrumental tracks. They're backed on most tracks by Russell Ferrante, Jeff Babko, Abraham Laboriel, and Toss Panos, identified as 'several studio musician heavyweights [who] were brought in to read a heavily doctored score with interpolations of everything from Stravinsky to Shania Twain (look for others)'. Two tracks feature members of Tortoise. Beck sings solo lead vocals on 'Acroyali/Standing in Motion' and 'Reflections of Passion', shares with Moore on an additional three, and doesn't appear at all on 'Nostalgia'.

Charlotte Gainsbourg

Charlotte Gainsbourg is a French/English actor and singer, the daughter of Beck influence Serge Gainsbourg and English actor/singer Jane Birkin. She and Beck began working together in 2009 as the two seemingly bonded over injuries. Gainsbourg suffered a life-threatening brain hemorrhage in 2007 after a water-skiing accident, and Beck endured a debilitating injury during the 2005 'E-Pro' video shoot. Their work together encompassed Gainsbourg recording 17 Beck written and produced songs, and two Beck-produced cover songs ('Le Chat Du Café Des Artistes' and 'Hey Joe'). While Beck (thankfully) didn't 'write female' for Gainsbourg as Prince did for Vanity 6, Jill Jones and other woman artists, it seems like a lost opportunity that Beck didn't produce more full-concept projects for like-minded female artists.

Charlotte Gainsbourg – IRM (2009)

Beck and Gainsbourg collaborated at Beck's house off and on during 2009 while both were in various stages of convalescence, which explains the title: *IRM* is a French acronym for *imagerie par résonance magnétique*, that is, an MRI (magnetic resonance imaging). According to Gainsbourg, Beck 'wrote everything and composed everything, but I think the fact that I was there influenced everything'. Beck's father David Campbell arranged the strings on several songs. The only song that found its way into Beck's set was 'Heaven Can Wait', performed in Paris on 2 July 2013 as a duet with Gainsbourg. An *IRM* limited edition was released in 2010. It included a second disc of seven remixes (see below) plus the exclusive 'IRM (DiskJokke Remix)' (8:32). The album was released on 7 December 2009 and hit 62 in the UK and 69 in the US, her highest-charting LP in both countries. A 'Heaven Can Wait' UK promo CD included three exclusive remixes, 'Time of the Assassins' promo CDs included five different mixes, and a 'Trick Pony' CD included four exclusive versions.

Charlotte Gainsbourg – Live at Sunset Sound UK promo CD / digital EP (2010)

Recorded on 29 October 2009 and broadcast on 17 January 2010 on KCRW Morning Becomes Eclectic, Beck produced this 14 June 2010 release.

Charlotte Gainsbourg – Sunset Sound Session 7" single (2010)

Beck produced these outtakes from the KCRW sessions, released in the US and UK on Record Store Day, 17 April 2010.

Charlotte Gainsbourg – Stage Whisper (2011)

Beck produced half of the 'Unreleased' studio disc on this 2011 cash-in holiday release. The second disc features five Beck-written *IRM* songs from June 2010 live shows, with a band that included Brian LeBarton, Bram

Inscore, and Eric Gardner. A deluxe edition DVD includes eight live Beck-written songs. 'Terrible Angels', which was released as a US, UK, and France single, was newly written for this release, while the other studio songs were outtakes from *IRM*. The four other studio songs have no Beck involvement. A 'Paradisco' single included four exclusive remixes.

Charlotte Gainsbourg – 'Hey Joe' 7" (2014)

'Hey Joe' (Billy Roberts) 4:52, 'Hey Joe (SebastiAn Remix)' (Billy Roberts) 3:50
Beck produced this one-off collaboration at the behest of *Nymphomaniac* director Lars Von Trier. The original version of the song appeared on the film soundtrack collection, with Beck on guitar and background vocals, and as the A-side of a 19 April 2014 Record Store Day single in Europe.

Thurston Moore – Demolished Thoughts (2011)
Beck produced this beautiful album in 2010 and early 2011, a change of pace for Beck fans used to Moore's abrasive side. Moore had 'trepidation' with the lyrics, which he called 'coded' and personal, seemingly in reference to his marriage with Sonic Youth bandmate Kim Gordon, which was in the process of coming apart; the group would disband in late 2011 and the couple divorce in 2013. Moore felt Beck was able to temper the downbeat mood: 'He gave it a lot of colour. And just by colouring it as such, it gave it a certain light and positivity, even though there's this line of sadness that goes through it'. The album, released on 24 May 2011, peaked on the UK chart at 119. Beck provides slight instrumentation on three of the nine tracks.

Stephen Malkmus and The Jicks – Mirror Traffic (2011)
Beck produced but doesn't appear on *Mirror Traffic*. Before working with Charlotte Gainsbourg, Beck called former Pavement frontman Malkmus and offered his services for the group's fifth LP. The rest of that band agreed and they recorded the LP in less than a week at Sunset Sound Studios. Malkmus credited Beck and engineer Darrell Thorp with giving the album an 'old-school controlled drum sound'. A clean version and a radio edit were released for the first single, 'Senator'. The album was first released in Japan on 17 August 2011.

Song Reader (2012)
At a time when Beck's health limited his ability to hit the road and perform his songs, this project allowed him to stay at home while his music hit the road to be performed by others. The 108-page *Song Reader* book, published by McSweeney's, offered sheet music for 20 songs, including beautiful cover art for each song, and an additional 41 song fragments. This project, released on 11 December 2012, harkens back to the earliest days of the music industry, in the late 19th century when sheet music was the coin of the realm,

before radio and the record industry in the 1920s squeezed out home (mainly piano) interpretations. The intent was to have people interpret the songs and share them online at the now-defunct *SongReader.net*. Beck recruited artists for the 20 songs that appear on the official release below, but you can find homemade versions of most songs online. A play, *Song Reader: The Musical*, with book and arrangements by Clandestine Art's Harvey Droke and Daniel Hornal, was performed at the Capital Fringe Festival in Washington, D.C. in July 2016.

Many of the 41 songs that don't appear on the CD are very fragmentary, although some, such as 'Won't You Fondle Me', are fleshed out lyrically. Many of the titles, such as 'Today I Had a Lot of Things to Do (But I Put Them All On Hold To Follow You)' read alarmingly like Morrissey titles.

Various Artists – Song Reader (2014)

Beck and film-music supervisor extraordinaire Randall Poster executive produced this collection of Beck-written songs from 2012's *Song Reader* sheet music collection. Beck couldn't find anyone to record 'Heaven's Ladder', so he recorded it himself (see *Modern Guilt* chapter). Beck has performed all of the songs live, but has mostly ignored the material except for three 2013 *Song Reader* events. Released on 28 June 2014, about four months after *Morning Phase*.

Sideman, Songwriter, Producer, Remixer

There's online information that Beck produced songs in the early and mid-1980s for Black Fag, a band that included his mom and performance artist Vaginal Davis, but there's no independent confirmation of the existence of this material. At the very least, I haven't heard it.

The Geraldine Fibbers – Get Thee Gone (1994)
'Blue Cross' 3:29: Guitar and vocals

The Jon Spencer Blues Explosion – Orange (1994)
'Flavor' (Jon Spencer, Beck Hansen, Russell Simins, Judah Bauer) 6:19: **Vocals**

The Jon Spencer Blues Explosion – Experimental Remixes (1995)
'Flavor Part 1 – Mike D' (Jon Spencer) 4:47: Remixed / reorganized / repeated / destroyed / simonized by Beck Hansen, Mario Caldato Jr., and Mike D.
'Flavor Part 2 – Beck & Mike D' (Jon Spencer, Beck Hansen) 4:09: Vocals and remixed / reorganized / repeated / destroyed / simonized by Beck Hansen, Mario Caldato Jr., and Mike D.

Nardwuar The Human Serviette 'Interview: Nardwuar Vs. Beck' – Skookum Chief Powered... Teenage Zit Rawk Angst! 0:28 (1995)
Professional instigator Narduwuar records a phone call with Beck and pisses him off in the process. The full version runs over 14 minutes and can be found online.

Forest For The Trees – Forest For The Trees (1997)
Beck producer/co-writer Karl Stephenson's band
'Infinite Cow' (Karl Stephenson) 3:10: Background vocals
'Fall' 4:33 (John Coz, Karl Stephenson, Mark Peterson, Mark Schultz): Harmonica; as on 'Loser', song samples Johnny Jenkins' 'I Walk on Gilded Splinters'.

Momus – Ping Pong (1997)

Kahimi Karie – Larme de Crocodile (1997).
'Lolitapop Dollhouse' (Nicholas Currie) 4:08
Harmonica; Scottish impresario/musician sampled Beck from a bootleg, which Beck's management approved. The backing track is the same on both LPs, with the respective artists adding vocals.

that dog. – Hear You Me: A Tribute to Mykel & Carli (1998)
'Silently' (Anna Waronker) 2:33
Banjo; Various artists tribute LP for Weezer fans killed in an after-concert car crash.

Amnesia – Lingus (1998)
'Drop Down' (Brad Laner) 5:10: Harmonica

Air 'Sexy Boy' single (1998)
'Sexy Boy (Sex Kino Mix by Beck)' (Air) 6:33: Remix; also on *Moon Safari* deluxe edition.

Björk 'Alarm Call' single (1998)
'Alarm Call (Bjeck Remix)' (Björk) 6:28: Remix; also on France 'Hunter' single.

Forest for the Trees – The Sound of Wet Paint (1999)
'Jet Engine' (5:44) (Karl Stephenson, Beck Hansen): Vocals

David Bowie 'Seven' (2000)
'Seven (Beck Mix #1)' (David Bowie) 3:44
'Seven (Beck Mix #2)' (David Bowie) 5:14
Mix #1 appeared on commercial Europe singles; Both mixes appeared on a UK promo single and the 2004 two-disc limited edition of Bowie's *Hours*....

Air – 10 000 Hz Legend (2001)
'The Vagabond' (Jean-Benoît Dunckel, Nicolas Godin, Beck Hansen) 5:37
Harmonica, vocals
'Don't be Light' (Jean-Benoît Dunckel, Nicolas Godin) 6:18
Vocals
'Don't be Light (Malibu Remix)' 5:21
'Don't be Light (Mr. Oizo Remix)' 4:17
Vocals; Beck's poem appears on the two remixes, available on Air's *Everybody Hertz* (2002), with four additional remixes that have no Beck involvement.

Futurama TV Show
'My Broken Friend' (Christopher Tyng, Eric Horsted, Ken Keeler)
Beck's disembodied head contributed vocals in Season three, Episode 13, 'Bendin' in the Wind', which aired on Fox on 22 April 2001. The episode was released on DVD on 7 March 2004.

Marianne Faithfull – Kissin' Time (2002)
'Like being Born' (Beck Hansen, Marianne Faithfull) 3:51: Co-production, guitar
'Nobody's Fault' 6:28: Co-production, guitar; version of 'Nobody's Fault but My Own'.
'Sex With Strangers' (Beck Hansen, Marianne Faithfull) 4:22: Co-production, Background Vocals, synthesizer, percussion
'Sex with Strangers (Sly & Robbie Sex Ref Mix)' (Beck Hansen, Marianne Faithfull) 4:56

'Sex with Strangers (Sly & Robbie Dub Mix)' (Beck Hansen, Marianne Faithfull) 4:29
Remixes appear on UK/Europe 'Sex with Strangers' single.

Pearl Jam – Ten Club PJ Merry Christmas 2002 7"
'Sleepless Nights' (Boudleaux Bryant, Felice Bryant) 3:21:Vocals, guitar
Duet with Eddie Vedder recorded live at The Wiltern Theater, Los Angeles, 26 February 2002 at a recording artists rights concert. A-side is a Pearl Jam cover of the Sonics' 'Don't Believe in Christmas'.

Charlie's Angels: Full Throttle Soundtrack – Pink featuring William Orbit (2003)
'Feel Good Time' (Beck Hansen, William Orbit) 3:46
Beck co-wrote and recorded this song for the film, but the release eventually bumped up against *Sea Change,* so he mixed it. His contributions to the song were removed and Pink vocals were added. There are a handful of remixes that also have no Beck involvement beyond songwriting, although some are confusingly done by the DJ duo Boris & Beck. Orbit leaked two remixes that feature both Beck and Pink vocals, but Beck's unreleased original (5:10) is worth searching out. Includes a sample of 'Fresh Garbage' by Spirit.

Macy Gray – The Trouble with Being Myself (2003)
'It Ain't the Money' (Beck Hansen, Macy Gray, Pharoahe Monch) 4:07: Guitar, backing vocals
'It Ain't the Money (Instrumental)' (Beck Hansen, Macy Gray, Pharoahe Monch) 4:07
'It Ain't the Money (A Cappella)' (Beck Hansen, Macy Gray, Pharoahe Monch) 4:07
Alternate versions appear on the US promo and UK single releases of 'It Ain't the Money'.

Sia – Colour the Small One (2004)
'The Bully' (Beck Hansen, Sia Furler, Jimmy Hogarth) 3:51
'The Bully (Instrumental)' (3:51)
On US promo CD *Strictly Background 4* (2005).
Loser – Kill the Moonlight (2006)
Loser was an early 1990s Beck band that included Steve Hanft (vocals), Mike Tolmin (bass), and Moses (drums). The 1997 CD soundtrack release for Hanft's film *Kill the Moonlight* included three Beck songs. This 2006 DVD/CD reissue expanded to include three Loser tracks from the film that weren't on the original CD.
Loser 'Born of Whiskey' (Loser) 2:10: Electric guitar, background vocals; different version on *1992 Tape*.

Loser 'Dad Came Home' (Loser) 2:05: Electric guitar; same version on *1992 Tape*.
Loser 'Fish Bait' (Loser) 2:28:Electric guitar; Instrumental

North American Halloween Prevention Initiative 'Do They Know It's Hallowe'en'? Single (2005)
'Do They Know It's Hallowe'en? (Original Version)' (Adam Gollner, Nick Diamonds) 5:58
'Do They Know It's Hallowe'en? (Radio Edit)' (Adam Gollner, Nick Diamonds) 3:55
'Do They Know It's Hallowe'en? (Disco D Remix)' (Adam Gollner, Nick Diamonds) 3:51
'Do They Know It's Hallowe'en? (Th' Corn Gangg Remix)' (Adam Gollner, Nick Diamonds) 4:54
Beck contributes a few lines of vocals among almost three dozen indie-rock and film luminaries, including Win Butler, Thurston Moore, Malcolm McLaren, and Elvira, who contribute to this Band-Aid parody.

The Avant Guards – Popadelic (2007)
'Knock-Knock Hello' (Matthew Tepper) 1:43: Vocals

Dr. Dog 'The Girl (Beck Remix)' 3:31 (2007)
Remix vinyl 7" of *We All Belong* (2007) album track.

The White Stripes 'Conquest' singles (2007)
Beck and Jack White co-produced four songs spread over three singles released in the US and UK on 31 December 2007. The songs were recorded in Beck's living room. Beck wasn't involved in 'Conquest', the Corky Robbins cover from the White Stripes' final LP *Icky Thump*. All five songs ended up on the 2008 US EP *Conquest*.
'It's My Fault for being Famous' (Jack White) 2:56: Piano
'Honey, We Can't Afford to Look This Cheap' (Jack White) 3:55: Slide Guitar
'Cash Grab Complications on the Matter' (Jack White) 3:37: **Stompin' And A Clappin'**
'Conquest (Acoustic Mariachi Version)' 3:37 (Corky Robbins) aka '**Conquest (Versiòn Acùstica De Mariachi)'** 3:37

Sia – Some People Have Real Problems (2008)
'Academia' (Sia Furler, Dan Carey) 3:16: Vocals, backing vocals
'Death by Chocolate' (Sia Furler, Greg Kurstin) 5:04: Backing vocals

Norah Jones – Chasing Pirates Remix EP (2009)
'Chasing Pirates (Droogs Remix)' (Norah Jones) 3:19

Remix by Beck, Brian LeBarton, and Drew Brown (Droogs collectively) of first single from *The Fall*.

Devendra Banhart 'Life During Wartime' (Todd Soldonz, Marc Shaiman, Beck Hansen) 4:47
Beck sings background vocals on the title song from Soldonz's 2009 film.

Jamie Lidell – Compass (2010)
Beck co-produced this 14-track LP, but it's unclear which tracks he worked on as the credits include three other artists on 'additional production'.
'I Wanna be Your Telephone' (Jamie Lidell) 3:30: Guitar

'You are Waking' (Jamie Lidell) 3:43: Guitar
'It's a Kiss' (Jamie Lidell) 3:47: Juno synth
'Compass' (Jamie Lidell) 5:33: Guitar, percussion
'Coma Chameleon' (Beck Hansen, Jamie Lidell) 3:21: Guitar, Juno synth
'Big Drift' (Jamie Lidell, Beck Hansen, Leslie Feist, Lindsey Rome) 4:45: Backing vocals

Jamie Lidell 'I Wanna Be Your Telephone' UK single (2010)
'I Wanna be Your Telephone (Tiga Party Like It's 19909 Remix)' (Jamie Lidell) 5:14: Guitar

James Lidell Website release (2010)
'Completely Exposed (Beck Remix)' (James Lidell) 3:13
'Big Drift 1982 (Krikor Remix)' (Jamie Lidell, Beck Hansen, Leslie Feist, Lindsey Rome) 7:02

The Jon Spencer Blues Explosion – Now I Got Worry Deluxe Edition (2010)
Expanded edition of 1996 LP
'Roosevelt Hotel Blues' (Jon Spencer, Judah Bauer, Russell Simins) 3:23: Keyboard

Lykke Li 'Get Some (Beck Remix)' (2010) 4:47
This was available as a stand-alone download at the RCRD LBL website before appearing as a digital download and on a bonus disc for Li's *Wounded Rhymes* (2011).

The White Stripes 'The Hardest Button to Button (Beck Remix)' 7" single (Jack White) 4:04 (2012)
Beck remixed this single from the defunct band's *Elephant*. It was released as part of White's Third Man Records Vault Package series, backed by a remix of The Dead Weather's 'Hang You from the Heavens'.

Karen Elson 'Gold Dust Woman' (Stevie Nicks) 5:42 (2012)
Beck produced and appeared on this track from supermodel/Jack White ex Elson. The song is on *Just Tell Me That You Want Me – A Tribute to Fleetwood Mac*.

Feist 'How Come You Never Go There (Beck remix)' (Feist) 3:10 (2012)
Remix of 2011 single and *Metals* LP track.

Dwight Yoakam – 3 Pears (2012)
Beck co-produced these two tracks with Yoakam.
'A Heart Like Mine' (Dwight Yoakam) 3:59: Handclaps
'Missing Heart' (Dwight Yoakam) 4:35

Bat for Lashes – The Haunted Man (2012)
'Marilyn' (Natasha Khan) 4:36: Guitar, synthesizer, beat programming, drum machine

JJ Doom – Bookhead EP and Key to The Kuffs 'Butter Edition' 2013)
Remix of track from Jneiro Jarel and MF Doom's 2012 *Key to the Kuffs*.
'Banished (Beck Remix)' (Daniel Dumile, Beck Hansen) 4:04: Vocals
Jenny Lewis – The Voyager (2014)
'Just One of The Guys' (Jenny Lewis) 3:51: Glockenspiel, bass, background vocals

M83 – Junk (2016) 'Time Wind' (feat. Beck) (Anthony Gonzalez, Beck Hansen, Justin Meldal-Johnsen) 4:09
A mid-tempo pop track from the French 'Midnight City' group featuring Beck on vocals. Beck sideman Meldal-Johnsen produced this and two other LPs for the band. Sounds like soundtrack fodder.

U2 'Lights of Home' 12" (2018)
'Lights Of Home' (Free Yourself / Beck Remix) (U2, Alana Haim, Danielle Haim, Este Haim, Ariel Rechtshaid) 3:46
Record Store Day April 2018 exclusive

U2 'Love Is Bigger Than Anything in Its Way (Beck Remix)' (U2) digital download 3:22 (2018): Keyboards, piano, programmed by Beck

Jenny Lewis – On the Line (2019)
Beck produced these tunes on the album that went top 40 in the US and UK.
'Do Si Do' (Jenny Lewis) 3:54: Piano, organ, synthesizer, background vocals
'Little White Dove' (Jenny Lewis) 4:49: Guitar, keyboards, background vocals
'Rabbit Hole' (Jenny Lewis) 2:46: Background vocals

Leonard Cohen – Thanks for The Dance (2019)
'The Night of Santiago' (Leonard Cohen, Adam Cohen) 4:15: **Jew's harp,**
acoustic guitar

**The Bird and The Bee – Interpreting the Masters Volume 2: A Tribute To
Van Halen** Japan CD (2019)
'Hot For Teacher' (Eddie Van Halen, Alex Van Halen, Michael Anthony, David
Lee Roth) 4:44
Spoken vocals

Remi Wolf – We Love Dogs! Remix EP (2021)
'Sauce' Beck Remix 3:24

Rahill (feat. Beck) 'Fables' (Rahill Jamalifard) 4:51
Habibi co-founder Rahill Jamalifard sings lead on this swirling slice of
psychedelic pop released in March 2023. Beck contributes guitar and
background vocals. A must listen.

Sources

A special note of thanks goes out to the following invaluable sources/databases:
Discogs (discogs.com)
Diskobox.org
Matecritic.com
Rock's Backpages
SecondHandSongs (secondhandsongs.com)
Setlist.fm, The Setlist Wiki
Whiskeyclone.net
WhoSampled (whosampled.com)

The creation of this book relied on multiple book, newspaper, magazine, and web sources. Sources for album review quotes are mentioned in the text. Direct quotes from Beck and others are pulled from multiple sources, typically the major publications that Beck has spoken with on a regular basis, such as *Rolling Stone*, *The Guardian*, *The New York Times*, *Q*, *Spin*, etc. Due to space considerations, only the above sources and books are listed here, but if you'd like more information on where something came from, drop me a line: arthur.lizie@gmail.com.

Any errors in the text are solely my responsibility. You can let me know about them, too.

Books
Beck., *Song Reader* (McSweeney's, 2012)
de Wilde, A., *Beck* (Chronicle Books, 2011)
Jovanovic, R., *Beck! On A River Backwards: The Story of Beck* (Fromm International, 2001)
Jovanovic, R., *Throwing Frisbees at the Sun: A Book About Beck* (Jawbone Press, 2015)
Martell, N., *Beck: The Art of Mutation* (Pocket Books, 2001)
Palacios, J. *Beck: Beautiful Monstrosity* (Boxtree, 2000)

Also available from Sonicbond Publishing ...

On Track series
Alan Parsons Project – Steve Swift 978-1-78952-154-2
Tori Amos – Lisa Torem 978-1-78952-142-9
Asia – Peter Braidis 978-1-78952-099-6
Badfinger – Robert Day-Webb 978-1-878952-176-4
Barclay James Harvest – Keith and Monica Domone 978-1-78952-067-5
The Beatles – Andrew Wild 978-1-78952-009-5
The Beatles Solo 1969-1980 – Andrew Wild 978-1-78952-030-9
Blue Oyster Cult – Jacob Holm-Lupo 978-1-78952-007-1
Blur – Matt Bishop – 978-178952-164-1
Marc Bolan and T.Rex – Peter Gallagher 978-1-78952-124-5
Kate Bush – Bill Thomas 978-1-78952-097-2
Camel – Hamish Kuzminski 978-1-78952-040-8
Caravan – Andy Boot 978-1-78952-127-6
Cardiacs – Eric Benac 978-1-78952-131-3
Eric Clapton Solo – Andrew Wild 978-1-78952-141-2
The Clash – Nick Assirati 978-1-78952-077-4
Crosby, Stills and Nash – Andrew Wild 978-1-78952-039-2
The Damned – Morgan Brown 978-1-78952-136-8
Deep Purple and Rainbow 1968-79 – Steve Pilkington 978-1-78952-002-6
Dire Straits – Andrew Wild 978-1-78952-044-6
The Doors – Tony Thompson 978-1-78952-137-5
Dream Theater – Jordan Blum 978-1-78952-050-7
Electric Light Orchestra – Barry Delve 978-1-78952-152-8
Elvis Costello and The Attractions – Georg Purvis 978-1-78952-129-0
Emerson Lake and Palmer – Mike Goode 978-1-78952-000-2
Fairport Convention – Kevan Furbank 978-1-78952-051-4
Peter Gabriel – Graeme Scarfe 978-1-78952-138-2
Genesis – Stuart MacFarlane 978-1-78952-005-7
Gentle Giant – Gary Steel 978-1-78952-058-3
Gong – Kevan Furbank 978-1-78952-082-8
Hall and Oates – Ian Abrahams 978-1-78952-167-2
Hawkwind – Duncan Harris 978-1-78952-052-1
Peter Hammill – Richard Rees Jones 978-1-78952-163-4
Roy Harper – Opher Goodwin 978-1-78952-130-6
Jimi Hendrix – Emma Stott 978-1-78952-175-7
The Hollies – Andrew Darlington 978-1-78952-159-7
Iron Maiden – Steve Pilkington 978-1-78952-061-3
Jefferson Airplane – Richard Butterworth 978-1-78952-143-6
Jethro Tull – Jordan Blum 978-1-78952-016-3
Elton John in the 1970s – Peter Kearns 978-1-78952-034-7
The Incredible String Band – Tim Moon 978-1-78952-107-8
Iron Maiden – Steve Pilkington 978-1-78952-061-3
Judas Priest – John Tucker 978-1-78952-018-7
Kansas – Kevin Cummings 978-1-78952-057-6
The Kinks – Martin Hutchinson 978-1-78952-172-6
Korn – Matt Karpe 978-1-78952-153-5
Led Zeppelin – Steve Pilkington 978-1-78952-151-1
Level 42 – Matt Philips 978-1-78952-102-3
Little Feat – 978-1-78952-168-9
Aimee Mann – Jez Rowden 978-1-78952-036-1
Joni Mitchell – Peter Kearns 978-1-78952-081-1
The Moody Blues – Geoffrey Feakes 978-1-78952-042-2
Motorhead – Duncan Harris 978-1-78952-173-3
Mike Oldfield – Ryan Yard 978-1-78952-060-6
Opeth – Jordan Blum 978-1-78-952-166-5
Tom Petty – Richard James 978-1-78952-128-3
Porcupine Tree – Nick Holmes 978-1-78952-144-3
Queen – Andrew Wild 978-1-78952-003-3
Radiohead – William Allen 978-1-78952-149-8
Renaissance – David Detmer 978-1-78952-062-0

The Rolling Stones 1963-80 – Steve Pilkington 978-1-78952-017-0
The Smiths and Morrissey – Tommy Gunnarsson 978-1-78952-140-5
Status Quo the Frantic Four Years – Richard James 978-1-78952-160-3
Steely Dan – Jez Rowden 978-1-78952-043-9
Steve Hackett – Geoffrey Feakes 978-1-78952-098-9
Thin Lizzy – Graeme Stroud 978-1-78952-064-4
Toto – Jacob Holm-Lupo 978-1-78952-019-4
U2 – Eoghan Lyng 978-1-78952-078-1
UFO – Richard James 978-1-78952-073-6
The Who – Geoffrey Feakes 978-1-78952-076-7
Roy Wood and the Move – James R Turner 978-1-78952-008-8
Van Der Graaf Generator – Dan Coffey 978-1-78952-031-6
Yes – Stephen Lambe 978-1-78952-001-9
Frank Zappa 1966 to 1979 – Eric Benac 978-1-78952-033-0
Warren Zevon – Peter Gallagher 978-1-78952-170-2
10CC – Peter Kearns 978-1-78952-054-5

Decades Series
The Bee Gees in the 1960s – Andrew Môn Hughes et al 978-1-78952-148-1
The Bee Gees in the 1970s – Andrew Môn Hughes et al 978-1-78952-179-5
Black Sabbath in the 1970s – Chris Sutton 978-1-78952-171-9
Britpop – Peter Richard Adams and Matt Pooler 978-1-78952-169-6
Alice Cooper in the 1970s – Chris Sutton 978-1-78952-104-7
Curved Air in the 1970s – Laura Shenton 978-1-78952-069-9
Bob Dylan in the 1980s – Don Klees 978-1-78952-157-3
Fleetwood Mac in the 1970s – Andrew Wild 978-1-78952-105-4
Focus in the 1970s – Stephen Lambe 978-1-78952-079-8
Free and Bad Company in the 1970s – John Van der Kiste 978-1-78952-178-8
Genesis in the 1970s – Bill Thomas 978178952-146-7
George Harrison in the 1970s – Eoghan Lyng 978-1-78952-174-0
Marillion in the 1980s – Nathaniel Webb 978-1-78952-065-1
Mott the Hoople and Ian Hunter in the 1970s – John Van der Kiste 978-1-78-952-162-7
Pink Floyd In The 1970s – Georg Purvis 978-1-78952-072-9
Tangerine Dream in the 1970s – Stephen Palmer 978-1-78952-161-0
The Sweet in the 1970s – Darren Johnson from Gary Cosby collection 978-1-78952-139-9
Uriah Heep in the 1970s – Steve Pilkington 978-1-78952-103-0
Yes in the 1980s – Stephen Lambe with David Watkinson 978-1-78952-125-2

On Screen series
Carry On… – Stephen Lambe 978-1-78952-004-0
David Cronenberg – Patrick Chapman 978-1-78952-071-2
Doctor Who: The David Tennant Years – Jamie Hailstone 978-1-78952-066-8
James Bond – Andrew Wild – 978-1-78952-010-1
Monty Python – Steve Pilkington 978-1-78952-047-7
Seinfeld Seasons 1 to 5 – Stephen Lambe 978-1-78952-012-5

Other Books
1967: A Year In Psychedelic Rock – Kevan Furbank 978-1-78952-155-9
1970: A Year In Rock – John Van der Kiste 978-1-78952-147-4
1973: The Golden Year of Progressive Rock 978-1-78952-165-8
Babysitting A Band On The Rocks – G.D. Praetorius 978-1-78952-106-1
Eric Clapton Sessions – Andrew Wild 978-1-78952-177-1
Derek Taylor: For Your Radioactive Children – Andrew Darlington 978-1-78952-038-5
The Golden Road: The Recording History of The Grateful Dead – John Kilbride 978-1-78952-156-6
Iggy and The Stooges On Stage 1967-1974 – Per Nilsen 978-1-78952-101-6
Jon Anderson and the Warriors – the road to Yes – David Watkinson 978-1-78952-059-0
Nu Metal: A Definitive Guide – Matt Karpe 978-1-78952-063-7
Tommy Bolin: In and Out of Deep Purple – Laura Shenton 978-1-78952-070-5
Maximum Darkness – Deke Leonard 978-1-78952-048-4
Maybe I Should've Stayed In Bed – Deke Leonard 978-1-78952-053-8
The Twang Dynasty – Deke Leonard 978-1-78952-049-1

and many more to come!

Would you like to write for Sonicbond Publishing?

At Sonicbond Publishing we are always on the look-out for authors, particularly for our two main series:

On Track. Mixing fact with in depth analysis, the On Track series examines the work of a particular musical artist or group. All genres are considered from easy listening and jazz to 60s soul to 90s pop, via rock and metal.

On Screen. This series looks at the world of film and television. Subjects considered include directors, actors and writers, as well as entire television and film series. As with the On Track series, we balance fact with analysis.

While professional writing experience would, of course, be an advantage the most important qualification is to have real enthusiasm and knowledge of your subject. First-time authors are welcomed, but the ability to write well in English is essential.

Sonicbond Publishing has distribution throughout Europe and North America, and all books are also published in E-book form. Authors will be paid a royalty based on sales of their book.

Further details are available from www.sonicbondpublishing.co.uk.
To contact us, complete the contact form there or
email info@sonicbondpublishing.co.uk